Microsoft® Word 6 FOR WINDOWS™

Tutorial & Applications

Connie Morrison &
Brenda Lewis

SOUTH-WESTERN EDUCATIONAL PUBLISHING

Dixie & Gayle   318-5185
8:15 - 8:30

Acquisitions Editor: Janie F. Schwark

Developmental Editor: Dave Lafferty

Design Coordinator: Darren Wright

Cover and Internal Designer: Lou Ann Thesing

Cover Illustration: Andrew Faulkner

Production Editor: Gayle J. Statman

ISBN: 0–538–63654–8
1 2 3 4 5 6 7 8 9 VH 02 01 00 99 98 97 96 95 94
Printed in the United States of America

I(T)P
International Thomson Publishing

South-Western Educational Publishing is a division of International Thomson Publishing Inc. The ITP trademark is used under license.

PREFACE

●●●●●●●●●●●●●●●●●●●●●●

Microsoft[1] *Word 6 for Windows*[2]: *Tutorial and Applications* introduces basic, intermediate, and advanced word processing features using Microsoft Word for Windows version 6 on an IBM or IBM-compatible personal computer. The text is designed for an introductory course at the secondary level, and it should serve as a convenient source of reference for users of Word for Windows.

Organization and Features of the Text

Each chapter builds on previously learned procedures. New concepts are introduced in logical progression; the chapters are sequenced in a building-block approach to maximize the use of the software commands and procedures.

- Chapters organized in a simple-to-complex order

- Basic word processing functions for keying and editing text

- Formatting features including annotations, find and replace, and sorting and calculating

- More advanced features including merging, multiple-column documents, and graphics and special effects.

- Emphasis on visual aids (the Toolbars and the ruler) and the mouse to execute word processing functions easily and quickly

- Numerous exercises introducing new concepts in step-by-step instructions

- Review activities and Create Your Own activities to reinforce concepts

- Exercises and applications all based on realistic documents used in businesses in the '90s (scripted copy and draft documents with proofreaders' marks included)

[1]Microsoft® is a registered trademark of Microsoft Corporation.
[2]Windows™ is a trademark of Microsoft Corporation.

Learning Aids in the Text

Each chapter offers carefully planned and detailed instruction for easy and effective learning. The following features are included:

- Chapter objectives

- Preparation steps

- Screen illustrations

- Margin illustrations

- Icon and key illustrations

- Chapter exercises titled for easy reference; step-by-step instructions

- Hints on how to complete procedures previously presented

- Tips for useful shortcuts

- Computer review activities

- Create Your Own activities for skills reinforcement and development of language arts skills

- Written review questions

- Reference questions; answers found in the Word documentation

- Key terms italicized in each chapter and defined in the Glossary

- Glossary

- Appendix

- Index

Instructor's Manual

Although this text can be used as a self-paced learning guide, a comprehensive instructor's manual provides the following:

- General suggestions for presenting the chapter

- Lesson enhancement suggestions, including troubleshooting suggestions and supplemental activities and information

- The estimated time for completion of each chapter

- Unit theory tests and unit computer activities

- Solutions for chapter exercises, chapter review questions, computer activities, unity theory tests, and unit computer activities

- Solutions Disk packaged with Template Disk

To the Student

This tutorial provides an easy introduction to Windows version 3.1 and basic word processing functions using Word. Upon completion of the text, you will be able to use proficiently many of the powerful features of Word for Windows version 6.

If this is your first experience using Windows, you will want to work through the Introduction before beginning Chapter 1. It provides information about using the Windows program, including opening and closing windows, moving and sizing windows, switching between windows, and changing drives and directories. If you are familiar with Windows, it is an excellent review of the fundamentals. If this is your first experience working with a mouse, or if you want to review the procedures and terminology for using a mouse, refer to Appendix A.

Table of Contents

PART I

BASIC WORD FEATURES

PART 2

FORMATTING

PART 3

EDITING, TABLES, AND MAIL MERGE

PART 4

ADVANCED WORD FEATURES

START-UP CHECKLIST

Microsoft Word for Windows version 6 is a full-featured word processor. It enables you to work efficiently and easily to produce professional results for a variety of documents containing text and graphics. The Microsoft Windows graphical environment makes the computer easier and more fun to use. Before you begin this course, the software must be installed properly. The following checklist will assist you in installing the software and using this textbook.

HARDWARE:

✔ PC with 386 or higher microprocessor

✔ Hard drive

✔ 1.2 or 1.44 MB floppy disk drive

✔ 4 MB of RAM for the basic program (8 recommended)

✔ 6 MB of hard disk space for basic features; 24 MB for complete installation

✔ EGA or VGA monitor

✔ Mouse

✔ Printer supported by Windows 3.1

SOFTWARE:

✔ Word for Windows version 6

✔ Windows 3.1

✔ DOS 3.3 or higher (6.0 or higher recommended)

✔ Data Disk (supplied with text)

✔ Formatted Student Disks

OPTIONAL SETUP INSTALLATIONS (FOR CHAPTERS 4, 12, 13, AND 14):

✔ Proofing Tools (Spelling, Grammar, Thesaurus, Hyphenation)

✔ WordArt

✔ Filters (for graphics) under Setup category of Converters, Filters, and Data Access

✔ Clip Art

INTRODUCTION TO WINDOWS

CHAPTER

I

Microsoft Word for Windows (referred to in this text simply as "Word") runs in the Windows environment. Windows provides a variety of features that enable you to manage your applications and files easily and efficiently. This introduction presents some basic features of the Windows 3.1 program (referred to in this text simply as "Windows."). You can use it for a review or go on to Chapter 1 if you are comfortable working with the Windows 3.1 program. Refer to Troubleshooting (Appendix C) on page 395 or ask your instructor for assistance if you encounter any problems as you work through the exercises in this introduction.

EXERCISE

I.1

Loading Windows

Read pages 1-20
Read Only

1. Load (start) Windows:

   a. At the DOS prompt, key **win**.

   b. Press (Enter).

2. Look at Figures I.1 and I.2. Your screen should look similar to one of these figures.

As you work through this introduction, your screens may look different from the ones illustrated. It is not necessary that screens match exactly.

Notice that Windows applications are graph-ics-oriented. All Windows programs use icons. An *icon* is a pictorial representation of a function or *window*.

IMPORTANT: If you need to exit Windows before completing this introduction, double-click ⊟ for the Program Manager, and click ⎯OK⎯ when you see the Exit Windows message box.

1

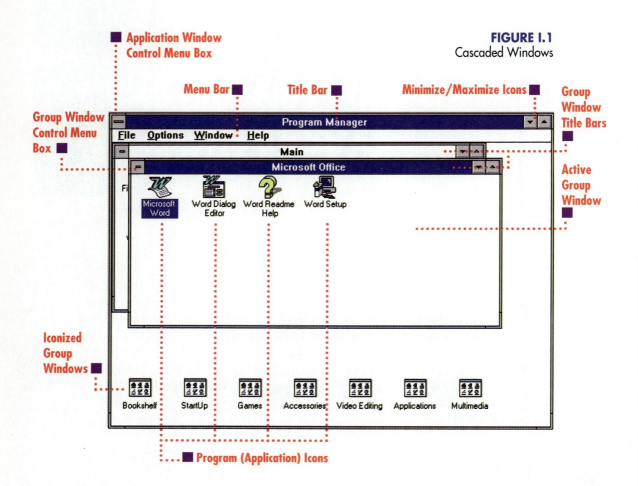

FIGURE I.1
Cascaded Windows

Application Window Control Menu Box

Menu Bar ■

Title Bar ■

Minimize/Maximize Icons ■

Group Window Title Bars

Group Window Control Menu Box ■

Active Group Window ■

Iconized Group Windows ■

■ **Program (Application) Icons**

Using Menus in Windows Applications

A *menu* in Windows applications can be opened and closed using either the keyboard or the mouse. In this text, mouse procedures will be used. If you prefer to use the keyboard, see Appendix F.

FIGURE I.2
Tiled Windows

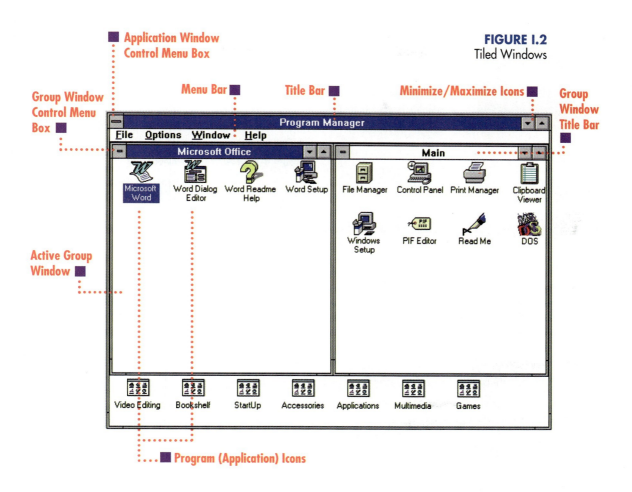

Application Window
Control Menu Box

Group Window
Control Menu
Box

Menu Bar

Title Bar

Minimize/Maximize Icons

Group
Window
Title Bar

Active Group
Window

Program (Application) Icons

EXERCISE

Opening and Canceling Menus

1. Open the Help menu (Figure I.3):

a. *Point* to the word *Help* in the *menu bar*.

b. *Click* the left mouse button.

IMPORTANT: In this text, when you see *click, double-click,* or *triple-click,* use the left mouse button unless otherwise instructed.

FIGURE I.3
Help Menu

Program Manager

<u>H</u>elp
<u>C</u>ontents
<u>S</u>earch for Help on...
<u>H</u>ow to Use Help
<u>W</u>indows Tutorial
<u>A</u>bout Program Manager...

2. Cancel the Help menu: click the word *Help* again.

I.3

Choosing Commands

• •

1. Open the Window menu.

HINT: *Click Window in the menu bar.*

Remember, your screen may not look exactly like the one illustrated in Figure I.4.

2. Choose the Accessories command: click the word *Accessories*.

The Accessories window opens on top of any other displayed windows, and the Accessories *title bar* is darkened to indicate that the Accessories window is the active group window.

FIGURE I.4
Window Menu

Program M:
Window Help
Cascade Shift+F5
Tile Shift+F4
Arrange Icons
1 Main
2 Microsoft Office
3 Multimedia
4 Applications
5 Bookshelf
6 Video Editing
7 Accessories
8 Games
✓9 StartUp

> **TIP**
>
> Windows applications have many keyboard shortcuts (such as (Shift) + (F5) for Window Cascade in Figure I.4). These shortcuts can be used in place of opening the menu to choose the command. (See Appendix F.)

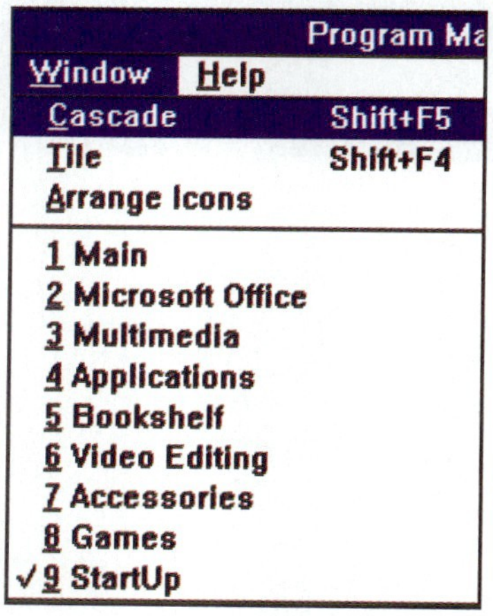

In the future, you will generally not be instructed to open a menu. You will see an instruction such as "Choose Window Accessories." In other words, do this: (1) click the word *Window* in the menu bar; and (2) click the word *Accessories* in the open Window menu. If you accidentally choose a command name followed by three dots (an ellipsis) and a box opens on your screen, click Cancel .

Using the Control Menu Functions in Windows Applications

Control menus are available for both application windows and group windows (document windows in Word). The Control menu box is used to access a Control menu similar to the one shown in Figure I.5. The Control menu box with the large hyphen ⊟ is for the application window, and the

Control menu box with the small hyphen ⊝ is for the group or document window. In this chapter, practice is provided using the mouse alternatives to the Control menu commands.

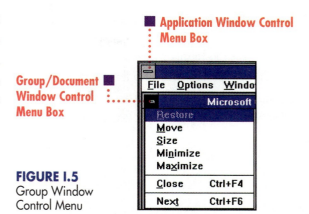

Application Window Control Menu Box

Group/Document Window Control Menu Box

FIGURE 1.5
Group Window Control Menu

EXERCISE 1.4

Moving Windows

Although exact positioning of windows is not required, you may occasionally want to reposition (move) a window to see another area of the screen more clearly.

1. Choose Window Main to activate the Main group window.

HINT: *Click Window in the menu bar; then click Main.*

2. Move the Main group window:

   a. Position the pointer on the Main group window title bar, as shown in Figure 1.6.

FIGURE 1.6
Drag the Title Bar to Move a Window

   b. Hold down the mouse button and *drag* the window down and to the right slightly (a shadowed outline of the entire window appears as you drag). Then release the mouse button. The window is now repositioned.

3. Point to the Main group window title bar again and drag the window back up and to the left, as close as possible to its original location, then release the mouse button.

EXERCISE 1.5

Sizing Windows

Although exact sizing of windows is not required, you may occasionally want to resize a window to see more of the contents of that window or other windows. If a *scroll bar* appears for a group window, the window is too small to view all the icons contained in the window. Resizing the window to a size large enough for all icons belonging in the window will make the scroll bar disappear.

1. Choose Window Games to activate the Games group window.

HINT: *Click Window; then click Games.*

2. Resize the Games group window from the top:

    a. Point to the top border (but not a corner) of the Games group window.

    b. When you see a two-headed vertical sizing arrow $\updownarrow$, drag the window up or down to a new size (a shadowed outline of the top border appears). Then release the mouse button.

3. Resize the window from the left:

    a. Point to the left border (not a corner) of the Games group window.

    b. When you see a two-headed horizontal sizing arrow $\leftrightarrow$, drag the window horizontally to a new size (a shadowed outline of the left border appears). Then release the mouse button.

4. Resize the window diagonally from a corner (not just horizontally or just vertically):

    a. Point to the corner where the top and left borders of the Games group window meet.

    b. When you see a two-headed diagonal sizing arrow $\searrow$, drag diagonally from the top left border to resize as closely as possible to the original size of the window (a shadowed outline of the top and left borders appears). Then release the mouse button.

EXERCISE

Maximizing and Restoring Windows

● ●

Group (or document) windows can be enlarged (maximized) to fill the application window. Application windows can be maximized to fill the screen.

1. Choose Window Accessories to activate the Accessories group window.

HINT: *Click Window; then click Accessories.*

2. Maximize the window: click the Maximize icon ⬚ for the Accessories group window (not the Program Manager window).

The group window fills the Program Manager application window and shares the Program Manager title bar as shown in Figure I.7.

3. Restore the Accessories group window to its

FIGURE 1.7
Maximized Accessories
Group Window

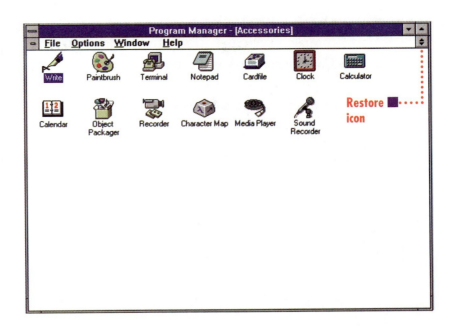

former size and location: click the Restore icon ⬍.

The Program Manager window now fills the screen.

4. Click ▲ for the Program Manager window.

5. Click ⬍ to restore the Program Manager to its former size and location.

E X E R C I S E

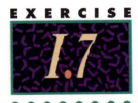

Iconizing and Restoring Windows

When you no longer need to work with a window, you can conserve screen space by *iconizing* (minimizing) it. Iconizing means to shrink a window to its smallest possible size; that is, to the size of an icon at the bottom of the screen, as shown in Figure 1.8. A label appears below each icon to help you identify the correct window. If you cannot see an icon after minimizing a window, another displayed window may be covering it. Choose Window Cascade to rearrange the windows, and you should see the icon for the minimized window.

FIGURE 1.8
Iconized Windows

1. Choose Window Games to activate the Games group window.

HINT: *Click Window, then Games.*

2. Minimize the Games group window: click the Minimize icon ▼ for the Games group window (not the Program Manager window).

The Games icon should now be at the bottom of the Program Manager window. If you cannot see, choose Window Cascade.

3. Restore the window to its former size and location: *double-click*.

4. Click ▼ for the Program Manager application window.

The Program Manager icon appears at the bottom of the screen, and all group windows are hidden.

5. Double-click to restore the Program Manager to its former size and location.

Activating (or Switching Between) Group or Document Windows

In the following exercise, you will use different methods to switch between windows. In each case, the newly activated window will have the darkened title bar.

EXERCISE

1.8

Activating Windows

1. Choose Window Main to activate the Main group window.

HINT: *Click Window; then click Main.*

The Main group window opens on top of the other windows, with the Main group window title bar darkened.

2. Click in a displayed portion of a window other than the currently active window (the one with the darkened title bar). A different window is now active.

3. Iconize all displayed group windows.

HINT: *Click ▼ for each group window.*

Each time you iconize, a different group window becomes active.

4. Double-click the following icons: Accessories, Main, and Games.

The window for the last icon you double-click becomes the active window. (If a window covers the icons at the bottom of the screen, choose Window Cascade, and then double-click the desired icons.)

Using Windows Applications

Using Windows allows you to *multi-task;* that is, to run more than one software application at a time.

The following three exercises, Exercise I.9 to Exercise I.11, should be completed in a single class session. You will need approximately ten minutes to complete them.

EXERCISE

I.9

Loading Applications from the Program Manager

● ●

1. Load the Print Manager application:

   a. Activate the Main group window.

HINT: *Click Window; then click Main.*

   b. Double-click the Print Manager icon 🖨.

The Print Manager window opens on top of the Program Manager window with the Print Manager title bar darkened.

2. Minimize the Print Manager window for later access.

HINT: *Click ▼ .*

3. Load the Calendar application:

   a. Activate the Accessories group window.

   b. Double-click the Calendar icon 🔢. The Calendar window opens, with its title bar darkened.

4. Iconize the Calendar window for later access.

5. Load Word for Windows:

   a. Double-click icons at the bottom of the screen until the window containing the Microsoft Word icon 📝 is active.

   b. Double-click 📝.

   c. If you see a Tip of the Day, click ▢ OK ▢.

d. If necessary, click ⬛ so that the Word application window fills the screen.

Because the Word for Windows application window is maximized, you cannot see the icons for the other two applications you opened and minimized, nor can you see the Program Manager window. Nevertheless, they are active in the background and can be accessed using one of the four methods presented in the following exercise.

EXERCISE

I.10 Switching Applications

● ●

1. Switch applications using the Control menu:

a. Click the Application Window Control menu box (the one with the large hyphen) ▭ once to open the Control menu.

b. Click *Switch To*. The Task List (Figure I.9) appears.

FIGURE I.9
Task List Window

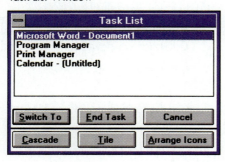

TIP

Ctrl + *Esc* is a shortcut for the Control menu Switch To command.

c. Double-click the application name *Calendar.*

The Calendar window opens on top of the Word window, with the Calendar window title bar darkened.

2. Switch back to the Word window (it is behind the Calendar window) by clicking in it.

Anytime you have overlapping windows, you can switch windows by clicking in the desired window.

3. Click 🔼 for the Word application window (the top right icon).

4. Double-click 🖨 at the bottom of the screen.

(If you cannot see the icon, drag the bottom of the Calendar window up to resize it so you can see the icon.) When you have iconized applications, you can switch by double-clicking the icon representing the application.

5. Switch windows by holding down *Alt* and pressing *Tab*.

Each time you press (Tab) with (Alt) held down, a rectangular box appears with the name of an application. When you release (Tab) and then (Alt), the application becomes active.

IMPORTANT: When key combinations are listed in this text (shown with a + symbol, such as (Alt) + (Tab)), hold down the first key listed and without releasing it, press the second key. Release both keys simultaneously.

EXERCISE I.11

Closing (Exiting) Windows Applications

1. If it is not already active, switch to the Calendar window.

HINT: *Press* (Alt) + (Tab).

2. Close the window using one of the following procedures:

- Choose the Exit command from the appropriate menu (the File menu in this case).

- Double-click the Application Window Control menu box ⊟.

> **TIP**
>
> (Alt) + (F4) is a keyboard alternative to double-clicking the Control menu box to close Windows or a Windows application.

3. If it is not already active, switch to the Print Manager window. Close the window.

4. If it is not already active, switch to the Word for Windows window.

EXERCISE I.12

Changing Drives and Directories

In most Windows applications (including Word), there are commands that open a *dialog box* in which you can change the drive and *directory*. The procedures to change the drive and directory are the same for floppy disk users and hard disk users. If you plan to work only from floppies, do Steps

FIGURE I.10
File Open Dialog Box for A Drive with Data Disk
Inserted

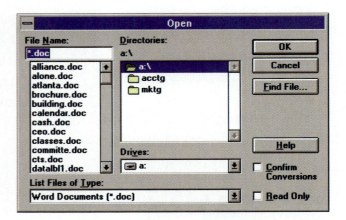

1–11. If you will be saving and opening
files on the hard drive, do Steps 12–21.

1. If necessary, load Word by double-clicking in the appropriate Program Manager group window.

2. Insert your *Data Disk* into the A drive.
(Substitute the appropriate drive letter for "a"
in all the following steps if your Data Disk is
in a drive other than A.)

3. Choose File Open. A dialog box similar to
the one shown in Figure I.10 appears,
although you still need to change drives.

4. Click the underlined down arrow to the right
of the Drives list box.

5. Click the a: to change to the A drive.

6. If a:\ is not *highlighted* in the Directories box,
double-click it to change to the root directory
on the A drive.

The dialog box should now look like Figure I.10.
Notice that there are several files listed in the File
Name list box.

7. Double-click the directory name **mktg** to
change directories again.

The path now reads a:\mktg. There is only one file
in this directory, **mktginfo.doc**, and there are
four subdirectories (*letters*, *memos*, *misc*, and *tables*).

8. Double-click the *subdirectory* name **letters**
to change directories again.

The path shown for the Directories box now reads
a:\mktg\letters, and a new file is listed
(**ltrstyle.doc**). To go to *lower* directory levels,
you must always double-click parent-level directories until you reach the desired level (for example,
you had to double-click the parent directory *mktg*
before you could access the subdirectory *letters*).

9. Double-click the *a:*.

Notice that you did not need to switch to the *mktg*
level in order to go up to the root level. You can go
to any displayed *higher* directory level without
having to switch to intermediate levels.

10. You do not need to open a file at this time, so
click Cancel .

11. Close Word for Windows.

HINT: *Double-click* ⊟.

Do Steps 12–21 *only* if you are using the hard
drive to do all your work in this text. Before beginning these steps, you will need to check with your

FIGURE I.11
File Open Dialog Box for the Datafile Subdirectory

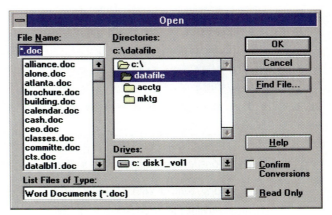

instructor for the location of your *Data Disk* files. Instructions are given for the directory *c:\datafile*. If necessary, make the appropriate substitutions for the *datafile* directory in Step 16.

12. If necessary, load Word by double-clicking ![icon] in the appropriate Program Manager group window.

13. Choose File Open. A dialog box similar to the one shown in Figure I.11 appears, although you need to change directories and possibly drives.

14. If the Drives list box does not show a drive name beginning with *c:,* click the underlined down arrow to the right of the Drives list box, then click the drive letter.

15. If *c:* is not *highlighted* in the Directories box, double-click *c:* to change to the root directory on the hard drive which has names for other directories.

16. Scroll, if necessary, to locate the directory name **datafile**. Then double-click *datafile* to change to that directory.

The dialog box should now look like Figure I.11. Notice that there are several files listed in the File Name list box.

17. Double-click the *subdirectory* name **mktg** to change directories again.

The path now reads *c:\datafile\mktg*. There is

only one file in this directory, **mktginfo.doc**, and there are four subdirectories (*letters, memos, misc,* and *tables*).

18. Double-click the subdirectory name **letters** to change directories again.

The path shown for the Directories box now reads *c:\datafile\mktg\letters* and a new file is listed (**ltrstyle.doc**). To go to *lower* directory levels, you must always double-click parent-level directories until you reach the desired level (for example, you had to double-click the parent directory *mktg* before you could access the subdirectory letters).

19. Double-click the *c:*.

Notice that you did not need to switch to the *mktg* level in order to go up to the root level. You can go to any displayed *higher* directory level without having to switch to intermediate levels.

20. You do not need to open a file at this time, so click ⌷ Cancel ⌷.

21. Close Word for Windows.

HINT: *Double-click* ⊟.

I.13

Closing (Exiting) the Windows Program

1. *Toggle* off all settings in the Options menu:

   a. Click Options to open the Options menu.

   b. Click on any setting with a check mark (such as the default Save Settings on Exit shown in Figure I.12). If no settings are checked, click Options again to cancel the menu.

FIGURE I.12
Save Settings on Exit Turned On

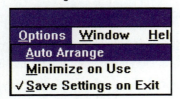

2. Close the Windows program properly by doing one of the following:

   ■ Choose File Exit Windows.

TIP

Alt + F4 is a keyboard alternative to double-clicking the Control menu box to close Windows or a Windows application.

   ■ Double-click the Application Window Control menu box ⊟.

3. Click [OK] in the Exit Windows confirmation dialog box (Figure I.13). You are returned to the *DOS* prompt.

FIGURE I.13
Exit Windows Dialog Box

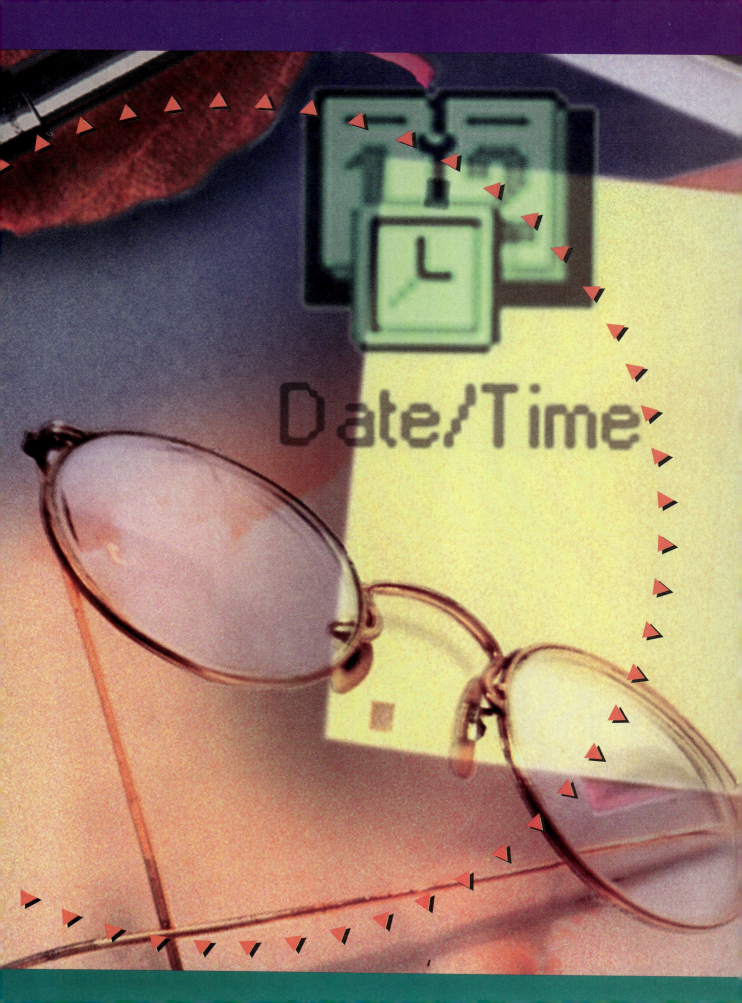

Date/Time

BASIC WORD FEATURES

CREATING A DOCUMENT

CHAPTER

1

OBJECTIVES
Upon completion of this chapter, you will be able to:

- Select the printer you will use to print a final copy.

- Enter text into a document.

- Perform an initial save of a document.

- Print a document.

- Clear the screen and begin a new document.

- Change line spacing.

- Turn on special characters.

- Move the insertion point in a document.

- Edit a document and re-save the file.

- Center text.

- Emphasize (format) text with bold, italic, and underline.

- Add the date automatically to a document.

Preparation

1. You will need a formatted *Student Disk* on which to store your files for this text. To keep files well-organized, you may want to create a subdirectory on the floppy disk for each chapter in this text (for example, *a:\chap01*). If you want to use the hard drive during a class session, you will need to create your own directory on the hard drive (for example, *c:\student*).

2. At the end of each class session, be sure to close Word and Windows properly (see the Introduction if you do not remember how to close applications). If you are using the hard drive to store your completed work, back up your files onto your formatted Student Disk, and erase your files from the directory you used on the hard drive.

Creating a Document

As you work through this chapter, refer to Figure 1.1 if you need help remembering the names of parts of the Word *window*.

At the beginning of each class session, *before* you begin working on new or existing documents, you need to *select* a printer. If you change printers after completing a document, you may see a totally different effect from the one you planned. For example, not all printers have the same *fonts*. If you plan your page layout very precisely, including placement of graphics, charts, and text, and then change your printer selection after completing your document, you may be disappointed: line lengths can change, forcing you to readjust the layout totally.

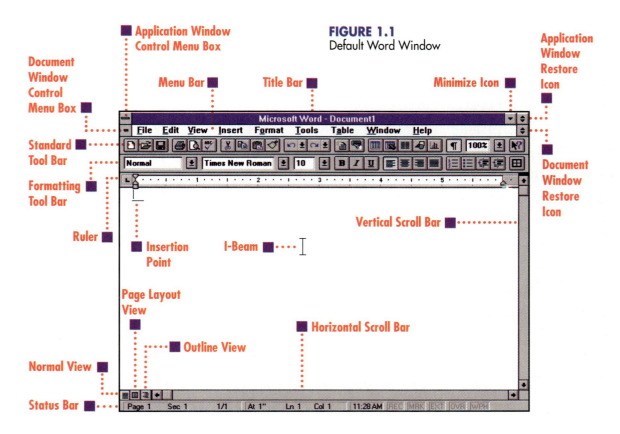

FIGURE 1.1
Default Word Window

Application Window Control Menu Box
Document Window Control Menu Box
Menu Bar
Title Bar
Minimize Icon
Application Window Restore Icon
Standard Tool Bar
Document Window Restore Icon
Formatting Tool Bar
Ruler
Vertical Scroll Bar
Insertion Point
I-Beam
Page Layout View
Horizontal Scroll Bar
Outline View
Normal View
Status Bar

EXERCISE 1.1

Loading Word and Selecting a Printer

IMPORTANT: In this text, when you see click, double-click, or triple-click, use the left mouse button unless otherwise instructed.

1. Load Windows: at the DOS prompt, key **win** and press (Enter).

2. Load Word for Windows:

   a. Skip to step c if the window containing the Microsoft Word *icon* 𝒲 is displayed. If you do not see 𝒲, *click* Window in the *menu bar* to open the Window *menu*.

   b. In the Window menu, click the name of the window that contains the 𝒲 icon.

   (If you still do not see the icon, repeat Steps a and b, clicking a different window name in the Window menu.)

   c. *Double-click* 𝒲.

   d. Click | **OK** | if you see a Tip of the Day.

3. Select the printer you will use to print your final document:

   a. Choose File Print.

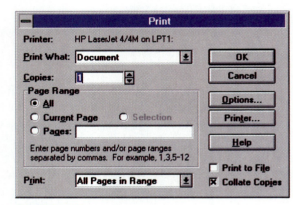

FIGURE 1.2
File Print Dialog Box

HINT: *Click the File menu name in the menu bar; then click the Print command name.*

The Print *dialog box* shown in Figure 1.2 will open.

   b. Click Printer. A dialog box similar to the one shown in Figure 1.3 appears.

   c. Click the name of the printer you will use to print your final document. (Skip to step e if

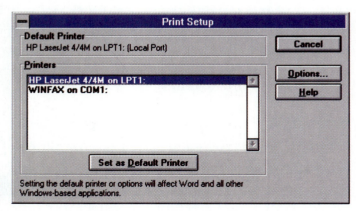

FIGURE 1.3
Print Setup Dialog Box

the *highlighted* printer is the one you will use to print the final document.)

d. If you changed printers in Step c, click Set as Default Printer.

1st assignment

e. Click [Close] (or [Cancel] if you

made no changes) to close the Print Setup dialog box.

f. Click [Close] (or [Cancel] if you made no changes) to close the Print dialog box.

EXERCISE 1.2

Entering Text in a Document

● ●

1. Click the underlined arrow next to the Font Size box on the Formatting *Toolbar* if the Font Size box shows the default 10 or any size other than 12. (If the Font Size box on the Formatting Toolbar shows 12, skip to Step 3.)

2. In the list box that opens, click 12 to make the text you key slightly larger and more readable on the screen.

Use a *font size* of 12 for all documents you key in this text unless otherwise instructed.

3. Key the following sentence, beginning at the *insertion point* (the blinking vertical line as shown in Figure 1.1). **It is important to remember to protect your skin from the sun's rays.**

Notice as you key that the insertion point moves to the right. If you make any errors while keying, press (**Backspace**) to correct them.

4. Press (**Space Bar**) twice.

5. Key the following sentence without pressing the Return ((**Enter**)) key.

Even during the winter months when

snow blankets the ground and clouds fill the sky, the sun can damage your skin.

Notice that text automatically moves to the next line as you key (this is known as *word wrap*).

6. Space twice and key the next three sentences, letting Word wrap the text at the end of each line.

Snow reflects up to 85 percent of the sun's rays. Even when it is cloudy, as much as 80 percent of the rays pass through the clouds. Downhill skiers are especially at risk when they ski at mountain resorts because the sun's rays are more intense at higher altitudes.

7. Press (**Enter**) once to end the document with a blank line.

You will generally end your documents by pressing (**Enter**) once. The blank line is necessary for proper spacing when you move or copy text at the end of a document (which you will do in Chapter 3).

EXERCISE 1.3

Saving and Printing a Document

It is a wise idea to save your work frequently—at least once every 15 minutes or so. Frequently saving provides protection against unexpected events such as power failures, so you will not have to start over completely. It also allows you to throw out your current version and return to the latest saved version, should you make errors that would take too much time to undo.

1. Complete your initial save of the document as follows:

   a. Click the Save icon on the Standard Toolbar 💾.

Because you have not yet named your document, the dialog box shown in Figure 1.4 appears. Your File Name box, Directories box, Drives box, and the path shown above the Directories box may be different.

   b. Insert your formatted Student Disk in the appropriate drive if you will be saving your work on a floppy disk.

   c. Change drives and directories until the path shown for the Directories box is the location in which your work will be saved (for example, *a:\chap01* or *c:\student\chap01*).

HINT: *Click the underlined arrow in the Drives box and click the desired drive. Double-click the drive letter in the Directories box; then, if necessary, double-click the desired directory and/or subdirectory.*

   d. Position the mouse pointer at the beginning of the entry in the File Name text box and click the left mouse button.

   e. Press ⟨Delete⟩ to erase the existing entry.

   f. Key the filename **chap1-1** (do not key a period or an extension; Word will automatically add the extension .DOC).

Filenames can be from one to eight characters in size. They cannot include spaces, periods, commas, or any of the following characters: * < > ? ; [ ] + = \ / :.

   g. Click ⟨ OK ⟩ to return to your document.

FIGURE 1.4
File Save As Dialog Box

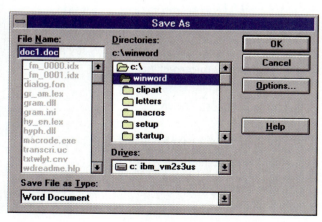

Notice that the *title bar* now shows the filename CHAP1-1.DOC.

2. Print your document as follows:

   a. Check to make sure your printer is on-line.

   b. Click the Print icon on the Standard Toolbar .

The document prints using the *default* Print settings. In the future, if you need to change settings such as the default printer, the number of copies, the specific pages to be printed, and so forth, choose File Print rather than clicking .

Editing a Document

Editing involves adding, deleting, and changing text in a document. In the following exercises, you will clear your screen, change to double spacing, key a new document, and save it. You will then edit, format, re-save, and print the final document.

EXERCISE

Clearing the Screen and Opening a New Document Window

Although you can open a new document window while a document is on the screen, it is usually best to save computer memory by clearing the screen (also known as closing the document windows).

1. Clear the screen by doing one of the following:

   ■ Choose File Close.

   ■ Double-click the Document Window Control menu box ⊟.

Notice that only the File and Help menus are available when you clear the screen.

> **TIP**
>
> Pressing **Ctrl** + **F4** is an alternative to double-clicking the Control menu box to close a document window.

2. Open a new document window: click the New icon on the Standard Toolbar ▯.

A new document window is now open, with "Microsoft Word" and a document number in the title bar.

Keying Your Second Document

1. Change to double spacing: hold down **Ctrl** and press **2**; then release **2** and **Ctrl**.

2. Click the underlined arrow next to the Font Size box on the Formatting Toolbar and click 12.

All paragraphs in your document will be double-spaced until you change this *paragraph format* again. In the future, you can press **Ctrl** + the number **1** for single spacing or **Ctrl** + **2** for double spacing.

IMPORTANT: When key combinations are listed in this text (shown with a + symbol), hold down the first key listed and without releasing it, press the second key. Release both keys simultaneously.

3. Press **Tab**; then key the first paragraph of the document (Figure 1.5).

Your line endings may be slightly different from those shown, but let Word wrap the text at the end of each line. Press **Backspace** to correct any errors.

4. Press **Enter** once to start a new paragraph.

In the future, to start new paragraphs, press **Enter** once if the text is double-spaced and twice if the text is single-spaced.

5. Press **Tab** and key the second paragraph. Press **Backspace** to correct errors (Figure 1.6 on page 25).

IMPORTANT: Do not press **Enter to end your document this time; you will add the blank line in Exercise 1.9.**

FIGURE 1.5
First Paragraph of Double-Spaced Document

> Recently I decided to look at careers in sports medicine. In the early '80s a doctor who treated professional sports players suddenly began treating many new patients for injuries resulting from aerobics, jogging, and floor exercise. Clinics began shifting the focus away from surgery and toward rehabilitation and education.

FIGURE 1.6
Second Paragraph of Double-Spaced Document

> *I carefully thought about that career for months, and I am positive that a career in sports medicine will be interesting and rewarding. The future is promising and challenging because the field of sports medicine is new and changing.*

6. Click 💾.

7. Save the document in the appropriate location for Student Disk files as **chap1-2**; then click ▭ OK ▭. The title bar now shows

CHAP1-2.DOC.

8. Print a copy of this first draft.

HINT: *Click* 🖨.

E X E R C I S E

Displaying Nonprinting Characters

Word considers characters to be letters, numbers, and graphics. These characters are visible on your screen just as they will look when printed. To simplify editing, you can also display (turn on) some special characters. These characters are known as nonprinting characters because the symbols representing them do not print.

1. Click the Show/Hide icon on the Standard Toolbar ¶. The icon should now be highlighted. (If it is not highlighted, click it again.)

2. Compare your document to Figure 1.7 on page 26.

The right arrow at the beginning of each para-

graph indicates where you pressed (Tab). Between each pair of words, a dot indicates where you pressed (Space Bar). At the end of the first paragraph is a paragraph mark (¶) indicating where you pressed (Enter) and started a new paragraph.

As you edit your documents, be careful that you do not accidentally erase nonprinting characters. If you should accidentally delete a nonprinting character, reinsert the character by pressing the appropriate key ((Tab), (Space Bar), or (Enter)). After you restore a paragraph mark by pressing (Enter), position the mouse pointer in the paragraph and click. Then reset any paragraph formatting such as line spacing.

FIGURE 1.7
Completed Document
with Nonprinting
Characters Displayed

→   Recently·I·decided·to·look·at·careers·in·sports·medicine.··In·the·early·'80s·a·doctor·

who·treated·professional·sports·players·suddenly·began·treating·many·new·patients·for·

injuries·resulting·from·aerobics,·jogging,·and·floor·exercise.··Clinics·began·shifting·the·

focus·away·from·surgery·and·toward·rehabilitation·and·education.¶

→   I·carefully·thought·about·that·career·for·months,·and·I·am·positive·that·a·career·in·

sports·medicine·will·be·interesting·and·rewarding.··The·future·is·promising·and·

challenging·because·the·field·of·sports·medicine·is·new·and·changing.¶
—

EXERCISE

Moving the Insertion Point

1. If you do not have a separate keypad on your keyboard for direction keys, turn off the numbers lock key.

2. Practice using the direction keys to move the insertion point through your document.

3. Practice using the following special key combinations to move the insertion point more quickly. (If you cannot remember these shortcuts later, you can always use the direction keys or simply click where needed.)

a. (Ctrl) + (End) (end of document)

b. (Ctrl) + (Home) (beginning of document)

c. (End) (end of line)

d. (Home) (beginning of line)

As an alternative to using the keyboard, you can move the mouse until the pointer (the *I-beam*) is at approximately the desired location and then click the left mouse button. (Clicking the left mouse button at a location is known as clicking an insertion point.)

4. Practice moving the mouse to position the I-beam and clicking an insertion point. (If necessary, after you click an insertion point, you can use the direction keys to position the insertion point exactly where needed for editing.)

EXERCISE

Correcting and Re-saving a Document

To correct errors or make other changes in your document, you first position the insertion point and edit as you want. Figure 1.8 illustrates the changes you will make to your document. The steps for

FIGURE 1.8
Document with Proofreaders' Marks

> Recently I decided to ~~look at~~ *pursue a* careers in sports medicine.
>
> In the early '80s a *doctor*^s who treated professional ~~sports~~ *football and tennis* players suddenly began treating many new patients for injuries resulting from aerobics, jogging, and ~~floor~~ *dance* exercise. Clinics began shifting the focus away from surgery and toward rehabilitation and education.
>
> I carefully thought about ~~that~~ *this* career for *several* months, and I am ~~positive~~ *confident* that a career in sports medicine will be interesting and rewarding. The future is promising and challenging because the field of sports medicine is new and *still* ~~changing~~ *developing*.

making these corrections are not in the order shown in the figure. Therefore, proofread carefully to be sure you make all necessary corrections. If you accidentally highlight text, simply position the mouse pointer somewhere in the text and click the left mouse button (click an insertion point) or press a direction key. If you accidentally delete the wrong text, click the Undo icon on the Standard Toolbar before you make any further edits.

1. Press (Ctrl) + (Home) to position the insertion point at the top of your document.

2. Position the insertion point at the end of the word "doctor" in the first sentence.

3. Key **s** to change the word to "doctors."

4. Position the insertion point between "for" and "months" in the first sentence of the second paragraph.

   `for months.`

5. Press (Space Bar) once; then key **several.**

6. Position the insertion point in the last sentence

and key **still,** as shown in Figure 1.8 (be sure to add a space).

7. Position the insertion point immediately ~~before~~ *after* "a" in the second sentence.

8. Press ◀ *Backspace* ~~twice~~ *once* to erase the letter and the following space.

9. Position the insertion point at the end of the word "careers" in the first sentence and press (**Backspace**) to delete the last letter.

Two shortcuts you will use in the following steps for deleting words are (**Ctrl**) + ◀ and (**Ctrl**) + (**Backspace**). If you cannot remember these shortcuts in the future, simply press (**Backspace**) or ◀ .

10. Position the insertion point at the ~~beginning~~ *end* of the word "positive" in the second paragraph.

Don't highlight *Doesn't work on mine*

11. Press (**Ctrl**) + ◀ *Backspace* to erase the word.

12. Key **confident** and add a space.

13. Position the insertion point at the end of the word "changing" in the last sentence (before the period).

14. Press (**Ctrl**) + (**Backspace**) to erase the word.

15. Space once and key **developing.**

16. Switch from the *INSERT* mode to the *OVERTYPE* mode and replace text:

   a. Position the insertion point at the beginning of the first "that" in the second paragraph.

   b. Double-click OVR on the status bar at the bottom of the window to turn on OVERTYPE (OVR is then highlighted).

   c. Key **this** to change "that" to "this".

   d. Double-click OVR to turn off OVERTYPE and return to the INSERT mode (OVR is no longer highlighted on the status bar).

17. Overtype "floor" with "dance" in the first paragraph (be sure to turn off OVERTYPE after you make the change).

In the following steps, the words you are going to use to replace "sports" happen to have more than six letters. If you were to turn on OVERTYPE and key all the replacement words ("football and tennis"), you would replace not only "sports" but also part of the following text, "players suddenly," as shown in Figure 1.9. Be sure to turn off OVERTYPE after replacing the original text; then finish keying the new text.

FIGURE 1.9
Text Overtyped in Error

professional·football·and·tennis|nly·began·

18. Overtype text of a different length:

   a. Position the insertion point at the beginning of the word "sports" in the second sentence.

   b. Double-click OVR to turn on OVERTYPE.

   c. Key **footba** (the first six characters of the replacement text).

   d. Double-click OVR to turn off OVERTYPE.

e. Finish keying the text: **ll and tennis.**

19. Use OVERTYPE to change "look at" to "pursue a" in the first sentence.

20. Proofread the document and correct any errors.

Your editing was extensive; therefore, you should save your work again. Because you have already completed your initial save and named your document, you will not see a dialog box.

21. Click 🖫.

EXERCISE

Sometimes gives a "go to Dialog" box, use scroll Bar and mouse.

Formatting a Document

● ●

Formatting involves changing the appearance of your document from the default settings. When you are keying new text, you must turn on the format, key the new text, and then turn off the format.

1. Press (Ctrl) + (Home) to position the insertion point at the beginning of your document.

2. Press (Enter) once to add a blank line. Then move the insertion point back to the top of the document.

To change *alignment* (a type of paragraph format), click the appropriate icon on the Formatting Toolbar (left, centered, right, justified). The selected format icon will be highlighted whenever the insertion point is anywhere within the paragraph to which the format has been applied.

3. Key a centered line in all capital letters:

a. Click the Center icon on the Formatting Toolbar ▤.

b. Press (Caps Lock).

c. Key the title: **SPORTS MEDICINE.**

4. End the centered, all-caps format:

a. Press (Enter) once.

b. Press (Caps Lock) to turn off all caps.

c. Click the Align Left icon on the Formatting Toolbar ▤ to end the centered format and return to the default left alignment.

5. Press (Ctrl) + (End) to position the insertion point at the end of your document.

6. If the Font Size box shows a size other than 12, click the arrow next to the Font Size box and click 12. (Whenever you press (Ctrl) + (End), be sure to check your *font size* before you key.)

7. Press (Enter).

8. Press (Ctrl) + (1) to change to single spacing.

To add any of the *character formats*—bold, italic, or underline—click the appropriate icon on the

Formatting Toolbar. More than one character format at a time can be applied to text (for example, a common combination is bold and italic).

9. Key bold text:

    a. Click the Bold icon on the Formatting Toolbar $\boxed{\mathbf{B}}$.

Notice that the icon for the selected format (bold) is highlighted on the Formatting Toolbar.

    b. Key your name.

Notice that the text appears bold on your screen. Word displays most formats just as they will print.

    c. Click $\boxed{\mathbf{B}}$ to turn off the format.

Notice that the icon on the Formatting Toolbar is no longer highlighted.

10. Press (**Enter**) for a new paragraph.

11. Italicize text:

    a. Click the Italic icon on the Formatting Toolbar $\boxed{I}$.

    b. Key your course name.

    c. Click $\boxed{I}$ to turn off the format.

12. Press (**Enter**) for a new paragraph.

13. Add an underlined date (note that Word has an automatic date function, so you do not have to key dates in your documents):

    a. Click the Underline icon on the Formatting Toolbar $\boxed{\underline{U}}$ to turn on the underline format.

    b. Choose Insert Date and Time.

FIGURE 1.10
Insert Date and Time Dialog Box

HINT: *Click Insert in the menu bar; then click Date and Time.*

A dialog box similar to the one shown in Figure 1.10 appears.

    c. Click on the desired date format (in this case, click on the one that has a format similar to March 23, 1994).

    d. Click $\boxed{\text{OK}}$. The current date appears in your document.

    e. Click $\boxed{\underline{U}}$ to turn off the underline format.

14. Press (**Enter**) to end the document with a blank line.

15. Add combination formats:

    a. Position the insertion point at the end of the word "be" in the second paragraph, and space once.

    b. Click $\boxed{\mathbf{B}}$; then click $\boxed{I}$.

Notice that both the Bold and the Italic icons are highlighted.

    c. Key **both** (the phrase then reads "will be ***both*** interesting and rewarding").

d. Click **B** and *I* to turn off the formats.

16. Proofread the document and if necessary, make further corrections.

17. Save the changes to your document and print a final copy.

HINT: *Click 💾; then click 🖨.*

18. Clear the screen.

HINT: *Double-click Ⓙ.*

No such Icon
use ⊟

COMPUTER ACTIVITIES

ACTIVITY 1

1. Open a new document window.

2. Check to be sure the printer you will use to print your document is selected.

3. Click 12 in the Font Size box.

4. Set the line spacing to double.

5. Key the document shown in Figure 1.11. Press (**Tab**) to begin the paragraph, and press (**Enter**) once to end the document. Use word wrap to end all lines except the last.

6. Proofread and correct all errors.

7. Save the document as **act1-1** in the appropriate location for Student Disk files. Print one copy and clear the screen.

FIGURE 1.11
Double-Spaced Paragraph

> Sports medicine is very popular and is growing rapidly. One of the trends that spurred from sports medicine is aggressive therapy. Aggressive therapy means that patients begin moving sooner after their injuries and that patients stay in condition during their recovery. For example, doctors used to think that patients recovering from reconstructive knee surgery needed to rest for 6 to 12 weeks before doing any vigorous exercise. Doctors now believe instead that aggressive exercise accelerates the healing process. Essentially, doctors believe the body likes the exercise during the healing process. Thus, in aggressive therapy patients may literally begin exercising as soon as they wake up after the surgery.

ACTIVITY 2

1. In a new document window, click 12 in the Font Size box.

2. Set the line spacing to double.

3. Key the document illustrated in Figure 1.12. Press **Tab** to begin each paragraph, and press **Enter** to end each paragraph. (Use word wrap to end all lines except the last line of each paragraph.)

4. Save the document as **act1-2** and print a copy of this first draft.

5. Make the corrections indicated in Figure 1.13. Position the insertion point at each place a correction needs to be made; then insert, overtype, or delete as necessary.

6. Proofread the document and make any other necessary corrections.

7. Save your changes, print a final copy, and clear the screen.

FIGURE 1.12
Rough Draft for Two Paragraphs

The average person's life expectancy is around 75 years. Most of us assume that as individuals grow older, their chances of dying increase. Contrary to that belief, some experts now think just the opposite. They believe that the likelihood of people dying actually decreases as they age, and that there is no limit on the length of human life. What this really means is that the older human beings get, the more likely they are to live even longer.

Based on some contemporary studies, several leading researchers now predict that in the next two generations humans will age slower and live longer. Their predictions are surprising. They speculate that today's 25-year-old adults will live to be 80 or 90. They further estimate that the young children today will probably live long past 100. Finally, they believe that the generation to be born after the year 2010 may live to be 150 years or older.

FIGURE 1.13
Document with Proofreaders' Marks

The average person's life expectancy is around 75 years. Most

of us assume that as individuals ~~grow older~~ _age,_ their chances of

dying increase. ~~Contrary to that belief,~~ _some_ ~~experts~~ _scientists are_ now

~~think~~ _saying_ just the opposite. They believe that the likelihood of

people dying actually decreases as they ~~age,~~ _grow older,_ and that there

is no _fixed_ limit on the length of _a_ human life. What this really

means is that the older human beings get, the more likely

they are to live ~~even~~ longer.

Based on some contemporary studies, several leading

researchers now predict that in the next two _or three_ generations

humans will age slower and live _much, much_ longer. Their predictions

are surprising. They speculate that today's ~~25~~ _30_-year-old

adults will live to be ~~80~~ _90_ or ~~90~~ _100_. They further estimate that

the young children today will probably live long past 100.

Finally, they believe that the generation to be born after

the year 2020 may live to be ~~150~~ _200_ years or older.

ACTIVITY 3

1. In a new document window, key the memo illustrated in Figure 1.14 on page 36 following
    these instructions:

a. Click 12 in the Font Size box.

b. Key **MEMORANDUM** in all capital letters, centered and bold. (Be sure to turn off the bold format after you key the title.)

c. Press **Enter** four times to leave three blank lines.

d. Turn on left alignment.

e. Key the first memorandum heading (**TO:**) in all caps using the all caps, bold, and italic formats; then turn off the formats.

f. Press **Tab** twice and key **Fitness Trainers.**

g. Press **Enter** twice.

h. Repeat Steps e–g for the other three memo headings (but press **Tab** only once for the other headings), keying the appropriate information for each heading.

i. Press **Enter** twice after the subject line.

j. Key the body of the memo. (Use word wrap to end each line, but press **Enter** twice to end each paragraph.)

k. After the last paragraph in the body of the memo, press **Enter** twice.

l. Key your initials, then press **Enter** once to end the document.

 IMPORTANT: For all letters and memos, substitute your initials for "smn."

2. Save the memo as **act1-3** and print a copy of this first draft.

3. Make the corrections indicated in Figure 1.15 on page 37. Position the insertion point at each place a correction needs to be made; then insert, overtype, or delete as necessary. (The memo is double-spaced to show the proofreaders' marks, but your memo should be single-spaced.)

4. Proofread the document and make any other needed changes.

5. Save your changes, print a final copy, and clear the screen.

FIGURE 1.14
Rough-Draft Memorandum

MEMORANDUM

TO: Fitness Trainers

FROM: Pat Swearingen

DATE: September 1, 19--

SUBJECT: Class Schedule

As we approach our grand opening day, I am completing the class schedule for the family lifestyle center. You will recall that when we met last week I asked you to think about whether we should offer classes on cooking and food labeling.

Do you think our family members will be interested in these classes?

Are these classes necessary, and will they complement our instruction on nutrition?

Should we offer more than one class on cooking and design the instruction for specific age groups?

I would like to hear your thoughts about these classes. I would also like to hear your suggestions for any other classes that you think we should offer. Please write down your thoughts and send them to me, or stop by my office at any time.

smn

FIGURE 1.15
Corrections to Memorandum

MEMORANDUM

TO: Fitness Trainers
FROM: Pat Swearingen
DATE: September 1, 19--
SUBJECT: Class Schedule

~~October 1~~   finalizing
As we approach our grand opening day, I am ~~completing~~ the
class schedule for the family lifestyle center. You will
                                              each of
recall that when we met last week I asked you to think
                        a   a class on
about whether we should offer classes on cooking and food
labeling.

Do you think our ~~family~~ members will be interested in these
classes?

Are these classes necessary, and will they complement our
                              class
~~instruction of~~ nutrition?

                                                   target
Should we offer more than one class on cooking and ~~design~~
                       to
the instruction ~~for~~ specific age groups?

                                      proposed
I would like to hear your thoughts about these classes.
I would also like to hear your suggestions for ~~any~~ other
classes that you think we should offer. Please write down
                                              any day this week
your thoughts and send them to me, or stop by my ofice ~~at~~
~~any time.~~

smn

CREATE YOUR OWN ∙∙∙∙∙∙∙∙∙∙∙∙

Suppose that you are one of the fitness trainers working for Pat Swearingen. Compose a response in memo format (see Figures 1.14 and 1.15). Give your own answers to the questions asked by Pat Swearingen. Offer your own personal thoughts on the classes that should be offered. Proofread and make any necessary corrections. Save your document, print a copy, and clear the screen.

Do not do these lessons.

REVIEW EXERCISES

TRUE / FALSE

Each of the following statements is either true or false. Indicate your answer on the left by circling T if the statement is true or F if the statement is false.

T **(F)** **1.** The printer selection can be changed either before or after the document is completed without affecting the layout.

(T) F **2.** Centering is a form of paragraph formatting.

T **(F)** **3.** As you key text, you must press **Enter** to end each line.

T **(F)** **4.** A filename cannot exceed six characters.

FILL IN THE BLANKS

Complete the following sentences by writing the correct word or words in the blanks provided.

5. To position the insertion point at the top of the document, press ____Ctrl____ + ____Home____.

6. To position the insertion point at the end of the document, press ____Ctrl____ + ____end____.

7. Press ____Format____ + ____Auto____ to single-space text; press ____Format____ + ____2ti 2____ to double-space text.

8. ____Wrap around____ is a Word feature that automatically starts a new line when text reaches the end of a line.

9. To select the printer to be used for the final copy, choose the ____Printer Setup____ command and click Printer.
____File, Print____

MATCHING

Find the icon on the right that matches the description on the left. Write the appropriate letter in the blank provided at the left margin.

_L_ **10.** Underline

_H_ **11.** New

_F_ **12.** Bold

_K_ **13** Save

_A_ **14.** Undo

_J_ **15.** Italic

_N_ **16.** Center

_E_ **17.** Print

_G_ _X_ **18.** Document
      Window Control
      Menu Box

_b_ **19.** Show/Hide

_c_ **20.** OVERTYPE

a. ⟨icon⟩

b. ¶

c. OVR

d. Ⓦ

e. ⟨printer icon⟩

f. **B**

g. Ⓙ - ▭

h. ▢   Start up Dialog

i. ▲

j. *I*

k. ⟨save icon⟩

l. U

m. ▼

REFERENCE QUESTIONS

Referring to the *Microsoft Word User's Guide,* write the answers to the following questions in the space provided.

1. If you want to be prompted for summary information when you first save a document, how can you turn on this option?

_____

_____

_____

2. What two options does Word provide to help you recover work if there is a power failure or other problem? "Undo"?

_____

_____

_____

SELECTING AND EDITING TEXT

OBJECTIVES
Upon completion of this chapter, you will be able to:

- Open (retrieve) previously created documents.

- Save a document with a new name.

- Move around in long or wide documents.

- Select (highlight) text.

- Edit selected text.

- Undo or redo edits.

Preparation

1. For the rest of this text you will be using two sets of files: *Data Disk* files (files prepared for this text) and your Student Disk. If you are using floppy disks, you should use two separate disks (there is not enough room on the Data Disk for all your work). If you are using the hard drive, you should use two different directories, one for accessing the data files and one for storing your work so you can back up just your own files at the end of each session. You may find it useful to make a subdirectory on your disks for each chapter in this text (for example, *a:\chap02* or *c:\student\chap02*).

2. If you are not using the hard drive to access the Data Disk files prepared for this text, insert your Data Disk in the appropriate floppy drive. If you are using the hard drive, the files IMMUNE.DOC, CALENDAR.DOC, NEWEQUIP.DOC, and WELLNESS.DOC should be located in the *c:\datafile* directory or the directory your instructor has designated for accessing Data Disk files.

3. Load Word. If ¶ is not *highlighted,* click it so that the nonprinting symbols will be displayed. Check your printer *selection.* You will not be instructed after this chapter to load Word or check Show/Hide and your printer selection.

4. At the end of each class session, be sure to close Word and Windows properly. If you are using the hard drive to store your completed work, back up your files onto your formatted Student Disk, and erase your files from the directory you used on the hard drive. (Do not erase the Data Disk files unless your instructor tells you to do so.)

Opening Files and Saving with a New Name

To prevent accidental changes to your Data Disk files, you will open Data Disk files and save them with new filenames.

EXERCISE

2.1

Opening Previously Saved Files and Saving with a New Name

● ●

1. Open (*retrieve*) a previously saved file:

   a. Click the Open icon on the Standard Toolbar. The Open dialog box appears (see Figure 2.1).

   b. Change to the drive and directory in which the Data Disk files prepared for this text are stored.

HINT: *To change drives, click the underlined arrow for the Drives box; then click the desired drive letter. To change directories, double-click the*

FIGURE 2.1
File Open Dialog Box

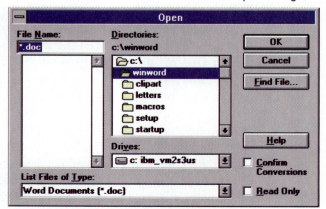

*drive letter in the Directories box; then dou-
ble-click the desired directory. If necessary,
double-click a subdirectory.*

c. Do one of the following to select and load
the file **immune.doc**:

■ Click the down arrow on the vertical *scroll
bar* in the File Name list box to *scroll*
through the list of filenames until you see
immune.doc. Double-click the filename
immune.doc (or click the filename once
and click OK).

■ Click in the File Name box and delete the
existing entry. Key **immune** (Word automatically looks for the .DOC extension, so
you only need to key an extension if it is
not .DOC), and click OK.

2. Save the file with a new name:

a. Choose File Save As. **Do not click the
Save icon** 🖫 **this time.**

In this case, you cannot use the icon. Choosing
File Save or clicking the Save icon automatically
resaves a file with exactly the same path (including

the filename), and the previous version of the file is
deleted. For previously saved files, no dialog box
appears on the screen when you choose File Save
or click the icon. You must use the File Save As
command and complete information in the dialog
box when you want to save a file with a new
name.

b. Place your Student Disk in the appropriate
drive. If necessary, change drives and
directories. If you are using the hard disk,
change to the appropriate drive and
directory for storing your work.

c. Click in the File Name box and delete the
existing entry.

d. Key **chap2-1** as the new filename, and
click OK. The document returns
with the new name on the title bar.

Working with Long or Wide Documents

▮n Chapter 1 you learned how to move the insertion point in short documents. In Exercises 2.2 to 2.5 you will learn some additional techniques for
positioning the insertion point that are especially useful in long or wide documents. Note that until Exercise 2.6, text should not be highlighted. If you accidentally highlight text, position the mouse pointer somewhere in the document
and click so that the text will no longer be highlighted. If you accidentally
delete or change text, immediately click the Undo icon.

Using the Vertical Scroll Bar

The vertical *scroll bar* (Figure 2.2) enables you to move long documents quickly through a window so that you can locate the desired position for the insertion point.

1. Look at the status bar and note the current position of the insertion point. Click the down scroll bar arrow five times. Each click on a scroll bar arrow represents one line.

As text farther down on the page comes into view, the insertion point disappears. Notice, too, that the status bar numbers disappear for "At," "Ln," and "Col." This serves as a reminder. As you *scroll,* the insertion point does not change. When you reach the desired location, you must click the left mouse button to set the new insertion point. (Remember that clicking the left mouse button in a document is known as clicking an insertion point.)

FIGURE 2.2
Vertical Scroll Bar

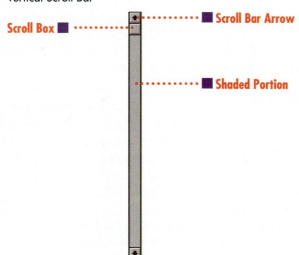

Scroll Box

Scroll Bar Arrow

Shaded Portion

If necessary, you can then use the direction keys to adjust the position of the insertion point.

2. Position the I-beam somewhere in the text in the current window, and click an insertion point. The status bar changes to show your new position.

3. Click the up scroll bar arrow until you see the top of your document again. Then click an insertion point at the beginning of the title.

4. Click the shaded area immediately below the scroll box. Each click on the shaded area represents approximately one window.

5. Click an insertion point somewhere in the text in the current window.

6. *Point* to the scroll box on the vertical scroll bar. Hold down the mouse button and *drag* the scroll box about halfway down the scroll bar (you will see a shadowed outline of the scroll box as you drag). Then release the mouse button.

The scroll box can be dragged to any location in the document (for example: top, bottom, a quarter of the way down, halfway down).

7. Click an insertion point somewhere in the text in the current window.

8. Drag the scroll box to the top of the scroll bar, and click an insertion point at the beginning of the title.

EXERCISE 2.3

Using the Horizontal Scroll Bar

FIGURE 2.3
Horizontal Scroll Bar

Shaded Portion

Scroll Bar Arrow

Scroll Box

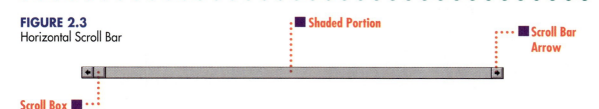

Depending on your monitor, window size, and the selected printer, the margins used in a document may cause some lines to be wider than the screen width. The horizontal scroll bar (Figure 2.3) enables you to scroll across a page. Once you have scrolled, you can click an insertion point at the desired location for editing or viewing.

1. Click an insertion point at the beginning of the second line of the second paragraph.

Notice that on the *ruler* (Figure 2.4), the left margin of your document is lined up with the zero position (the number 0 is not displayed). Notice also the column number on the status bar.

2. Click the right scroll bar arrow on the horizontal scroll bar three times.

The document scrolls a short distance across the window. The insertion point does not change, but the ruler shifts slightly to show that you are now farther across the page.

3. Click a new insertion point somewhere in the displayed text. Notice the new column number on the status bar.

4. Drag the scroll box approximately halfway across the horizontal scroll bar.

It is possible that no text will show because your document is not wide enough, but the ruler shifts (or disappears, if you scroll far enough) to show that you are farther across the page. Remember, though, that the insertion point does not move unless you click an insertion point (notice that the column number has not changed).

5. Click the light gray shaded area immediately to the right of the horizontal scroll box.

Clicking the shaded area scrolls approximately one window to the right. Again, however, the column number does not change because you have not clicked an insertion point.

6. Scroll back to the left edge of your document. Then click an insertion point at the beginning of the title (scroll up if necessary).

FIGURE 2.4
Ruler

EXERCISE 2.4

Using the Go To and Go Back Features

"EDIT"

1. Go to page 3:

   a. Double-click the page number on the status bar (the mouse shortcut for the Edit Go To command). The dialog box shown in Figure 2.5 appears.

   b. If necessary, click Page in the Go to What list box.

   c. Key **3** in the Enter Page Number text box; then click Go To. *OK*

FIGURE 2.5
Edit Go To Dialog Box

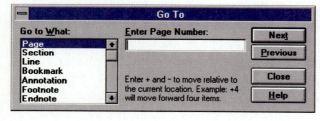

> **TIP**
>
> **F5** is another shortcut for the Edit Go To command.

   d. Click [**Close**]. The insertion point is now at the top of page 3, and the status bar shows your new position.

Mine doesn't

2. Press the Go Back key (**Shift** + **F5**).

   Each time you press **Shift** + **F5**, you go back one position. Word can remember up to three previous locations for the insertion point. The insertion point is now at the top of page 1 again (your position before going to page 3).

EXERCISE 2.5

Changing the Screen View Size

1. Choose View Full Screen.

As shown in Figure 2.6, all screen elements (menu bar, Toolbars, and so forth) disappear, except for your text and a single icon. This allows you to see more of your document, although you still cannot see the full page width very well because this is a wide document.

2. Click a new insertion point somewhere in your document.

FIGURE 2.6
Full Screen Display

STRENGTHENING·YOUR·IMMUNE·SYSTEM¶

¶

→   There·are·many·reasons·why·you·should·eat·well·and·exercise·regularly,·but·did·you·
know·that·improving·your·immune·system·was·one·of·them?··Recent·studies·indicate·that·regular·
exercise,·a·healthy·diet,·and·reduced·emotional·stress·also·help·toughen·the·immune·system·for·
people·of·all·ages.¶

→   As·people·age,·their·immune·systems·weaken·and·become·less·effective·in·protecting·the·
body·against·bacteria·and·viruses.··As·a·result,·older·people·are·more·susceptive·to·getting·
infections·and·infectious·diseases.¶

→   There·is·one·advantage·that·age·has·for·the·immune·system.··One·of·the·functions·of·the·
immune·system·is·to·maintain·a·record·of·various·bacteria·or·viruses·that·the·body·encounters.··
When·the·bacteria·or·virus·enters·the·body·a·second·time,·the·immune·system·can·recognize·it·
and·begin·attacking·it·immediately.··This·is·why·vaccinations·work.··For·example,·w[Full]·
immune·system·encounters·a·vaccine·for·a·polio·virus,·it·remembers·the·virus·so·that····fight·
it·immediately·if·it·is·ever·encountered·again.¶

3. Click the Full Screen icon 🔲. All screen elements return. Notice that the insertion point is at the new position.

4. Locate the *Zoom Control* box on the Standard Toolbar (it currently shows 100 percent). Click the underlined down arrow next to the Zoom Control box.

A shortcut menu (Figure 2.7) opens with the most common screen view sizes. (For custom screen view sizes, you must either key a measurement in the Zoom Control box or choose the View Zoom command.)

5. Click Page Width.

Your screen automatically adjusts to the size necessary to see the full width of the page (92 percent in this case). This view change makes it easier to move the insertion point to the correct location for editing or viewing.

6. Click a new insertion point somewhere in your document.

7. Open the Zoom Control shortcut menu again and change back to 100 percent. Notice that the insertion point is at the new location.

8. Click an insertion point at the beginning of the title (scroll if necessary).

FIGURE 2.7
Zoom Control Menu

Selecting and Editing Text

Selecting text is also known as *highlighting* blocks of text. A block of text can be a single character, several characters, a word, a phrase, a sentence, one or more paragraphs, or even the entire document. Once you *select* text, you can replace it, delete it, format it, move it, copy it, and so on. If you accidentally select the wrong text in the following exercises, click an insertion point somewhere so no text will be highlighted. If you make an accidental change as you select text (other than saving, which cannot be undone), click ⌐↶⊡ immediately after you complete the action.

EXERCISE

Selecting Blocks of Text by Dragging the Mouse

Exercises 2.7 to 2.9 present shortcuts for selecting text with the mouse. If you cannot remember a shortcut, drag across the desired text as explained in the following steps.

1. Move the I-beam mouse pointer until it is at the beginning of the first paragraph, following the tab symbol.

2. Hold down the mouse button and drag through the space after "but" in the same sentence; then release the mouse button. The phrase is now selected, as shown in Figure 2.8.

3. Press (**Delete**). The selected phrase is deleted.

4. The phrase should actually not be deleted. Click the *Undo* icon on the Standard Toolbar

⌐↶⊡. The phrase is restored and is still highlighted.

5. You change your mind and decide to keep your edit. Click the *Redo* icon on the Standard Toolbar ⌐↶⊡. The phrase is deleted again.

6. Bring back the phrase again: click ⌐↶⊡ one more time.

7. Click an insertion point somewhere in your document, or simply press a direction key on your keyboard. The phrase is now *deselected*.

8. Drag across the phrase "people of all ages" (do not include the period) at the end of the first paragraph, and press (**Delete**). Select and delete the word "for" (but not the period).

FIGURE 2.8
Selected Phrase

¶

→ There·are·many·reasons·why·you·should·eat·well·and·exercise·regularly,·but·did·you·

The last sentence now ends ". . . the immune system."

9. Save your change.

HINT: *Click 💾 because you do not need to give the document a new name again.*

EXERCISE

Selecting Blocks of Text with the Click-(Shift)-Click Method

1. Select a phrase:

a. Scroll left, then down to the fourth paragraph. Click an insertion point at the beginning of the phrase that begins: "even though the strength . . ."

The insertion point marks where you want the selection to begin. No text should be selected yet.

b. Without holding down the mouse button, move the mouse until the I-beam is just before the word "the" at the end of the line.

age[the·

c. Hold down (Shift), and click. Release the mouse button, then (Shift).

The phrase "even though the strength of the immune system declines with age," is now selected. (If it is not, click an insertion point again at the beginning of the phrase, and (Shift)-click at the end.)

Click-(Shift)-click is especially useful in long documents. You can click, scroll down with the down scroll bar arrow as far as necessary, and (Shift)-click to end your selection.

2. Add the bold and underline formats to the selected text.

HINT: *Click 🅱, then click 🅤.*

The phrase would look better with no formats. Clicking the Undo icon ↶⬍ would allow you to undo only the last format you applied. The Undo feature, however, has an attached list that allows for multiple undos.

Practice on theirs

3. Undo both the underline and the bold formats at the same time:

a. Click the underlined arrow next to the Undo icon.

A list box similar to the one shown in Figure 2.9 opens. It shows actions that can be undone, with the most recent action you have performed (adding the underline format) listed first. You can drag down the Undo list as far as desired, but you must start at the top of the list and cannot skip any

FIGURE 2.9
Undo List Box

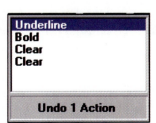

items between the top of the list and where you want to stop undoing.

b. Drag down to highlight Underline and Bold (not Clear). When you see Undo 2 Actions, release the mouse button. The bold and underline formats are removed.

You want to keep the formats after all. Clicking the Redo icon  would allow you to restore only one undone action. The Redo feature, however, also has an attached list that allows for multiple redos.

4. Redo to restore both formats:

a. Click the underlined arrow next to the Redo icon.

A list box similar to the one shown in Figure 2.10 opens, showing actions you have undone that can be redone. The most recent action that was

FIGURE 2.10
Redo List Box

undone (Bold, in this case) is listed first. Again, you can drag down the list as far as desired, but you must start at the top of the list, and you cannot skip any items.

b. Drag down to highlight Bold and Underline. When you see Redo 2 Actions, release the mouse button. The formats are restored.

5. Use the Undo list box to undo the Underline and Bold formats (not the Clear) one more time; then click an insertion point to deselect all text.

EXERCISE

2.8 Selecting Words, Sentences, and Paragraphs with the Mouse

1. Scroll up, position the I-beam anywhere on the word "toughen" in the second sentence of the first paragraph, and double-click. The word is selected.

2. Key **strengthen**.

When you select text, it is not necessary to press ⟨Delete⟩ before you key replacement text. As soon as you begin keying new text, the old text is automatically deleted. It is only necessary to press

hot of mine

⟨Delete⟩ if you want to erase text without replacing it with new text.

IMPORTANT: Be cautious when text is selected. Pressing a key can delete the selection. If you accidentally erase text, be sure to click  immediately.

3. Position the I-beam anywhere on the first sentence of the second paragraph. Hold down

FIGURE 2.11
Selected Sentence

> → As·people·age,·their·immune·systems·weaken·and·become·less·effective·in·protecting·t body·against·bacteria·and·viruses.··As·a·result,·older·people·are·more·susceptive·to·getting·

(Ctrl) and click. Release the mouse button, then (Ctrl). The sentence is selected, as shown in Figure 2.11.

not mine
4. Double-click ⌷OVR⌷ in the status bar to turn on OVERTYPE (⌷OVR⌷ is then highlighted).

5. Key the following text: **Immune systems weaken**.

When text is selected and you turn on OVERTYPE to key new text, rather than being pushed to the right, the selected text is immediately deleted, and the following text is replaced as you key. The result is shown in Figure 2.12. When text is selected, be sure you do not turn on OVERTYPE.

FIGURE 2.12
Sentence Overtyped in Error

Immune·systems·weaken|ople·are·

Each character you overtyped is considered an action. To undo, you must use the list box.

6. Undo the overtyping:

a. Click the underlined down arrow next to ⌷∧⌷⌷⬍⌷.

b. Drag down the list until all the "Typing" actions (approximately 21) with single letters or spaces are highlighted (do not highlight Typing "strengthen" or Clear).

c. Release the mouse button. The original sentence should be restored and still highlighted.

7. Click an insertion point to deselect the sentence, then double-click ⌷OVR⌷ to turn off OVERTYPE (⌷OVR⌷ is no longer highlighted).

8. Scroll down to the paragraph on the second page that begins "Research shows that lifestyle . . ."

not mine
9. Position the I-beam anywhere in the paragraph, and *triple-click*. The paragraph is selected.

10. Press (Delete) to delete the paragraph; then save your work.

E X E R C I S E

Selecting Text with the Mouse Using the Selection Bar

Practice on their machine

The *selection bar* (Figure 2.13) is an invisible area just to the left of the left margin.

1. Scroll to the top of the document and click an insertion point.

FIGURE 2.13
The Selection Bar

Selection ■ · · · · · ↗
Bar Arrow

→ There·∶
know·that·imp
exercise,·a·hea
→ As·peo
body·against·b
infections·and·

The dotted line drawn on this illustration does not appear on your screen. This dotted line indicates the invisible area of the selection bar.

2. Select a line:

a. Move the I-beam to the left of the first line of the first paragraph until you see the arrowhead pointer pointing upward and toward the right, as shown in Figure 2.13.

b. Click once. The first line is selected.

3. Click an insertion point to deselect this text.

4. Scroll down to the paragraph on the third page that begins "Doctors and hospitals . . . ."

5. Select a paragraph:

a. Move the I-beam to the selection bar anywhere next to the paragraph.

b. When you see the arrowhead pointer, double-click. The paragraph is selected.

6. Press (Delete) to delete the paragraph.

Note that in the future you can select multiple lines or paragraphs by simply dragging down the selection bar as far as needed.

7. Select the entire document:

a. Move the I-beam to the selection bar.

b. When you see the arrowhead pointer, triple-click. The entire document is highlighted. ("At," "Ln," and "Col" in the status bar will be blank.)

8. Change the document to single spacing.

HINT: *Press* (Ctrl) + (1).

9. Undo this change so that the document is again double-spaced.

10. Click an insertion point to deselect all text; then save your document.

11. Print the document.

HINT: *Click the Print icon* 🖨 .

12. Clear the screen.

HINT: *Double-click the document Control menu box* ⊟ .

COMPUTER ACTIVITIES

ACTIVITY 1

1. Open the Data Disk file **calendar.doc**. Save the file on your Student Disk or in the appropriate student directory on the hard drive with the new name **act2-1**.

2. Add emphasis by selecting text and formatting it according to the following instructions. Then save and print the document and clear the screen.

   a. Format the title bold.

   b. Format the three different days and dates bold and underline. (You will need to scroll to the third day and date.)

   c. Format the words "Location:" and "Program:" for each of the three dates bold.

HINT: *If you double-click, the colon is not included, so drag across the text.*

   d. Format the program names "Wellness of Body and Mind," "Increase Your Personal Power," and "Smart Moves for Fitness" italic. (Do not italicize the semicolons.)

ACTIVITY 2

1. Open the Data Disk file **wellness.doc**. Save the file in the appropriate location with the new name **act2-2**.

2. Make the following changes to the document in order. Then save and print the document and clear the screen.

   a. In the first sentence of the fifth paragraph (beginning "To implement . . ."), change "programs" to "program."

   b. In the third sentence of the first paragraph, change "colleagues" to "co-workers."

   c. Format the title of the document bold.

   d. In the second sentence of the third paragraph (beginning "Wellness programs offer . . ."), correct "excercise."

   e. In the sixth paragraph, (beginning "Although wellness programs. . ."), italicize the phrase "two or three times."

   f. In the same paragraph, change "group life" to "group-life."

TIP

Remember that you can use the Zoom Control box Page Width setting for wide documents.

g. In the fourth sentence of the first paragraph, italicize "as high as 10 percent of all payroll costs." (Be sure not to italicize the period.)

h. In the same paragraph, change "50 percent" to "60 percent."

i. In the third paragraph (beginning "Wellness programs ..."), change "drug and alcohol addiction" to "substance abuse."

HINT: *If the phrase is split between two lines, use click-(Shift)-click to select it.*) *not in min*

j. Delete the last paragraph of the document.

k. In the fourth sentence of the first paragraph, correct "businesess."

ACTIVITY 3

1. Open the Data Disk file **newequip.doc**. Save the file in the appropriate location with the new name **act2-3**.

2. Add the bold format to "MEMORANDUM," "TO:," "FROM:," "DATE:," and "SUBJECT:." (Note that formatted text may take more space. If the date shifts to the right, delete a tab.)

3. Change "August 28" to "September 4" on the dateline. Be sure to substitute the current year for -- whenever it is used in a document in this text.

4. Make the other changes shown in Figure 2.14 on page 55.

5. Add two returns at the bottom of the memo, and key your initials on the next-to-last line.

6. Save the changes, print one copy, and clear the screen.

FIGURE 2.14
Edits to NEWEQUIP.DOC

MEMORANDUM *bold*

bold

TO: All Fitness Trainers

FROM: Pat Swearingen, Manager

DATE: ~~August 28, 19--~~ *September 4*

SUBJECT: ~~Installation~~ *Fitness* New Equipment

For many months we have anticipated the opening of the new *Family*
fitness facility in Columbus, and we are now counting down
the days for our grand opening on October 1. Today we
received confirmation that the fitness equipment for the
facility will be delivered on September 11. All equipment
will be assembled and installed as quickly as possible ~~next~~ *that*
week ~~and then~~ *then* we will test and inspect each piece of
equipment to make sure it is functioning *properly and* safely.

Please review the equipment list that was distributed at our
last *staff* meeting and let me know immediately if you know of any
equipment needs that are not included in the list. If
necessary, we can still purchase needed equipment, but I
must receive your requests for additional equipment no later
than September 7. *in order to ensure delivery by October 1*

Initials

CREATE YOUR OWN ••••••••••••

The following is a list of words that are frequently misused. To illustrate the correct use of each word, write a sentence for each of the words listed. If you are not sure about the proper use of a word, refer to a dictionary or an office reference manual for clarification. When you finish, select each word you defined and add the bold format. Proofread and make any necessary changes, print one copy, and clear the screen. Keep this list for your future reference.

EXAMPLE: advice/advise
I received some sound advice from my counselor.
We advise our second-year students to participate in a work/study program.

accept/except   farther/further
alright/all right   good/well
can/may   it's/its
sometime/some time   passed/past
lay/lie   principal/principle

REVIEW EXERCISES

TRUE / FALSE

Each of the following statements is either true or false. Indicate your answer on the left by circling T if the statement is true or F if the statement is false.

T **F** 1. To save a file with a new name, choose the File Save command. *SAVE AS*

T **F** 2. An invisible area just to the left of the left margin that is used for selecting text with the mouse is called the mouse bar. *Selection BAR*

T F 3. Once text has been selected, it can be formatted, deleted, or replaced.

T **F** 4. Word can remember up to five *3* previous locations of the insertion point.

T F 5. Highlighting blocks of text is called selecting.

T F 6. A single selected character is a block of text.

T F 7. When you begin keying text at the beginning of a selected block of text, the old text is automatically deleted, and the new text is inserted.

T F 8. Scrolling with the mouse does not move the insertion point. *Have to click to move*

T **F** 9. To retrieve a file, select the desired file in the Retrieve dialog box. *"Open File"*

T F 10. To hide all screen elements except your text and a single icon, choose View Full Screen.

T F 11. You can change the screen view to any size with the Zoom Control shortcut menu.

T **F** 12. You can undo or redo only a single action. *on pallet can*

MATCHING

Find the key(s) or icon on the right that matches the description on the left. Write the appropriate letter in the blank provided at the left margin.

_I_ **13.** Open

_J_ **14.** Redo

_E_ **15.** Full Screen

_b_ **16.** Document Window Control menu box

_F_ **17.** Print

_G_ **18.** Undo

_C_ **19.** Go Back

_H_ **20.** Save

a. ⬍

b. ⬜

c. (Shift) + (F5) — go Back

d. (F5)

e. ▣

f. 🖨

g. ↺⬇

h. 💾

i. 📂

j. ↻⬇

REFERENCE QUESTIONS

Referring to the _Microsoft Word User's Guide,_ write the answers to the following questions in the space provided.

1. Assume that you are opening a document that you worked with in your last class session. How can you tell Word to resume work with the insertion point moved to the location in the document where it was when you closed the document?

_____

_____

_____

2. Name one way to reopen a document quickly without using the Open dialog box.

The Icon of 🖫 _____

_____

_____

MOVING AND COPYING TEXT

CHAPTER

3

OBJECTIVES
Upon completion of this chapter, you will be able to:

- Move text using the Toolbar icons and the Windows Clipboard.

- Drag text to move it to a new location.

- Copy text using the Toolbar icons and the Windows Clipboard.

- Drag text to copy it to another location.

- Use the Edit Repeat feature to repeat the copy process.

- Use the Undo feature to undo the move and copy processes.

Preparation

1. To complete the chapter activities, you will need to access the Data Disk files WELCOME.DOC, FORM.DOC, and SCHEDULE.DOC and your Student Disk file CHAP2-1.DOC.

2. Remember to save frequently as you work. You may not be reminded to save until all work is completed for a file.

3. If you make mistakes as you work with the exercises in the chapter, remember to click ⟲⏬ immediately after completing the action.

4. At the end of each class session, be sure to close Word and Windows properly. If you are using the hard drive to store your completed work, back up your files onto your formatted Student Disk, and erase your files from the directory you used for storing your files on the hard drive. (Do not erase the Data Disk files unless your instructor tells you to do so.)

Moving Text Within a Document

Text can be moved from one location to another in a document using icons on the Standard Toolbar plus the Windows *Clipboard* or by dragging the text.

EXERCISE 3.1

Moving Text with the Toolbar Icons and the Clipboard

In Exercises 3.1 and 3.3, you will use the Toolbar and the Windows Clipboard. The Windows Clipboard is a temporary storage area for text that you want to move (cut) or copy and then paste in another location. Be cautious about cutting or copying to the Clipboard. Pasting the contents of the Clipboard does not delete the contents of the Clipboard. Each time you store something new in the Windows Clipboard, however, the item stored there previously is automatically deleted. Clicking ⌐ ⊡ immediately after cutting or copying to the Clipboard restores the original contents of the Clipboard.

1. Key the paragraphs shown in Figure 3.1 as follows:

   a. Click the underlined arrow next to the Font Size box on the Formatting Toolbar and click 12.

   b. Click ≣ and **B**, press **Caps Lock**, and then key the title.

   c. Click **B** and press **Caps Lock**. Then press **Enter** four times and click ≣.

   d. Key the three paragraphs using word wrap. Correct your errors as you key. Press **Tab** at the beginning of each paragraph. Press **Enter** twice between paragraphs and once after the last paragraph.

   e. Proofread the document and make any necessary corrections.

   f. Save the document in the appropriate location for Student Disk files as **chap3-1**.

2. Move text from the document to the Clipboard:

   a. Position the mouse pointer in the selection bar next to the tab preceding the first paragraph.

   b. Drag down the selection bar to select the first paragraph, including the preceding tab and the two paragraph marks following the paragraph. Figure 3.2 illustrates your selection.

   c. Click the Cut icon on the Standard Toolbar ✂. The text is removed from the screen and stored in the Windows Clipboard.

FIGURE 3.1
Text for CHAP3-1.DOC

FITNESS, NUTRITION, AND WELLNESS

In addition to strenuous exercise, America's fitness obsession focused on eating well and reducing body fat. During the '80s, everybody talked about fitness. The fitness craze brought us aerobic and step workouts, dance exercise, and fitness videos. In the '90s, people are still very concerned about fitness and nutrition, but now they are also talking about wellness.

Initially this often meant avoiding cholesterol and fatty foods and sometimes going on fad diets to achieve thin bodies. Eventually, though, the quest for proper nutrition and fitness led to eating smart.

Wellness is the fitness of both the body and the mind. It is the interaction of mental, emotional, and physical states. Numerous books and articles were published on this topic.

3. Although it is not necessary to open the Clipboard each time you store items in it, you may want to check the Clipboard before transferring its contents to a new location as follows:

   a. Press (Alt) + (Tab) to switch to the Windows Program Manager. (After switching, release (Tab) and then (Alt).)

   b. If necessary, click Window in the menu bar, and click Main to activate the window.

FIGURE 3.2
Selected Text and Nonprinting Characters to be Moved

¶
¶
→ In·addition·to·strenuous·exercise,·America's·fitness·obsession·focused·on·eating·well·and·reducing·body·fat.··During·the·'80s,·everybody·talked·about·fitness.··The·fitness·craze·brought·us·aerobic·and·step·workouts,·dance·exercise,·and·fitness·videos.··In·the·'90s,·people·are·still·very·concerned·about·fitness·and·nutrition,·but·now·they·are·also·talking·about·wellness.¶
¶

FIGURE 3.3
Viewing the Clipboard Contents

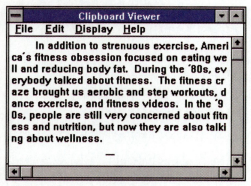

c. Double-click the Clipboard Viewer icon 📖. The paragraph you cut is now shown in the Clipboard (Figure 3.3).

d. Click the Maximize icon ▲ in the Clipboard window to see more of the contents of the Clipboard.

e. Close the Clipboard application window.

HINT: *Double-click* ⊟.

f. Press **Alt** + **Tab** to switch back to Word. (After switching, release **Tab** and then **Alt**.)

4. Paste (transfer) the contents of the Clipboard back into your document:

a. Click an insertion point at the left margin (preceding the tab symbol) of the second

paragraph (beginning "Wellness is the fitness …").

b. Click the Paste icon on the Standard Toolbar 🗒. The paragraph that begins "In addition to …" is now the second paragraph, as shown in Figure 3.4.

5. Undo both the cut and the paste as follows:

a. Click the underlined down arrow next to the Undo icon ↶↓.

Notice that the top of the list box contains two items, Paste (the most recent action) and Cut. (Your list box may show different items below Paste and Cut.)

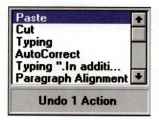

b. Drag to select both Paste and Cut.

When you release the mouse button, the paragraph beginning "In addition to …" is again the first paragraph (it is still highlighted).

6. Select the last sentence in the first paragraph (it begins: "In the '90s …").

FIGURE 3.4
Paragraph Pasted to New Location

→ Initially·this·often·meant·avoiding·cholesterol·and·fatty·foods·and·sometimes·going·on·fad·diets·to·achieve·thin·bodies.··Eventually,·though,·the·quest·for·proper·nutrition·and·fitness·led·to·eating·smart.¶   --
¶
Pasted Paragraph ■ → In·addition·to·strenuous·exercise,·America's·fitness·obsession·focused·on·eating·well·and·reducing·body·fat.··During·the·'80s,·everybody·talked·about·fitness.··The·fitness·craze·brought·us·aerobic·and·step·workouts,·dance·exercise,·and·fitness·videos.··In·the·'90s,·people·are·still·very·concerned·about·fitness·and·nutrition,·but·now·they·are·also·talking·about·wellness.¶
¶
→ Wellness·is·the·fitness·of·both·the·body·and·the·mind.··It·is·the·interaction·of

7. Cut the sentence and paste it immediately after the tab symbol at the beginning of the third paragraph (just before "Wellness is the fitness …").

8. Space twice to adjust the spacing between the two sentences. The third paragraph should now begin as in Figure 3.5.

9. Select the first sentence ("In addition to …"). Do not include the tab symbol in your selection. Your selection should look like that in Figure 3.6.

10. Cut the sentence and paste it following the tab symbol for the third paragraph.

11. You pasted to the wrong location. Open the Undo list box and drag to select both Paste and Cut. The sentence returns to its original location at the top of the document.

12. Cut the sentence again and paste it following the tab symbol for the second paragraph. The second paragraph should now look like Figure 3.7.

FIGURE 3.5
Sentence Pasted to New Location

→ In·the·'90s,·people·are·still·very·concerned·about·fitness·and·nutrition,·but·now· they·are·also·talking·about·wellness.·Wellness·is·the·fitness·of·both·the·body·and·the· mind.··It·is·the·interaction·of·mental,·emotional,·and·physical·states.··Numerous·books· and·articles·were·published·on·this·topic.¶

FIGURE 3.6
Selected Sentence without Tab Character

→ In·addition·to·strenuous·exercise,·America's·fitness·obsession·focused·on·eating· well·and·reducing·body·fat.·During·the·'80s,·everybody·talked·about·fitness.··The·fitness·
¶

FIGURE 3.7
Completed Second Paragraph

→ In·addition·to·strenuous·exercise,·America's·fitness·obsession·focused·on·eating· well·and·reducing·body·fat.·Initially·this·often·meant·avoiding·cholesterol·and·fatty·foods· and·sometimes·going·on·fad·diets·to·achieve·thin·bodies.··Eventually,·though,·the·quest· for·proper·nutrition·and·fitness·led·to·eating·smart.¶
¶

EXERCISE 3.2

Dragging Text to a New Location

1. Move the second paragraph:

a. Select the second paragraph (beginning "In addition to …").

Include the paragraph mark above the second paragraph and the paragraph mark at the end of the second paragraph in the selection. Do not include the paragraph mark below the second paragraph. Your selection should look like that in Figure 3.8.

b. Point to the selection and hold down the left mouse button.

FIGURE 3.8
Selected Paragraph to Be Dragged

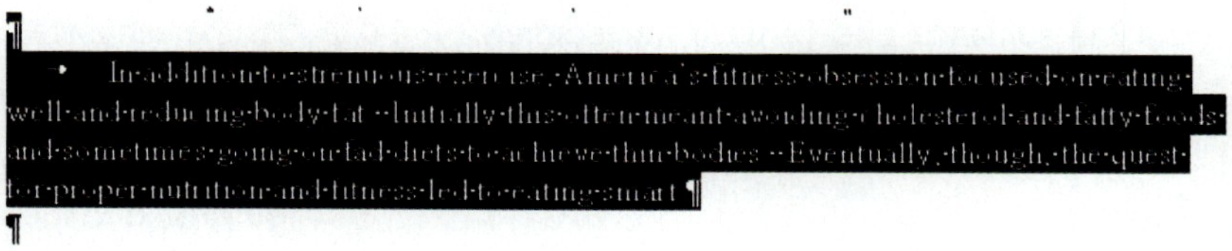

In addition to strenuous exercise, America's fitness obsession focused on eating well and keeping body fat minimal; this often meant avoiding cholesterol and fatty foods and sometimes going overboard in efforts to have thin bodies. Eventually, though, the quest for proper nutrition and fitness led to creating smart

An arrowhead, a small dotted box, and a dotted insertion point will be displayed.

   c. Drag the dotted insertion point to the last paragraph mark in the document.

The selected paragraph is now the final paragraph in the document. This procedure is called *drag and drop.*

2. Click ⌐⏷⏷ (you do not need to open the list) to undo this move.

3. Select the last sentence in the document. (Include the period but do not include the preceding spaces or the following paragraph mark.) Drag-and-drop the sentence as the last sentence in the first paragraph.

4. Click an insertion point at the beginning of the sentence to deselect the text; then space once.

5. Save the changes to your document, print one copy, and clear the screen.

HINT: *Click* 🖫 *, click* 🖶 *, then double-click* Ⓙ *.*

Copying Text Within a Document

Copying text involves the same steps as moving text, except that the selected text remains in its original location and a copy of the selected text is placed in the new location. After inserting a copy, you can repeat the copy as many times as you want until another command is used.

EXERCISE

3.3

Copying Text Using the Windows Clipboard

● ●

1. Key the paragraphs shown in Figure 3.9 as follows:

   a. Click 🗋.

b. Click the underlined arrow next to the Font Size box on the Formatting Toolbar, and click 12.

c. Key a centered title in all capital letters with the bold format. Then press **Caps Lock** and click **B** to turn off the formats.

d. Press **Enter** four times and change to left alignment.

e. Key the instruction; then press **Enter** twice.

f. Key the questions (plus the responses for Questions 1 and 4). You will need to press **Tab** after each number and before each response.

FIGURE 3.9
Handwritten Text for CHAP3-2.DOC

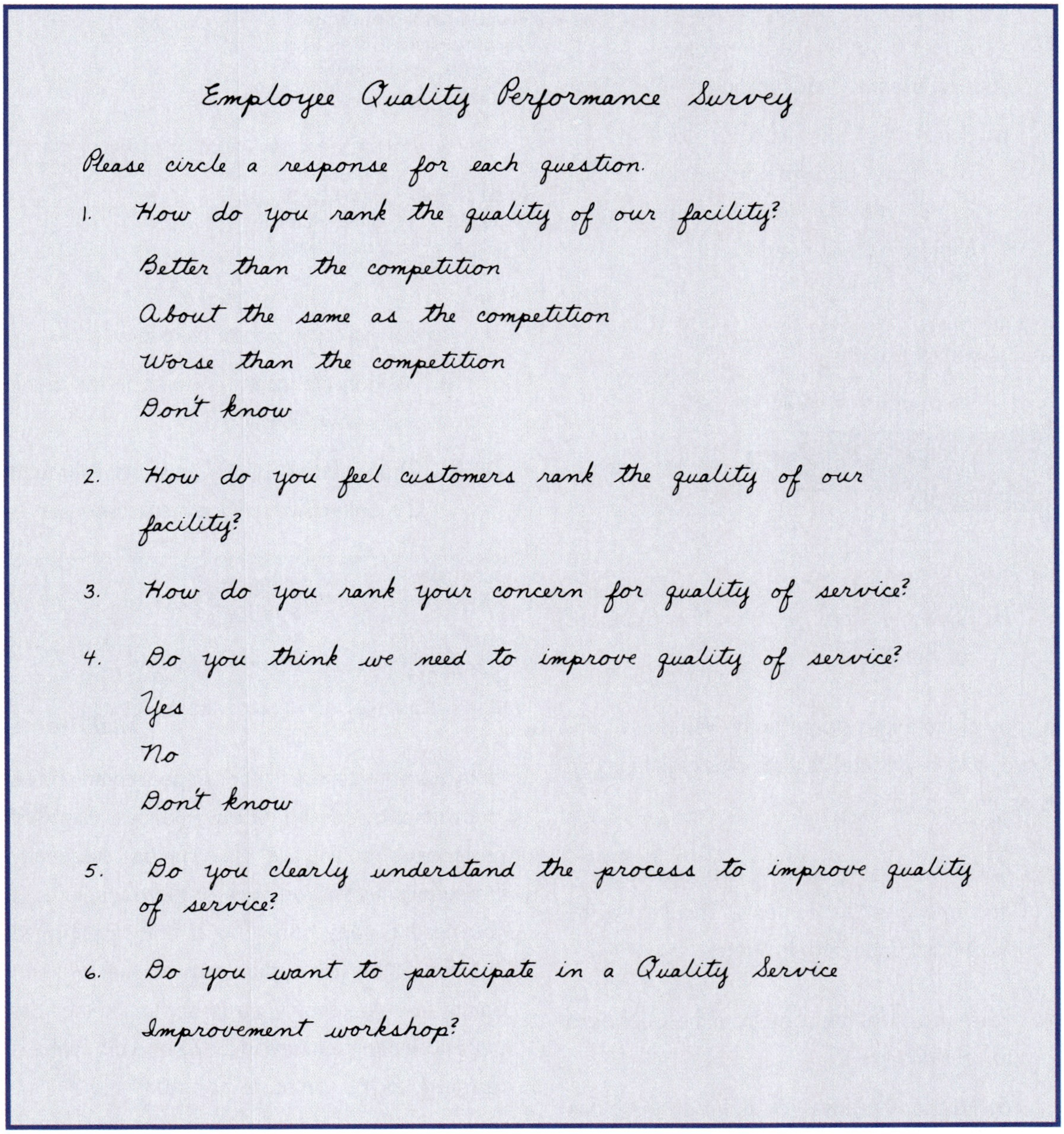

Employee Quality Performance Survey

Please circle a response for each question.

1. How do you rank the quality of our facility?
   Better than the competition
   About the same as the competition
   Worse than the competition
   Don't know

2. How do you feel customers rank the quality of our facility?

3. How do you rank your concern for quality of service?

4. Do you think we need to improve quality of service?
   Yes
   No
   Don't know

5. Do you clearly understand the process to improve quality of service?

6. Do you want to participate in a Quality Service Improvement workshop?

g. Be sure to end the document with a blank line.

h. Proofread the document and make any necessary corrections.

i. Save the document in the appropriate location for student files as **chap3-2**.

2. Copy text to the Clipboard as follows (remember as you do these steps that if you make a mistake, you can use the Undo function):

a. Select the four choices for Question 1 plus the paragraph mark directly above the choices. (See Figure 3.10.)

FIGURE 3.10
Text Selected for Copying

b. Click the Copy icon on the Standard Toolbar.

A copy of the text is stored in the Windows Clipboard, and the selected text remains highlighted in its original position.

3. If you want to, open the Clipboard application and view its contents. Then close the Clipboard and return to Word.

4. Paste (transfer) the copy from the Clipboard to your document:

a. Position the insertion point on the blank line below Question 2. No text should be selected now.

b. Click the Paste icon on the Standard Toolbar. You now have two sets of identical responses as shown in Figure 3.11.

FIGURE 3.11
Copied Text

1. → How·do·you·rank·the·quality·of·our·facility?¶
¶
→ Better·than·the·competition¶
→ About·the·same·as·the·competition¶
→ Worse·than·the·competition¶
→ Don't·know¶
¶
2. → How·do·you·feel·customers·rank·the·quality·of·our·facility?¶
¶
→ Better·than·the·competition¶
→ About·the·same·as·the·competition¶
→ Worse·than·the·competition¶
→ Don't·know¶

5. Repeat the copy process as follows:

a. Position the insertion point on the blank line below Question 3.

b. Choose Edit Repeat. Questions 1 through 3 should now have identical responses.

TIP

F4 is a shortcut for Edit Repeat.

Note that you can use the Edit Repeat command as many times as desired for an action you have just performed. You will use this command frequently throughout this text for many of Word's features. If you need a copy and have already performed another action (other than moving the insertion point), you can simply paste again. (Remember that information remains in the Clipboard until it is replaced, so you can paste it over and over.)

EXERCISE

3.4

Dragging to Copy Text to a New Location

1. Drag to copy text as follows:

   a. Scroll down so that Question 4 is toward the top of the screen.

   b. Select the three choices for Question 4 plus the paragraph mark directly above the choices. (See Figure 3.12.)

   c. Position the pointer on the selection and hold down **Ctrl** and the left mouse button.

   The arrowhead, the small dotted box, and the dotted insertion point are displayed.

   d. Without releasing **Ctrl** or the mouse button, drag the dotted insertion point to the blank line below Question 5.

FIGURE 3.12
Selected Text for Which
Copy is to be Dragged

4. → Do·you·think·we·need·to·improve·quality·of·service?¶
¶
   → Yes¶
   → No¶
   → Don't·know¶
¶

   e. Release the mouse button; then release **Ctrl**.

You now have two identical responses. The copy is highlighted. (See Figure 3.13.)

FIGURE 3.13
Text Dragged and Copied

4. → Do·you·think·we·need·to·improve·quality·of·service?¶
¶
   → Yes¶
   → No¶
   → Don't·know¶
5. → Do·you·clearly·understand·the·process·to·improve·quality·of·service?¶
   → Yes¶
   → No¶
   → Don't·know¶
¶

2. With the copy still selected, hold down **Ctrl** and drag another copy of the responses to the blank line below Question 6.

Questions 4 through 6 should now have identical responses.

3. Save the changes, print one copy, and clear the screen.

COMPUTER ACTIVITIES

ACTIVITY 1

1. Open **chap2-1.doc** from your Student Disk, and save it as **act3-1** (remember to use File Save As and not the Save icon).

2. Format the title bold.

3. Move the ninth paragraph (beginning, "Proper nutrition can . . .") to the top of the document (be sure to include the paragraph mark that follows in your selection).

4. Undo the move.

5. Move the paragraph so that it precedes the eighth paragraph (beginning "How the mind . . .").

6. Position the insertion point on the paragraph mark below the title, and press **Enter** to add an additional blank line.

7. Select the phrase "genetic and environmental factors" in the third sentence of the last paragraph.

8. Copy the phrase to the first blank line under the title. It will be a subtitle for the document.

9. Change the subtitle to initial caps except for the word "and." Center and italicize the subtitle.

HINT: Use OVR.

10. Save the changes to your file, print one copy, and clear the screen.

ACTIVITY 2

1. Open the Data Disk file **welcome.doc**. Save the file on your Student Disk or in the appropriate student directory on the hard drive with the new name **act3-2a.**

2. Make the changes indicated in Figure 3.14 on pages 69–71. Be sure to include the paragraph mark below the topic to be moved in your selection. Adjust spacing if necessary.

3. Save and print your letter; then clear the screen.

4. Open the Data Disk file **form.doc**. Save the file with the new name **act3-2b.**

FIGURE 3.14
Edits for ACT3-2.DOC

NATIONAL FAMILY HEALTH AND FITNESS CLUB
6000 Lakeview Plaza Boulevard
Worthington, Ohio 43085-1152

March 2, 19—

Ms. Shelley Azano

Apartment 262

112 Bluewing Court

Columbus, OH 43235-0786

Dear Ms. Azano:

new member

Welcome! You have joined nearly one million *other* members
nationwide. Technological awareness and the highest *fitness*
training standards have made National Family Health and
Fitness Club America's leading health and fitness facility.

Our devotion to promoting lifetime wellness and more than
two decades
~~twenty years~~ of experience enable us to provide you a
comprehensive family fitness facility. National Family
Health and Fitness Club offers you everything you need from
fitness training to cooking classes to family counseling.
We have designed our facility and services to help you meet
all your health and fitness needs. Here are just some of
the services you can take advantage of as a National Family
Health and Fitness Club member.

Continued on next page

move topic to next page

References for New Membership *underline*

Save $~~15~~ 20 off your monthly fee each time you refer a new member to us. Use the enclosed form to let us know about relatives and friends who are interested.

Three Columbus Locations *underline*

We know you have a busy schedule, so we are open from 6 a.m. to 10 p.m. seven days a week. We have three convenient locations: 6000 Lakeview Plaza Boulevard in Worthington, 1180 Wyandot Place in Hillard, and 98 Shannon Drive in Reynoldsburg.

Focus on Fitness Training *underline*

Each facility employs more than 25 *certified* fitness trainers, each ~~very well~~ qualified to appraise your health and fitness levels and recommend appropriate exercise programs. Our fitness trainers are available at all times to answer your questions and assist you with your training needs.

Educational Programs and Workshops *underline*

Over the years we have learned that your needs go beyond exercise. Throughout the year we offer a variety of programs at no extra charge to you. For example, you can enroll in classes for cooking, food labeling, and prenatal *and postnatal* education.

Continued on next page

Nutrition Consultants _____ *underline*

To assist you with weight management, each facility employs a full-time nutrition consultant. These nutrition consultants will counsel you about the relationship of nutrition and fitness, encouraging a healthy lifestyle.

Insert "References for New Membership" topic here

We provide all of this to help you achieve a healthy lifestyle consistent with proper nutrition and fitness. It is our hope that you will take advantage of all the equipment and services available to you. We are confident that National Family Health and Fitness Club can help you shape a lifetime of health. Please let us know if you ever have concerns or suggestions.

Sincerely,

Juanita Crisanti
Director

smn

Enclosure

5. Copy the form to be attached to your letter. Include the first blank line below the dashed line in your selection, and insert the first copy on the second blank line below the dashed line. Repeat the copy process three times for a total of five forms.

6. Save your changes, print one copy, and clear the screen.

ACTIVITY 3

1. Open the Data Disk file **schedule.doc**. Save the file with the new name **act3-3**.

2. Copy the lines for "Date," "Time In," "Trainer," and "Time Out," plus the first three blank lines below them to the ending paragraph mark.

3. If necessary, deselect the copy. For the copy, delete the information that follows "Time In," "Trainer," and "Time Out" (do not delete the date or any tab symbols).

4. Copy the blank set plus the first three blank lines below it three additional times, so that you have a total of five sections for data, with the first completed.

5. Complete the last four sections using the data shown in Figure 3.15. Look at the tabs in the first section to see where data should be keyed; then click an insertion point at each position where data is to be keyed (do not add tabs). Leave 10/10 as the date for all sections.

6. Rearrange the form (move data) so the form is in correct alphabetical order by last name.

7. Save the form, print a copy, and clear the screen.

FIGURE 3.15
Data To Complete ACT3-3.DOC

Trainer: Ogg
Time In: 1 p.m.
Time Out: 10 p.m.

Trainer: Rose
Time In: 10 a.m.
Time Out: 7 p.m.

Trainer: Emi
Time In: 8 a.m.
Time Out: 5 p.m.

Trainer: Jones
Time In: 5 p.m.
Time Out: 10 p.m.

CREATE YOUR OWN • • • • • • • • • • •

1. Key a "To Do" list of all the activities, projects, assignments, responsibilities, etc., that you must carry out tomorrow. Your list might include class assignments, after school practices, personal errands such as buying school supplies or picking up clothes at the cleaners, and social activities. Make your list as complete and as accurate as you can. Save and print this list.

2. Prioritize your list of activities and commitments by selecting and moving text to place the activities in order of importance. The most important activity should be listed first. For example, completing a class assignment that is due the following day may be your top priority tomorrow. The least important activity should be moved to the bottom of the list. For example, it may not be absolutely necessary that you pick up your clothes at the dry cleaners tomorrow.

3. Save your revised list, print a copy, and clear the screen. Use the list to help plan your day.

REVIEW EXERCISES

TRUE / FALSE

Each of the following statements is either true or false. Indicate your answer on the left by circling T if the statement is true or F if the statement is false.

T F **1.** When text is copied, the selected text remains in its original location, and a copy is placed in a new location.

T F **2.** Text that is cut or copied with the Cut or Copy icon is temporarily stored in the Clipboard.

T **F** **3.** You must open the Clipboard before pasting its contents.

T **F** **4.** The contents of the Clipboard are deleted when they are pasted.

T **F** **5.** You cannot use the Undo feature once text has been pasted.

T **F** **6.** You cannot use the Undo feature for text that has been dragged to a new location.

MATCHING

Find the icon on the right that matches the description on the left. Write the appropriate letter in the blank provided at the left margin.

_F_ **7.** Copy

___ **8.** Paste

_C_ **9.** Cut

_b_ _a_ **10.** Undo

a. ⤺ ⬓	**d.** →
b. ⤼ ⬓	**e.** 📂
c. ✂	**f.** 📋

REFERENCE QUESTIONS

Referring to the *Microsoft Word User's Guide,* write the answers to the following questions in the space provided.

1. What can you do if you do not want Word to adjust spaces automatically when you cut and paste text?

    Format, Paragraph, Spacing, #, OK

    _____

    _____

2. If you are pasting from another Word document or from another application, what command can you use to create a link that allows automatic updates to the pasted material?

    _____

    _____

    _____

SPELLING,
GRAMMAR,
THESAURUS

OBJECTIVES
Upon completion of this chapter, you will be able to:

■ Check spelling for individual words or for an entire document.

■ Correct grammatical errors.

■ Use the Thesaurus to find alternate words.

Preparation

1. Each of the three features presented in this chapter, Spelling, Grammar, and Thesaurus is an optional installation to be chosen during Word setup. Your instructor will let you know which sections of this chapter (if any) you will need to skip. Each feature is presented separately, so if you do not have one of them installed, you can still work with the other features presented in the chapter.

2. Remember to proofread your work. Although the spelling checker and the grammar checker are tools that will assist you in correcting errors, they cannot find and correct all errors.

3. To complete the chapter activities, you will need to access the Data Disk files BUILDING.DOC, SURVEY.DOC, REVIEW.DOC, CLASSES.DOC, and CTS.DOC.

4. Remember to save frequently as you work. You will not be reminded to save until all work is completed for a file. If you make mistakes as you work with the exercises in the chapter, remember to click ⟲⬇ immediately after completing the action.

5. At the end of each class session, be sure to close Word and Windows properly. If you are using the hard drive to store your completed work, back up your files onto your formatted Student Disk, and erase your files from the directory you used on the hard drive. (Do not erase the Data Disk files unless your instructor tells you to do so.)

Checking Spelling in a Document

Word has a standard dictionary that you can use to check your spelling. You can check the spelling of one word, of a selected portion of a document, or of the entire document. In addition to spelling errors, Word locates repeated words and capitalization errors. Word allows you to add words to its standard dictionary (CUSTOM.DIC) or to custom dictionaries that you create (see Appendix D). You can also have Word correct misspellings automatically.

E X E R C I S E

Checking the Spelling of Single Words

Each time you load Word and plan to use the spelling checker, you should check the settings in the Spelling category of the Tools Options dialog box. If you or students in other classes have used the spelling checker, these settings may have been changed.

FIGURE 4.1
Spelling Category of the Tools Options Dialog Box

1. In a new document window, choose Tools Options and click the Spelling folder tab.

As shown in Figure 4.1, Always Suggest, From Main Dictionary Only, and CUSTOM.DIC should be turned on (with an *X* in the check box). Words in UPPERCASE and Words with Numbers should be turned off.

```
┌─────────────────────────────────────────────────────────────┐
│ ▬                           Options                           │
│  ┌─────────┬──────────┬──────────────┬──────────────────┐    │
│  │ Revisions │ User Info │ Compatibility │ File Locations │    │
│  ├─────────┼──────────┼──────────────┼──────────────────┤    │
│  │ View    │ General  │ Edit         │ Print            │    │
│  ├─────────┼──────────┼──────────────┼──────────────────┤    │
│  │ Save    │ Spelling │ Grammar      │ AutoFormat       │    │
│  └─────────┴──────────┴──────────────┴──────────────────┘    │
│  ┌─Suggest───────────────────────────┐   ┌──────────┐        │
│  │ ☒ Always Suggest                  │   │    OK    │        │
│  │ ☒ From Main Dictionary Only       │   └──────────┘        │
│  ├─Ignore─────────────────────────────   ┌──────────┐        │
│  │ ☐ Words in UPPERCASE   ┌─────────────┐│  Cancel  │        │
│  │ ☐ Words with Numbers   │Reset Ignore All└──────────┘        │
│  ├─Custom Dictionaries────────────────   ┌──────────┐        │
│  │ ☒ CUSTOM.DIC                      │   │   Help   │        │
│  │                                   │   └──────────┘        │
│  │                                   │   ┌──────────┐        │
│  │                                   │   │  New...   │        │
│  │                                   │   ├──────────┤        │
│  │                                   │   │  Edit     │        │
│  │                                   │   ├──────────┤        │
│  │ Language: [none]         ▼        │   │  Add...   │        │
│  │                                   │   ├──────────┤        │
│  │                                   │   │  Remove   │        │
│  └───────────────────────────────────┘   └──────────┘        │
└─────────────────────────────────────────────────────────────┘
```

2. If necessary, click check boxes to turn them on or off until your settings match those shown in Figure 4.1.

For the exercises in this chapter to work properly, the command box, Reset Ignore All, should be dimmed. If it is not dimmed, Word remembers all words for which you or another student has already chosen Ignore All and will skip over those words.

3. If Reset Ignore All is not dimmed, click it. Then click Yes at the message about deleting the current list of ignored words.

4. Click [**OK**] to return to your document window.

5. Key the following sentence: **The Word spelling checker allows me to quickly check the spelling of words I am unsure of, such as "receive" and "relevent."**

6. Select the word "receive."

HINT: *Double-click the word.*

7. Click the Spelling icon on the Standard Toolbar ☑.

Word determines that the word is spelled correctly, so instead of a dialog box, you see a message indicating that Word has finished

FIGURE 4.2
Message That Selection Has Been Checked

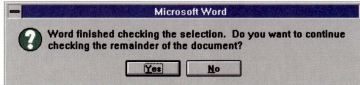

checking the selection and asking if you want to continue checking the remainder of the document (Figure 4.2).

8. Click No to end the spelling check.

9. Select the word "relevent" and click ☑.

Word determines that the word is not spelled correctly and displays the Spelling dialog box (Figure 4.3). Word suggests "relevant" in the Change To box and has no other suggestions in the Suggestions box.

10. Because the suggested spelling is the correct spelling, click Change.

FIGURE 4.3
Dialog Box Displayed When Word Finds a Misspelled Word

11. When you see the message asking if you want to continue checking the remainder of the document, click No to end the spelling check.

The word "relevent" should now be changed to "relevant."

12. Clear the screen (you do not need to save this document).

Checking the Spelling of an Entire Document

In this exercise you will check the spelling for an entire document. If no text is selected, Word will automatically check the spelling of the entire document when you click ✓. If you want to check the spelling of a portion of a document rather than the entire document, simply select the text to be checked, and click ✓.

As you use the spelling checker, the document scrolls so you can see how a word flagged in the Spelling dialog box is used in the document. If necessary, you can drag the dialog box out of the way to see more of the document.

Figure 4.4 illustrates the options you have for checking spelling.

- Ignore—skips the flagged (highlighted) word.

- Ignore All—skips the flagged word in all documents until you restart Word or click Reset Ignore All in Tools Options. Used for correctly spelled instances of names, acronyms, initials, and technical terms that are not in Word's main dictionary. Note, however, that Word will stop when the capitalization for the same word is different. (For example, Word will stop at both "boyd" and "Boyd.")

FIGURE 4.4
Suspected Error Highlighted in Document Pane and Displayed in Dialog Box

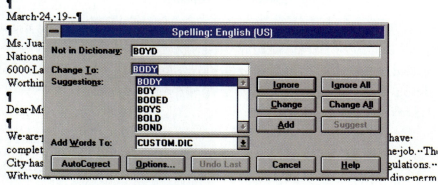

- Change—changes the flagged word to the entry in the Change To box or to the entry selected in the Suggestions box.

- Change All—same as Change, but changes the flagged word throughout the document. Use this option cautiously so that you do not change a word that requires a different correction. (For example, if Word flags "procede," in one case the correct spelling may be "proceed," but in another case in the same document the correct spelling may be "precede.")

- Add—adds the word to either CUSTOM.DIC (the default dictionary) or a dictionary you create. Because you may be sharing your computer with other students, you will not be instructed in this text to add words to a dictionary. Your instructor will assist you in creating your own custom dictionary (rather than using the default dictionary) if there is sufficient space on the hard drive for adding words that you frequently use.

- Suggest—dimmed because Always Suggest is selected in Tools Options.

- AutoCorrect—adds the word to a list of corrections that Word will make automatically in all documents. Again, however, because you may be sharing a computer, you will not use this option.

- Options—opens the Spelling category of the Tools Options dialog box.

FIGURE 4.5
Repeated Word Error

- Undo Last—currently dimmed because you have made no corrections. If you accidentally change the spelling of a word incorrectly, click this option.

As the spelling in your document is being checked, Word also checks for instances of double words. As shown in Figure 4.5, the Not in Dictionary box changes to the Repeated Word box. Click Delete when you do accidentally repeat words. Click Ignore if the repeated word should not be deleted. (For example, sometimes a side heading is repeated as the first word of the paragraph that follows it; in such cases the repeated word should not be deleted.)

As shown in Figure 4.6 on page 82, Word also checks for capitalization errors. The Not in Dictionary box changes to the Capitalization box.

Occasionally, no word in the Suggestions box is correct, or no suggestion is available. You can click in the Change To box, key your own correction, and then click Change or Change All to make the change in the document.

Sometimes during the spelling check, you may notice other changes you want to make in the document pane. You can click in the document pane to interrupt the spelling check temporarily.

FIGURE 4.6
Capitalization Error

After making the desired change, click Start in the dialog box.

1. Open the Data Disk file **building.doc**. Save the file on your Student Disk or in the appropriate student directory on the hard drive with the new name **chap4-1**.

2. Skip this step if you are continuing immediately after completing Exercise 4.1. If you are not continuing from Exercise 4.1, choose Tools Options, change settings in the Spelling category to match Figure 4.1, and click **OK**.

3. Click [ABC✓]. The dialog box shown in Figure 4.4 appears.

4. Make the following changes:

    a. Click Ignore All for "BOYD," "Juanita," "Crisanti," and "Lakeview."

    b. When "the" is highlighted in the document, and the Not in Dictionary box changes to the Repeated Word box (see Figure 4.5), click Delete to delete the second occurrence.

    c. When "adition" is flagged, click Change All to allow Word to change all instances to the suggested "addition."

    d. For "authzation," no suggestions are given. Click in the Change To box, change the entry to **authorization**, and click Change or Change All.

    e. For "procede," click Change so only this one instance will be changed to the suggested "proceed."

    f. For "scedule," click in the document pane to interrupt the spelling check. Change "scedule" to **schedule**, add a space, and key the word **to**. After making this correction, click Start to resume the spelling check.

    g. Click Ignore All for "Boyd."

    h. For "TOtal,"(Figure 4.6), click Change to accept Word's suggestion for the capitalization error.

    i. Click Ignore All for "CFM."

j. Click Change or Change All to accept Word's suggestions for the following: "exisiting," "ADd," and "exisitng."

k. For "wde," click in the Change To box, change the entry to **wide**, and click Change or Change All.

l. Click Change or Change All to accept Word's suggestion for "Sincerly."

m. Click Ignore All for "smn."

5. When the message is displayed indicating that the spelling check is completed, click $\boxed{\text{OK}}$.

6. If space permits, add one or two blank lines below the date but do not let the document wrap to a second page.

7. Save the changes, print one copy, and clear the screen.

Checking Grammar in a Document

It is common for proofreaders to check a document only for misspelled words. Good proofreading skills, however, include reading for content; that is, checking to be sure each sentence makes sense. For example, have you accidentally keyed "there" rather than "their" or "has" rather than "had"? Word can help you to locate such errors. With the Tools Grammar feature, Word flags sentences that may not follow standard rules of grammar and offers suggestions for changes. You can also check your spelling with the Tools Grammar command (to save time, you will disable this option for this exercise). You can check the grammar for the entire document or select a portion of the document and check the grammar. If necessary, you can drag the dialog box out of the way to see more of the document text.

E X E R C I S E

4.3

Checking Grammar

1. Open the Data Disk file **survey.doc**, and save it in the appropriate location for student files as **chap4-2**.

The comments in this exercise were keyed exactly as written by the consumer. It will be your job to clean up the grammatical errors.

2. Choose Tools Options and click the Grammar folder tab.

A dialog box similar to Figure 4.7 appears, although you will change some options for this exercise.

FIGURE 4.7
Grammar Category of the Tools Options
Dialog Box

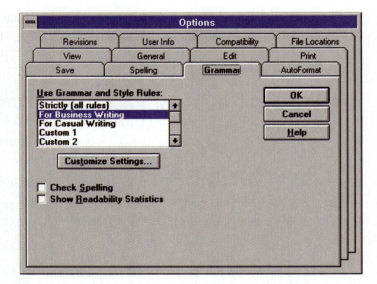

3. If necessary, click For Business Writing in the Use Grammar and Style Rules list box.

4. Turn off the default options Check Spelling (you will check the spelling later) and Show Readability Statistics (you do not need this information).

In addition to selecting an option under Use Grammar and Style Rules, Word allows you to customize which rules should be observed in the grammar and style check. For this exercise, however, leave the default settings (do not click Customize Settings). If any errors described in the following steps are not flagged, make a note of them and correct the errors after the grammar check is completed.

5. Click [**OK**].

Figure 4.8 illustrates options for a grammar check.

FIGURE 4.8
Grammar Dialog
Box with
Suspected Error
in Sentence
Highlighted

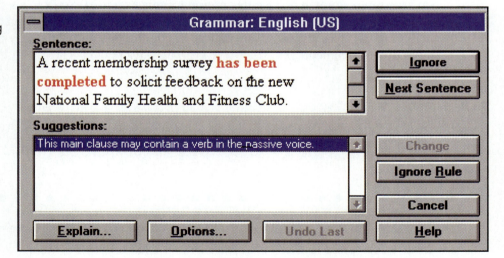

- Ignore—skips to the next suspected grammatical error without making a change.

- Next Sentence—skips to the next sentence without making a change.

- Change—replaces the highlighted error in the document pane with the highlighted suggestion. (Note that sometimes you have more than one suggestion, as shown in Figure 4.9. Click the correct suggestion before you click Change.)

- Ignore Rule—skips all future suspected violations of a rule in a document (such as passive voice).

- Explain—opens a dialog box to explain the rule listed under Suggestions.

- Options—opens the Grammar category of the Tools Options dialog box.

- Undo Last—reverses accidental changes.

If Change is dimmed in the dialog box when a suspected error is highlighted in the Grammar dialog box (Figure 4.10 on page 86), click in the document pane. After making the correction, click Start to resume the grammar check.

6. Choose Tools Grammar, and make corrections as follows (do not make other corrections until after the grammar check):

   a. If you want to, when the first suspected error ("has been completed") is highlighted, click Explain to read about passive voice errors. Then double-click the explanation's Control menu box to return to the grammar check.

   b. Click Ignore Rule so passive voice errors will no longer be flagged. (If you want, you can change these sentences after you complete the grammar check.)

FIGURE 4.9
Highlighted Grammatical Error with Two Suggested Replacements

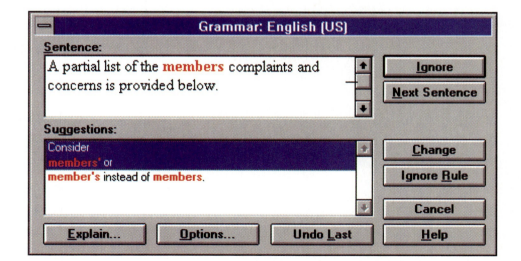

FIGURE 4.10
Dimmed Change
Option

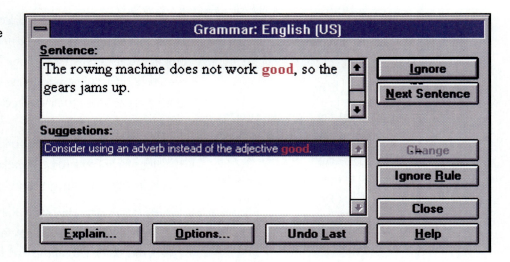

Grammar: English (US)

Sentence:

The rowing machine does not work **good**, so the gears jams up.

Ignore

Next Sentence

Suggestions:

Consider using an adverb instead of the adjective **good**.

Change

Ignore Rule

Close

Explain...   Options...   Undo Last   Help

c. Click Change to change "members" to **members'** (the first choice).

d. When "good" is highlighted, click in the document pane, change "good" to **well**, and click Start. (Click Start for all future steps in which you make changes directly in the document pane.)

e. Change "jams" to **jam** (the second choice).

f. Delete "up" in the document pane.

g. Click Ignore for "too" because it is correctly used.

h. Click Change to change "colors" to **color**.

i. Change "pedals" to **pedal** (the second choice).

j. Change "easy" to **easily** in the document pane.

k. Change the double negative "don't use none" to **don't use any** in the document pane.

l. Click Change to change "don't" to **do not**.

m. Change "there" to **they are** in the document pane.

n. Click Change to change "Its" to **It's**.

o. Click Change to change "an" to **a**.

p. Make this change to correct the run-in sentence in the document pane: **in the locker rooms and charge less for each locker?**

q. Click Change to change "has" to **have**.

r. Click Change to change "don't" to **do not**.

7. When you see a message that the grammar check is complete, click ⬚ **OK** ⬚.

8. If the spelling checker is available, do a spell-check now to correct any misspelled words. If the spelling checker is not available, scroll and manually correct the two errors ("protein" and "February").

9. Proofread the document. Notice that there

are some errors the grammar check and spelling check did not correct.

10. In the second complaint, change "week" to **weak**.

11. In the eighth complaint, change "two" to **too**.

12. In the tenth complaint, change "facilities to not stay" to **facilities do not stay**.

13. For consistency with the rest of the document (contractions were spelled out), change "It's" in the seventh complaint to **It is**.

14. Save your changes, print one copy, and clear the screen.

Using the Thesaurus

A good writer must be able to keep the attention of the reader. This means knowing who will be the intended audience and using language appropriate for that audience. Using the Word *Thesaurus,* you can replace a word in your document with a synonym that is more appropriate, easier to understand, or simply different (to avoid overusing a word). You can choose a replacement from the Meanings list box; the Replace with Synonym list box; or, by clicking Look Up, from different lists. You can also replace for a selected group of words (Activity 3) and you can replace words with antonyms.

EXERCISE

4.4

Selecting Alternative Words Using the Thesaurus

1. In a new document window, key the following paragraph. (Use the 12-point font size and press **Tab** to begin the paragraph.)

Sports psychology is another area that has grown in the last decade. Sports psychologists used to work only with professional athletes. Today, however, sports psychologists also work with recreational exercisers to help them set goals, build self-esteem, and improve motivation.

2. Proofread and correct errors. Save the file as **chap4-3**.

3. Position the insertion point in the word "area" in the first sentence, and choose Tools Thesaurus.

The Thesaurus dialog box (Figure 4.11) is displayed, with the word "area" in the Looked Up box. Notice that the highlighted word in the Meanings list box ("region") is also highlighted in the Replace with Synonym list box.

FIGURE 4.11
Thesaurus Dialog Box

4. Click "field" in the Meanings list box.

Notice that "field" is also highlighted in the Replace with Synonym list box.

5. Click "sphere" in the Replace with Synonym list box.

Notice that the Meanings list box does not change.

6. Click "domain" in the Replace with Synonym list box. Then click Look Up.

Notice that "domain" is now in the Looked Up box, and different lists appear in the Meanings and Replace with Synonym list boxes.

7. Open the Looked Up list box.

HINT: *Click the underlined arrow.*

You should see the current term ("domain") plus any previous terms that were looked up. In this case, "area" is also displayed (Figure 4.12).

8. Click "area."

The original dialog box returns with "area" in the Looked Up box and "region" highlighted in the Meanings and Replace with Synonym list boxes.

FIGURE 4.12
Opened List Box in Thesaurus Dialog Box

Words Previously Looked Up

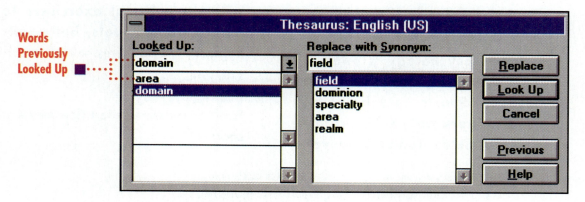

9. Instead of selecting an alternative word in the dialog box as a replacement for "area," click Cancel .

10. Position the insertion point in the word "only" in the second sentence. Choose Tools Thesaurus.

11. Click "exclusively" in the Replace with Synonym box; then click Replace.

The sentence should now read: "Sports psychologists used to work exclusively with professional athletes."

12. Position the insertion point in the word "recreational" in the third sentence. Choose Tools Thesaurus.

Word does not have a synonym for "recreational" but lists "Related Words" in the Meanings list box (Figure 4.13).

13. Click Look Up to display lists of related words.

14. Click "relaxation" in the Replace with Synonym list box; then click Replace.

FIGURE 4.13
When No Direct Synonyms Are Available, Look Up Related Words

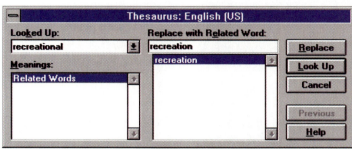

The middle part of the sentence should now say ". . . work with relaxation exercisers . . . ."

15. You decide the original word sounds better. Click [icon] so that the phrase again reads ". . . work with recreational exercisers . . . ."

16. Position the insertion point in the words "grown" and "build." Replace each with your choice of an appropriate word from the Thesaurus dialog box.

17. Save the changes, print one copy, and clear the screen.

COMPUTER ACTIVITIES

ACTIVITY 1

(The Spelling feature must be installed in order for you to do this exercise.)

1. Open the Data Disk file **review.doc**, and save it in the appropriate location for Student Disk files as **act4-1**.

2. With the insertion point positioned at the beginning of the document, complete a spelling check for the entire document. When Word suggests changes in the Spelling dialog box, use the following guidelines:

   a. Ignore all suggestions to change Scheiber. It is spelled correctly as written.

   b. Accept the suggested changes for misspelled words.

   c. Delete any repeated words.

   d. Change "gns" to **gains**.

   e. Switch to the document pane and change facilities closing ina" to **facilities now closing in on a**.

   f. Correct any capitalization errors.

3. Save the changes to the document, print one copy, and clear the screen.

ACTIVITY 2

(The Grammar feature must be installed in order for you to do this exercise.)

1. Open the Data Disk file **classes.doc** and save it in the appropriate location for Student Disk files as **act4-2**.

2. With the insertion point positioned at the beginning of the document, start a grammar check. When Word suggests changes in the Grammar dialog box, do the following:

   a. If the Spelling option is turned on, ignore the suggested spelling for Ike and Gibson. The name is correct as written.

   b. In the first paragraph, change "realizes" to **realize**.

   c. Change "this" to **these**.

   d. Change "too" to **to**.

   e. Change "whom" to **who**.

f. Change "is" to **are**.

g. Change "Once the number of participants has been identified" to **Once we identify the number of participants**.

h. Change "a" to **an**.

3. Save the changes to the document, print one copy, and clear the screen.

ACTIVITY 3

(The Thesaurus feature must be installed in order for you to do this exercise.)

1. Open the Data Disk file **cts.doc** and save it in the appropriate location for Student Disk files as **act4-3**.

2. Use the Thesaurus to look up synonyms for the following words. Replace each word with an appropriate synonym.

a. In the first sentence of the first paragraph, change "originally."

b. In the first sentence of the second paragraph, change "usually."

c. In the first sentence of the third paragraph, change "Although."

d. In the same sentence, change "clear."

e. In the same sentence, change "repeated."

f. In the second sentence of the third paragraph, select the entire phrase "As a result" and select a replacement.

3. Save the changes to the document, print one copy, and clear the screen.

CREATE YOUR OWN ● ● ● ● ● ● ● ● ● ● ●

Write two or more paragraphs about your career objectives and how you plan to attain them. Be specific about skill development, curriculum choices, and plans for work experience.

Check what you have written using the spelling checker and the grammar checker, then proofread and correct any additional errors.

Identify at least three words in your paragraphs that should be more precise, and at least one word that should be changed for variety. Use the Thesaurus to look up synonyms (or antonyms) to improve your writing.

Save your document, print one copy and file it for future reference. This information may be helpful in the future when you apply for a job or prepare college applications.

REVIEW EXERCISES

TRUE / FALSE

Each of the following statements is either true or false. Indicate your answer on the left by circling T if the statement is true or F if the statement is false.

(T)   F   **1.**   Word can also check for spelling errors during a grammar check.

T   (F)   **2.**   Word cannot undo corrections made during a spelling check.

(T)   F   **3.**   To look up a synonym for a word, you must select the word.

(T)   F   **4.**   Once you have chosen to skip all occurrences of a correctly spelled name in a document, Word skips all occurrences regardless of capitalization.

FILL IN THE BLANKS

Complete the following sentences by writing the correct word or words in the blanks provided.

5.   To skip all occurrences of a word listed in the Not in Dictionary box of the Spelling dialog box, click ___Ignore all___.

6.   To skip one occurrence of a word listed in the Not in Dictionary box of the Spelling dialog box, click ___Ignore___.

7.   To correct all misspellings of a word, click ___Change all___ in the Spelling dialog box.

8.   To correct a single misspelling of a word, click ___Change___ in the Spelling dialog box.

9.   If you accidentally change the spelling of a word to an incorrect spelling, click ___undo last___ in the Spelling dialog box.

10.   To check the grammar in a document, choose the ___tools ✓ grammar options___ or Icon ___ command.

REFERENCE QUESTIONS

Referring to the *Microsoft Word User's Guide,* write the answers to the following questions in the space provided.

1. What can you do if you do not want Word to display a list of suggested corrections when you are checking the spelling of a document?

   always suggest

2. How can you decrease the number of rules for a grammar check so only the most basic rules are checked?

   Tools, Grammar, Options

P A R T

2

FORMATTING

FORMATTING

CHAPTER 5

OBJECTIVES

Upon completion of this chapter, you will be able to:

- Change the printing direction to landscape orientation.
- Use Print Preview to check page layout and change margins.
- Insert section breaks.
- Center a page vertically.
- Change paragraph alignment.
- Apply character formats using the Toolbar and the Font dialog box.
- Change the font and font size.
- Adjust spacing between characters.
- Change the case of selected text.

Preparation

1. To complete the chapter activities, you will need to access your Student Disk files ACT3-1.DOC and ACT2-2.DOC.

2. Remember to save frequently as you work. You will generally not be reminded to save until all work is completed for a document.

3. If you make mistakes as you work with the exercises in the chapter, remember to click ⟲⬚ immediately after completing the action.

4. At the end of each class session, be sure to close Word and Windows properly. If you are using the hard drive to store your completed work, back up your files onto your formatted Student Disk, and erase your files from the directory you used on the hard drive. (Do not erase the Data Disk files unless your instructor tells you to do so.)

Introduction

Word offers a number of types of formats. Figure 5.1 on page 100 illustrates the formats you will work with in this text. It is important to recognize how they differ.

Document and Section Formats

Document formats apply to an entire document. You can position the insertion point anywhere in a document to change a document format. For portions of a document, you can divide the document into sections and change the document formats for each individual *section*.

EXERCISE

Changing Document Formats

Portrait orientation (the default) is also called vertical orientation; it prints with the short edge of the page at the top. *Landscape orientation* is also called horizontal orientation; it prints sideways with the long edge of the page at the top. In the following steps you will create a flyer using landscape orientation.

Landscape Orientation

Portrait Orientation

FIGURE 5.1
Formats Used in This Text

Format Type	Examples	Instructions
Document	Margins, columns, paper size, page orientation, page numbers, headers and footers	Position the insertion point anywhere in the document, and apply the desired document format.
Section	Same as Document	Position the insertion point where you want to change a portion of the document, choose Insert Break, select the type of section break, and click OK. Then move the insertion point to the desired section, and apply the desired document format to the section.
Paragraph	Line spacing, alignment, tabs, indents, borders, bullets, numbered paragraphs, space between paragraphs, drop caps	For existing text, position the insertion point anywhere in the paragraph (or select a group of paragraphs), and apply the desired format. For new text, turn on the format (it will stay in effect until you change the format).
Character	Font, font size, font style (bold and/or italic, underline, etc).	For existing text, select the text to be formatted and apply the format. For new text, turn on the format (it will stay in effect until you turn it off).
Miscellaneous	Change case, page breaks, footnotes, NEWLINE, annotations, tables, frames, hyphenation	Varies

IMPORTANT: Before you set document formats, de-select all text. When text is selected, Word creates a new section and applies the format to the text in the selected section.

1. Change the page orientation:

a. In a new document window, choose File Page Setup.

HINT: *Click File, then Page Setup.*

b. Click the Paper Size folder tab to display the dialog box shown in Figure 5.2.

c. Click the Landscape option button. Do not click [OK] yet; you will change margins in another portion of the Page Setup dialog box.

2. Change margins:

a. In the Page Setup dialog box, click the Margins folder tab to display the dialog box shown in Figure 5.3.

The default top and bottom margins are 1 inch, and the default left and right margins are 1.25 inch. When you switched to landscape orientation, however, Word automatically reversed the settings.

b. Click in the text box for Top.

c. Delete the current entry and key the number 1. (It is not necessary to key the inch symbol; Word will automatically use inches.)

FIGURE 5.2
Paper Size Category of File Page Setup Dialog Box

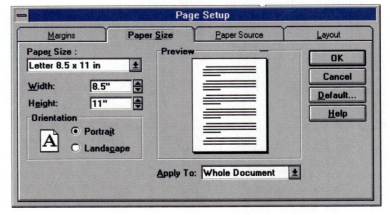

FIGURE 5.3
Margins Category of File Page Setup Dialog Box

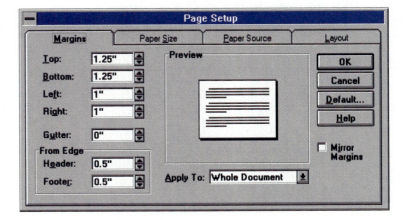

d. Change the Bottom text box to **1**.

e. Click [OK].

3. Click the underlined arrow for the Font Size box on the Formatting Toolbar, and click 12.

4. Key the document shown in Figure 5.4. (Press (Enter) twice to leave blank lines where shown.)

5. Spell-check your document. Then proofread and correct any additional errors.

6. Save the document as **chap5-1**. Do not print or clear the screen yet.

FIGURE 5.4
Flyer Text

```
HEALTH AND FITNESS EXPO

Los Angeles Convention Center

June 28-30

America's Largest Exhibition for Wellness of Body and Mind

Displays and Demonstrations of Hundreds of Products

A Look at Innovative Fitness Equipment for the Future

Seminars and Films

For more information call or write:
Health and Fitness Expo, Inc.
9600 Jeronimo Road, Suite 400
Irvine, CA  92718-4401

(714) 555-0101
(714) 555-3465
FAX (714) 555-0367
```

EXERCISE

5.2

Previewing a Document and Adjusting Document Formats

To see what a document with landscape orientation will look like when printed, switch to *Print Preview*. Print Preview is a reduced view of the layout of a completed page or pages, including such things as page orientation, margins, page breaks, columns, and page numbering. It is a good idea to preview your document and make adjustments before you print it to avoid excessive reprinting.

1. Click the Print Preview icon on the Standard Toolbar ▣.

Your screen should look similar to Figure 5.5, but do not be concerned if your screen is different.

2. Magnify a portion of your screen as follows:

    a. If the Magnifier icon ▣ is not highlighted, click it.

    b. Move the mouse until the pointer is on the document. If the pointer is not a magnifying glass pointer, click once.

    c. Move the pointer to the bottom of the document and click.

The screen enlarges to show the bottom portion of your document at 100 percent. You can magnify any portion of your document in Print Preview to edit specific portions.

FIGURE 5.5
Document with
Landscape
Orientation in
Print Preview

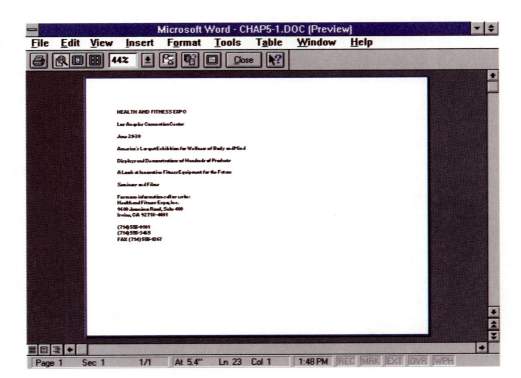

d. Click again on your document. It should return to its original size.

e. Click to change from the magnifying glass pointer to the text pointer (the I-beam).

f. Position the I-beam toward the top of the document, and click.

3. Change to a multiple-page view as follows:

a. Click the Multiple Pages icon 🔳. A grid should appear.

b. Drag down and across the grid until it shows 3 x 4 Pages. Then release the mouse button.

Notice that the view size of your document is reduced. If this document had multiple pages, you could have dragged the grid to display as many pages as you wanted at the same time so that you could check their layout. You will probably want to use this feature whenever you have multiple-page documents.

c. Click the One Page icon 🔳.

With One Page selected, Word sizes the screen to show an entire page. Note that One Page is the default Print Preview setting. You should select it each time you finish working in Print Preview so that any other documents you work with will be displayed at this setting. (Word remembers the most recent Print Preview setting and uses it for all documents until the setting is changed again.)

4. Use the full screen to display your document as follows:

a. Click the Full Screen icon 🔳.

All screen elements except the document and the Toolbar disappear. The document is slightly enlarged because there is more screen space available.

b. Click 🔳 again to return to your previous screen size and restore all the screen elements.

5. Zoom to the desired size as follows:

a. Click the underlined arrow next to the Zoom Control box.

As in Normal View, this shortcut menu lists the most common view sizes (for custom sizes, you can key a measurement in the text box).

b. Click 75%. Your document is enlarged.

c. Open the Zoom Control shortcut menu again, and click Whole Page. Your screen should return to its previous size.

6. Adjust margins in Print Preview as follows:

a. If the rulers are not displayed, click the View Ruler icon 🔳.

b. Click at the beginning of the title. Notice the current measurement for "At" in the status bar.

c. Position the pointer toward the top of the white portion of the vertical ruler at the left edge of the screen.

d. When you see a small, two-headed arrow, drag down the ruler a short distance; then release the mouse button. There should be a new measurement for "At."

e. This time, hold down (Alt) and the mouse button and drag (measurements are displayed). When you see 2" in the shaded portion, release the mouse button and (Alt).

Do not be concerned if your position is not exactly 2 inches. You changed your top margin to make the document look more attractive. If your document does not look approximately centered vertically, drag up or down the vertical ruler again until you are satisfied with the vertical appearance of your document. Note that you can also adjust the bottom margin by dragging from the bottom of the vertical ruler.

f. Position the pointer on the left edge of the horizontal ruler. When you see a two-headed arrow, drag to the right a short distance.

g. Repeat Step f until the longest line in your

document looks approximately centered horizontally.

Note that you can also adjust the right margin by dragging from the right edge of the horizontal ruler.

7. Choose File Save to save the changes to your document.

8. Click the Print icon 🖨 to print a copy of your document.

9. Click [**Close**] to return to Normal View.

10. If the ruler is not displayed below the Formatting Toolbar, choose View Ruler to restore it. Then save your document again.

11. Clear the screen.

EXERCISE

Working with Sections

Generally, you will use the same document formats for the entire document. Occasionally, however, you may want a portion of your document (a title page, for example) to have different formats, such as different margins or vertical centering. If you want a document to have some formats apply to the entire document and some formats apply to particular sections, you should do the following: (1) insert the section breaks; (2) set the formats to be applied to the entire document; and (3) reopen the

Page Setup dialog box and set the section formats.

1. Open **act3-1.doc** from your Student Disk and save it as **chap5-2**.

2. Insert a section break so that your title page will start on a separate page and will have a different format than the rest of the document:

a. With the insertion point at the top of the

FIGURE 5.6
Insert Break Dialog Box

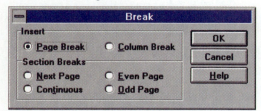

document, choose Insert Break. The dialog box shown in Figure 5.6 appears.

b. Under Section Breaks, click Next Page; then click OK.

You should now see a double line across your screen with the words "End of Section" (Figure 5.7).

FIGURE 5.7
Section Break Inserted

―――――――――――――End of Section―――――――――――――
STRENGTHENING·YOUR·IMMUNE·SYSTEM¶
Genetic·and·Environmental·Factors¶

3. Click an insertion point on the section marker so that the text you key will be in the new section you created.

4. Key **STRENGTHENING YOUR IMMUNE SYSTEM**.

Notice that the text is centered and bold. The paragraph in which the insertion point was positioned when you created the section break was double-spaced, centered, and bold, so the text in the new section will also be double-spaced, centered, and bold unless you change it.

5. Press (Caps Lock) and click **B** to turn off the all caps and bold formats (but leave the double-spaced and centered formats).

6. Press (Enter) four times and key your name.

7. Press (Enter) and key your course title.

8. Press (Enter) four times and insert the current date.

HINT: *Choose Insert Date and Time.*

9. Press (Enter) to end the title page with a paragraph break.

10. Change the margins for the entire document (not just the title page section):

a. Choose File Page Setup.

b. Click the Margins folder tab if it is not bold.

c. Change all margins to 1 inch.

d. Click the underlined arrow for the Apply To list box and click Whole Document.

e. Click OK.

11. Center just the title page section vertically:

a. Move the insertion point up into the title page section.

b. Choose File Page Setup.

c. Click Layout. The dialog box shown in Figure 5.8 appears.

d. Click the underlined arrow for the Vertical Alignment list box and click Center.

e. If necessary, click the underlined arrow for the Apply To list box and click This Section.

f. Click OK.

12. Click 🔍. Notice that your title page is centered vertically.

FIGURE 5.8
Layout Category of File Page Setup
Dialog Box

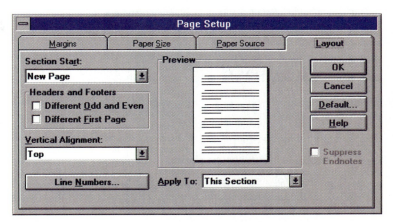

13. Click the Page Forward icon ⯯ on the vertical scroll bar.

Notice that the first page of the document is not centered vertically because you set the centered format for only the section containing the title page.

14. Click ⎍ Close ⎍.

15. Save your document, print a copy, and clear the screen.

Paragraph and Character Formats

Unlike document and section formats, *paragraph* and *character formats* can be applied to more specific portions of text. A paragraph format is applied to an entire *paragraph* and cannot be applied to a portion of a paragraph (for example, you cannot single-space part of a paragraph and double-space the rest). Character formats can be applied to as much text as desired, from a single *character* to the entire document. As Figure 5.1 states, paragraph and character formats can be added either before or after you key text.

E X E R C I S E

Formatting Paragraphs

1. Click ⎕ to open a new document window.

2. Click the underlined arrow next to the Font

Size box on the Formatting Toolbar and click 12.

3. Press (Ctrl) + **2** to set the double-spaced paragraph format.

4. Key **MEMORANDUM** and press (Enter) twice.

5. Key the memo headings and the information following the headings as shown in Figure 5.9. Press (Tab) as needed to align the text following the memo headings. Press (Enter) once after each heading line.

6. Key the first paragraph in the body of the memo (beginning "At our staff meeting . . .") but do not press (Enter).

This paragraph still has the double-spaced format because paragraph formats remain in effect until you change them.

TIP

A quick way to restore all paragraph formats to the defaults is to press the Reset Paragraph key, (Ctrl) + (Q).

7. With the insertion point anywhere in the paragraph you keyed, press (Ctrl) + the number (1) to change to the single-spaced paragraph format.

8. If necessary, move the insertion point to the end of the paragraph.

9. Press (Enter) twice and key the remainder of the memo, pressing (Enter) twice between paragraphs.

10. Press (Enter) twice after the last paragraph, key your initials, and press (Enter) once to end your document with a blank line.

11. Spell-check your document; then proofread and correct any additional errors.

12. Save the memo as **chap5-3**.

13. Move the insertion point to the top of your document. Move the insertion point through your memo.

HINT: *Use the direction keys on your keyboard.*

Notice that all paragraphs have the left alignment format (even left margins but ragged right margins). The Align Left icon on the Formatting Toolbar [≡] is highlighted.

14. Scroll up and position the insertion point anywhere in the title, "MEMORANDUM."

15. Click the Center icon [≡].

The title paragraph is now centered, and [≡] is highlighted on the Formatting Toolbar.

16. Position the insertion point anywhere in the first paragraph of the body of the memo. Choose Edit Repeat (or simply click [≡] again).

The first paragraph is centered (Figure 5.10), and [≡] is highlighted.

17. Position the insertion point anywhere in the second paragraph and click the Align Right icon [≡].

Chp. 5 - 3

FIGURE 5.9
Memorandum Text

MEMORANDUM

TO: All Fitness Trainers
FROM: Ike Gibson
DATE: Current Date
SUBJECT: Nutrition Classes

At our staff meeting last week, many of you expressed a need
to know more about the nutrition classes we will offer next
quarter.

Weight Management will help individuals identify their recommended
weight. The focus will be on sound advice for exercise and diet
programs that will help individuals add or take off pounds
to achieve ideal body weight.

Cooking for Good Health will provide tips on selecting and
preparing food. Participants will learn about the nutritional
benefits of a variety of foods from organic products to frozen
dinners. The focus will be on making good choices, cooking foods
properly, and creating wholesome menus.

Reading Food Labels will be a short class defining the information
included in food labels and explaining its relevance to diet.

Value of Vitamins will explore the advantages and disadvantages
of supplementing diets with vitamins. The benefits of each
vitamin will be described.

FIGURE 5.10
Centered Paragraph

At·our·staff·meeting·last·week,·many·of·you·expressed·a·need·to·know·more·about·the·
nutrition·classes·we·will·offer·next·quarter.¶
¶

All lines of the paragraph are now right-aligned, with even right margins but ragged left margins (Figure 5.11). **2** is highlighted.

18. Select the last three paragraphs to be formatted at one time.

HINT: *Drag down the selection bar.*

19. Click the Justify icon [≡]; then click to deselect the paragraphs. (Formats are often easier to see in deselected text.)

All lines (except the last) of all three paragraphs are now *justified*, or even on both sides (Figure 5.12). [≡] is highlighted. Extra white space has

been added between words as needed to extend each line to the right margin.

The memo would obviously look better if all paragraphs in the body of the memo had the same alignment.

20. Select all five paragraphs in the body of the memo (do not select the title or the portion with the memo headings and information).

21. Click [≡].

Notice that Word does not spread out the last line of any paragraph.

22. Save the changes to your memo, but do not print or clear the screen yet.

FIGURE 5.11
Right-Aligned
Paragraph

        ¶
Weight·Management·will·help·individuals·identify·their·recommended·weight.··The·focus·
will·be·on·sound·advice·for·exercise·and·diet·programs·that·will·help·individuals·add·or·
take·off·pounds·to·achieve·ideal·body·weight.¶

FIGURE 5.12
Justified Paragraphs

Cooking·for·Good·Health·will·provide·tips·on·selecting·and·preparing·food.··Participants·
will·learn·about·the·nutritional·benefits·of·a·variety·of·foods·from·organic·products·to·
frozen·dinners.··The·focus·will·be·on·making·good·choices,·cooking·foods·properly,·and·
creating·wholesome·menus.¶
¶
Reading·Food·Labels·will·be·a·short·class·defining·the·information·included·in·food·
labels·and·explaining·its·relevance·to·diet.¶
¶
Value·of·Vitamins·will·explore·the·advantages·and·disadvantages·of·supplementing·diets·
with·vitamins.··The·benefits·of·each·vitamin·will·be·described.¶

EXERCISE

5.5

Adding Character Formats

To add character formats to new text, you simply turn on the format, key the text, and turn off the format. For existing text, however, you must first

select the text and then apply the desired format or formats.

1. Select the title, "MEMORANDUM."

2. Click $\boxed{I}$ on the Formatting Toolbar to add the italic format.

3. Select the memo headings "TO:," "FROM:," "DATE:," and "SUBJECT:" and click $\boxed{\textbf{B}}$ to add the bold format.

4. If necessary, delete tabs after the memo headings to align information following the headings properly.

The title would look better if it were bold and underlined.

5. Remove a character format:

a. Select the title MEMORANDUM. Notice that $\boxed{I}$ is highlighted.

b. Click $\boxed{I}$. The format is removed and the icon is no longer highlighted.

> **TIP**
>
> A quick way to remove multiple character formats from selected text is to press the Reset Character key, (Ctrl) + (Space Bar).

> **TIP**
>
> (Ctrl) + (D) is a shortcut for the Format Font command.

6. Click $\boxed{\textbf{B}}$ and $\boxed{\underline{U}}$ to format the title.

7. Select the words "Weight Management" in the second paragraph.

8. Choose Format Font. If the Font folder tab is not bold, click it.

The dialog box shown in Figure 5.13 appears. Notice that the Bold and Italic formats that you apply using the Formatting Toolbar are listed under *Font Style*. Notice also the additional formats that are not available on the Formatting Toolbar: Color, Strikethrough, *Superscript*, *Subscript*, *Hidden*, Small Caps, and All Caps. You will not be applying these formats in this text directly from this dialog box, but you may want to make a note of where they are found for future reference.

9. Click the underlined arrow for the Underline list box.

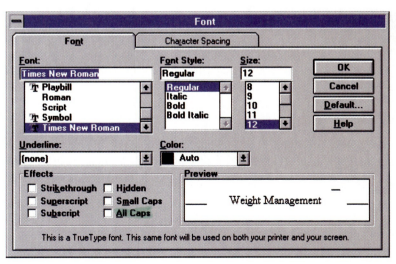

FIGURE 5.13
Font Category of Format Font Dialog Box

10. Click Words Only and click OK .

The words "Weight Manage-
ment" are underlined, but
the space between them is not (move the insertion
point if necessary to see this format).

Weight·Management·

11. Add the Words Only format to the class titles at the beginning of the next three paragraphs.

12. Save the changes to your document, print a copy, and clear the screen.

Working with Fonts, Font Sizes, Character Spacing, and Case

In Exercises 5.6 and 5.7, you will create samples of *fonts* and *font sizes* that you can save and use for future reference. In Exercise 5.8 you will experiment with increasing and decreasing spacing between characters. Finally, in Exercise 5.9 you will learn a way to change the case of selected text quickly.

EXERCISE

5.6 Changing the Font

1. Open a new document window.

2. Center the following title in bold: **FONTS SAMPLE FOR THE X PRINTER** (substitute your selected printer's name for the X).

3. Press **Enter** four times.

4. Turn off caps and the bold format, and change to left alignment.

HINT: *Press* **Caps Lock** *, click* **B** *, and click* ▤ *.*

5. Click the underlined arrow for the Font box and click Arial.

Note that as you use fonts, they appear at the top of this list box. You may have to scroll to locate some fonts.

6. Key the following sentence: **This is an example of Arial 10 point text**.

(If the Font Size box on the Formatting Toolbar shows a size other than 10-point, substitute the appropriate size throughout this exercise.)

7. Press **Enter** twice.

8. Open the Font list box again and click Courier New.

9. Key the following sentence: **This is an example of Courier New 10 point text**.

10. Press (Enter) twice.

11. Open the Font list box again and click Times New Roman.

12. Key the following sentence: **This is an example of Times New Roman 10 point text**.

13. Press (Enter) twice.

14. Continue the list, selecting several more fonts

that are available for your selected printer (or key a sentence for each available *font*, if you want).

Use fonts that are preceded by *TT* or a printer symbol. Fonts without these symbols are not designed for keying ordinary text. Some additional fonts may not be suitable; you will discover which ones are not suitable as you key.

15. Delete any lines with unreadable text and make a note of those fonts so you do not use them in the future.

16. Save your document as **fonts**, print a copy, and clear the screen.

Note the fonts that print with the best quality. In the future you may want to select a font that is easy to read on the screen and prints well.

EXERCISE

5.7 Changing Font Size

Each font has a list of available font sizes. Font sizes are measured in *points*. There are approximately 72 points to an inch. Character widths vary from font to font, as is evident in your FONTS printout. Small font sizes (such as 6- or 8-point) are often used for captions and for footnote reference numbers, but they are difficult to read on the screen. Font sizes of 10- and 12-point are used most frequently for keying ordinary text. You may want to use a slightly larger *font size* for side headings, titles, and letterheads.

1. Open a new document window.

2. Center the following title in bold: **POINT SIZES**.

3. Press (Enter) four times.

4. Turn off caps and the bold format, and change to left alignment.

5. If it is not already selected, click the underlined arrow for the Font box and select the Times New Roman font.

6. Click the underlined arrow for the Font Size box and click 8.

7. Key **Times New Roman 8 point** and press (Enter).

8. Change to 10-point, key **Times New Roman 10 point**, and press (Enter).

9. Change to 12-point, key **Times New Roman 12 point**, and press (Enter).

10. Click in the Font Size text box, key **15**, and click an insertion point back on the blank line below the 12-point line.

 IMPORTANT: When you key a font size rather than selecting a font size from the list, the insertion point remains in the Font Size box. You must click back in the document where you want the change to begin.

11. Key **Times New Roman 15 point** and press (Enter).

You can key any size in the Font Size box, including half sizes. Note, however, that occasionally if you use a font size that is not listed, the final document may not have the desired appearance.

12. Key one or two more lines for the Times New Roman font, using larger point sizes, such as 18, 24, or 30.

13. Select the Arial font and key several lines, using some of the same font sizes you used for Times New Roman. Compare the Times New Roman and Arial sets.

14. Select the Courier New font and key several lines in various sizes. Compare them to the Times New Roman and Arial sets.

15. If you want to, create sets of various font sizes for other fonts available for your printer.

16. Save the document as **points**, print one copy, and clear the screen. File the FONTS and POINTS printouts for future reference.

TIP

In future documents, to use a font or font size for the entire document other than the default 10-point Times New Roman, select the beginning paragraph mark and make the desired change.

EXERCISE 5.8

Character Spacing

Spacing between characters is determined by the font designer. In some cases, however (as with proportional fonts like Times New Roman), font size and/or certain character formats such as italics or bold/italics may result in unattractive spacing. In other cases, you may want to increase (expand) or decrease (condense) the space between characters deliberately to give a stronger visual impact to the text (for example, in posters or flyers). Word offers two ways to adjust the spacing. With TrueType fonts or similar scalable fonts, you can turn on *kerning* and Word will automatically make slight adjustments in the spacing between certain letter pairs for fonts over a certain size. This adjustment is so slight, however, that in the following exercise you will instead manually adjust the spacing after a selected character by the amount you specify.

Practice

1. Open a new document window and key **WORD FOR WINDOWS VERSION 6**.

2. Select the line and change the font and font size to 16-point Arial. Then deselect the line to see the format.

Notice that the letter "W" is quite close to the "I" in "WINDOWS."

3. Expand character spacing:

a. Select the first letter "W" in "WINDOWS."

b. Choose Format Font.

c. Click the Character Spacing folder tab to display the dialog box shown in Figure 5.14.

d. Click the underlined arrow for the Spacing list box and click Expanded.

Notice the By boxes. The first allows you to specify by how much you want to expand or condense character spacing (the default is 1 point). The second allows you to specify vertical position (you will not change this option in this text.)

e. Erase the current entry in the By box and key **3**, then click OK.

The space between the "W" and the "I" is expanded by 3 points. Now, however, there is too much space between the "W" and the "I."

4. With the "W" still selected, choose Format Font.

5. Key **2.5** in the By box (replacing 3 pt), and click OK.

FIGURE 5.14
Character Spacing Category of Format Font Dialog Box

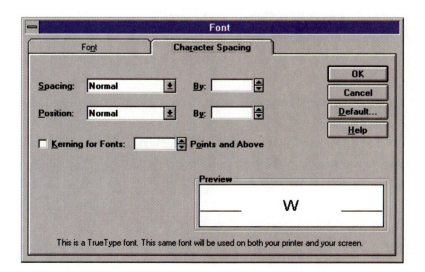

Besides expanding or condensing the spacing between a selected pair of characters, you can expand or condense character spacing for an entire line.

6. Condense character spacing:

   a. Select the entire line and choose Format Font.

Notice that the Spacing box is currently blank because part of the selection is expanded and the rest is normal.

   b. Open the Spacing box and click Condensed.

Changing the Case

· ·

1. Move the insertion point to the end of the line and press **Enter** twice.

2. Copy the line:

   a. Select the first line, including the ending paragraph mark.

   b. Click 📋.

   c. Click on the second blank line.

   d. Click 📋; then press **Enter**.

3. Select the first line and choose Format Change Case. The dialog box shown in Figure 5.15 appears.

4. Click Title Case; then click ⬚ **OK** ⬚.

c. Key **1.5** in the By box. Then click ⬚ **OK** ⬚ to condense spacing between characters by 1.5 points.

Tight spacing sometimes makes text look nicer, but in this case the text is too crowded.

7. With the entire line still selected, expand the spacing by 6 points, then click **B**.

Expanding the spacing spreads the words out across the line. The added bold format creates a very strong visual effect within a document.

Only the first letter of each word is now capitalized.

5. Select the second line.

6. Choose Format Change Case, click lowercase, and click ⬚ **OK** ⬚. The entire line should be lowercase.

FIGURE 5.15
Format Change
Case Dialog Box

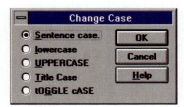

7. Copy the selected lowercase line to the second blank line.

8. Select the third line (the copy) and choose Format Change Case.

9. Click UPPERCASE; then click [OK]. The last line should be in all capitals.

Besides changing the case of lines, you can change case for individual words.

TIP

Shift + **F3** is a shortcut for quickly changing the case of selected text.

10. Select the word "For" in the first line and change it to lowercase.

11. Clear the screen (you do not need to save this document).

COMPUTER ACTIVITIES

ACTIVITY 1

1. Open **act2-2.doc** from your Student Disk and save it as **act5-1**.

2. Add a Next Page section break at the top of the document. Then click on the section mark and create a title page for the new section as follows:

   a. Change the font to 16-point Arial.

   b. Key **EMPLOYEE WELLNESS PROGRAMS** in all caps (keep the centered, bold format).

   c. At the end of the title, change the font to 14-point Times New Roman. Then press **Enter** four times.

   d. Key your name (without the all caps and bold formats) and press **Enter**.

   e. Key your course title and press **Enter** four times.

   f. Insert the current date, then press **Enter** once to end with a paragraph break.

   g. Move the insertion point up into the title page and center the page vertically. (Remember that Apply To should be This Section.)

3. Save the changes to the document.

4. Check the document in Print Preview, print a copy, close Print Preview, and clear the screen.

ACTIVITY 2

1. Open **chap5-1.doc** from your Student Disk and save it as **act5-2**.

2. Center each line of the flyer.

HINT: *Triple-click in the selection bar to select the entire document.*

3. Change the first line to 18-point Arial bold.

4. Change the second and third lines of text to 14-point Courier New bold.

5. Change the rest of the document to 14-point Times New Roman (do not apply the bold format this time).

6. Apply the italic format from "For more information . . ." to the end of the document; then deselect.

7. Center the document vertically.

8. In Print Preview, change the top margin to approximately 1 inch.

HINT: *Hold down* **Alt** *as you drag on the vertical ruler.*

9. Drag to the left on the horizontal ruler until the longest line in the document looks centered (you will probably have to release and drag several times to get this correct).

10. Save the document and print a copy.

11. If you want to, experiment with different fonts, character spacing, and margins (save the document with a new name first).

12. Clear the screen.

ACTIVITY 3

1. Open **chap5-2.doc** from your Student Disk and save it as **act5-3**.

2. Change the first line to 16-point Arial bold.

3. With the first line still selected, expand the spacing by 3.0 points.

4. Change the rest of the title page to 14-point.

5. Save the changes, check the document in Print Preview, print a copy, close Print Preview, and clear the screen.

CREATE YOUR OWN

Write a formal announcement to notify your family and friends of your upcoming graduation. Include the name of your school and be specific about the date, time, and location for the graduation ceremony.

Be creative. Use a variety of fonts and point sizes to enhance the text. If necessary, adjust the spacing between characters, and center the page vertically. If your printer has the capability, consider formatting the announcement for odd-size stationery by changing the width and height measurements in the Paper Size portion of the Page Setup dialog box.

R EVIEW E XERCISES

TRUE / FALSE

Each of the following statements is either true or false. Indicate your answer on the left by circling T if the statement is true or F if the statement is false.

(T)   F   1. To underline words but not the space between words, click the Underline icon on the Formatting Toolbar.

T   (F)   2. You cannot edit text in Print Preview because the text is too small to read.

(T)   F   3. When you turn on kerning, Word automatically adjusts spacing between certain letter pairs for fonts over a certain size.

(T)   F   4. You cannot use a font size that is not listed in the Font Size list box.

FILL IN THE BLANKS

Complete the following sentences by writing the correct word or words in the blanks provided.

5. To create a title page with different formats than the rest of the document, insert a Next Page section break with the _____Page Break_____ command.

6. To center a section vertically, choose the _____Insert Break Only_____ command, click Layout, and change the vertical alignment.

7. To change the direction of printing (orientation), choose the _____Format_____ command, click Paper Size, and click Portrait or Landscape.

8. To change character spacing, choose the _____Font_____ command, click Character Spacing, select Expanded or Condensed in the Spacing box, and key an amount in the By box.

MATCHING

Find the key(s) or icon on the right that matches the description on the left, and write the appropriate letter in the blank provided at the left margin.

_G_ **9.** Print Preview

_D_ **10.** Single-space

_I_ **11.** Double-space

_H_ **12.** Align Left

_C_ **13.** Center

_B_ **14.** Align Right

_J_ **15.** Justify

a. **Ctrl** + **S**

b. ▤

c. ▤

d. **Ctrl** + the number **1**

e. **Ctrl** + **D**

f. 🖨

g. 🔍

h. ▤

i. **Ctrl** + **2**

j. ▤

REFERENCE QUESTIONS

Referring to the _Microsoft Word User's Guide,_ write the answers to the following questions in the space provided.

1. Without opening the Font Size box, how can you quickly change to a larger or smaller point size?

   Zoom Control ?

2. How do you convert pitch (characters per inch) used on typewriters to point size?

   Font, Character spacing

PAGE BREAKS, HEADERS AND FOOTERS, FOOTNOTES

OBJECTIVES
Upon completion of this chapter, you will be able to:

- Insert and delete hard page breaks.

- Attach page numbers to the document.

- Add headers and footers.

- Add footnote references to text.

Preparation

1. To complete the chapter activities, you will need to access the Data Disk files MEMBERS.DOC, EXERCISE.DOC, and REMEDIES.DOC and your Student Disk files ACT3-2A.DOC, ACT5-1.DOC, and ACT5-3. DOC.

2. Remember to save frequently as you work. You will generally not be reminded to save until all work is completed for a document.

3. If you make mistakes as you work with the exercises in the chapter, remember to click ⟲⊞ immediately after completing the action.

4. At the end of each class session, be sure to close Word and Windows properly. If you are using the hard drive to store your completed work, back up your files onto your formatted Student Disk and erase your files from the directory you used on the hard drive. (Do not erase the Data Disk files unless your instructor tells you to do so.)

Page Breaks

As you key text, Word automatically begins new pages when needed (inserts *soft page breaks*). You can also break pages manually (insert *hard page breaks*).

EXERCISE 6.1 Adding Hard Page Breaks

· ·

1. Open **act5-3.doc** from your Student Disk and save it as **chap6-1**.

2. Move the insertion point to the third page:

  a. Double-click the page number on the status bar.

  b. Click Next twice.

  c. Click [**Close**].

> **TIP**
>
> A shortcut to move down or up one page at a time is (Alt) + (Ctrl) + (Page Down) or (Alt) + (Ctrl) + (Page Up).

3. Click the up scroll bar arrow once.

Notice the thin dotted line across the screen. This is a soft page break that Word automatically inserted at the end of the page (Figure 6.1). (The text above and below the page break may vary.)

FIGURE 6.1
Soft Page Break

unhealthy·diet,·and·stress·weaken·the

| → Survey·results·indicate·that·a·l

4. Move the insertion point to the top of the second page:

  a. Double-click the page number on the status bar. *Doesn't show on screen*

  b. Click Previous.

  c. Click [**Close**].

5. Click an insertion point to the left of the tab of the second paragraph (beginning "As people age...").

6. Insert a page break:

  a. Choose Insert Break.

  b. With Page Break selected in the Break dialog box, click [**OK**].

The page breaks immediately before the insertion point. The hard page break is indicated by the dotted line and the words "Page Break" (Figure 6.2). Page breaks that you insert are known as hard page breaks.

7. Move the insertion point to the left of the tab

FIGURE 6.2
Hard Page Break

exercise,·a·healthy·diet,·and·reduced·emotional·stress·also·help
·································Page·Break·································

| → As·people·age,·their·immune·systems·weaken·and·beco

TIP

 Ctrl + **Enter** is a shortcut to insert a hard page break.

for the paragraph that begins "Fortunately, even though ..." and insert a page break.

8. Move the insertion point to the left of the tab for the paragraph that begins "Survey results ..." and insert a page break.

9. Press **Enter** to create a blank line, and move the insertion point to the blank line.

10. Key an underlined subheading, **Exercise**.

11. Move the insertion point to the left of the tab for the paragraph that begins "Proper nutrition ..." and insert a page break.

12. Press **Enter** to create a blank line, and move the insertion point to the blank line.

13. Key an underlined subheading, **Nutrition and Stress**.

14. Move the insertion point to the left of the tab for the last paragraph that begins "In summary ..." and insert a page break.

15. Press **Enter**, and move the insertion point to the blank line.

16. Key an underlined subheading, **Conclusion**.

17. Move the insertion point to the top of the document.

18. Scroll down through the document and notice that all page breaks are now hard page breaks (except the section break below the title page).

EXERCISE

✓

6.2   Deleting Hard Page Breaks

Soft page breaks cannot be deleted. Hard page breaks, are removed like normal characters.

1. Move the insertion point to page 3.

HINT: *Double-click the page number on the status bar, key* **3**, *click Go To, and click* [**Close**]. *Don't use*

Just put cursor on line, Hit "Delete"

2. Move the insertion point up one line, to the hard page break above the paragraph that begins "As people age . . ."

3. Press (Delete). The hard page break is deleted.

4. Move the insertion point down to the next hard page break and delete it.

5. Scroll through your document. You should now have hard page breaks only above the underlined subheadings.

6. Save the changes to your document, print a copy, and clear the screen.

Page Numbering

Page numbers can be added to a document either by using the Insert Page Numbers command or by adding a *header* or *footer* containing a page number. You will work with headers and footers later in the chapter. Using the Insert Page Numbers command is a quick way to add page numbers that do not need accompanying text.

EXERCISE

6.3 Adding Page Numbers with the Insert Page Numbers Command

• •

1. Open the Data Disk file **members.doc** and save it in the appropriate location for Student Disk files as **chap6-2**.

2. Switch to Print Preview. If necessary, click ▣ to display a single page. Change the left

and right margins to 1.25 inches, then close Print Preview.

HINT: *Hold down* (Alt) *and drag on the horizontal ruler.*

FIGURE 6.3
Insert Page Numbers Dialog Box

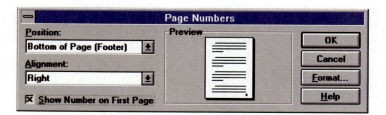

3. Choose Insert Page Numbers. The Page Numbers dialog box (Figure 6.3) appears.

4. If necessary, select Bottom of Page (Footer) in the Position list box.

5. Select Center in the Alignment list box.

6. If an *X* appears in the check box for Show Number on First Page (the default), click the check box to turn off the option, because you do not want a page number on the first page.

7. Click [**OK**].

Page numbers will be added to each page when the document is printed, although they cannot be seen on the screen at this time in Normal View.

EXERCISE

6.4

Viewing Page Numbers in Print Preview

1. With the insertion point at the top of the document, click [🔍].

A reduced view of the first page is displayed. Notice that there is no page number on the first page.

2. Click the Page Forward icon on the vertical scroll bar [▼].

Notice the centered page number at the bottom of page 2 (Figure 6.4). (If you want to see the page number more clearly, click [🔍] if necessary to highlight the icon; then click on the page number until it is magnified.)

3. Click [▼] again and notice the page number on page 3.

Page numbers are document formats and apply to the entire document (except the first page when you have turned off the option).

FIGURE 6.4
Page Number in Print Preview

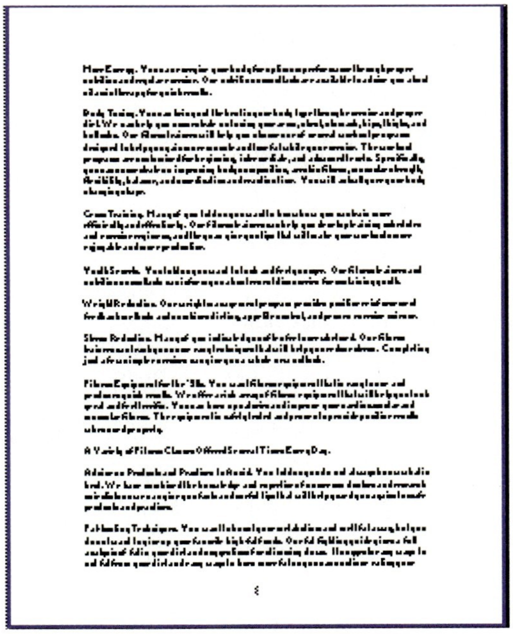

[Figure showing a reduced page of text with a page number centered at the bottom]

4. Click [**Close**].

EXERCISE 6.5

Viewing and Editing Page Numbers in Page Layout

View

In _Page Layout,_ a full page is displayed, with elements (such as page numbers, footnotes, and page breaks) displayed as they will be printed. Like Print Preview, Page Layout has rulers for adjusting margins, and it has the Page Forward and Page Back icons on the vertical scroll bar to allow you to move quickly from one page to the next or previous page. Page Layout, however, is slower than Normal View and should be used for last-minute adjustments rather than for keying and editing text.

1. Click the Page Layout View icon 📄 on the horizontal scroll bar at the bottom of the page.

The document switches to Page Layout View

(Figure 6.5). (If the first page is not displayed, press **Ctrl** + **Home**.)

2. Click ▼ twice, and click the up scroll bar arrow until you see a dimmed page number on page 2 (a dimmed item cannot be edited).

3. Click ▼ again and see the dimmed page number on page 3.

4. Change the page numbers from center alignment to right alignment:

   a. Choose Insert Page Numbers.

   b. Select Right in the Alignment list box.

   c. Click **OK** .

FIGURE 6.5
Document in Page Layout View

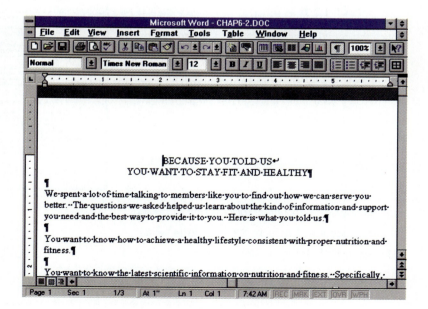

5. Scroll to the right on page 3 and notice that the page number is now at the right.

6. Click the Page Back icon on the vertical scroll bar ⬆ and notice that the page number on page 2 is also right-aligned.

Remember that page numbers are document formats, so changing the page number format on one page changes it on all pages.

7. Click the Normal View icon on the horizontal scroll bar (F5) to return to a normal view of your document.

8. Save and print your document, but do not clear the screen yet.

IMPORTANT: Do not save your work for the remainder of this exercise.

9. Switch to Page Layout View and scroll to the page number on the second page.

10. Double-click the dimmed page number.

The Header and Footer Toolbar and a dotted footer *pane* appear (Figure 6.6). (Note that the position of the Toolbar may vary and you may also see the header pane for page 3.) A page number is considered to be a header or footer.

11. If necessary, drag the title bar for the Header and Footer Toolbar to move it up out of the

footer pane so that you can see all changes to the footer pane.

12. Drag across the page number to select it. A shaded frame appears around the number.

13. Position the mouse pointer on the page number. When you see a four-headed arrow, drag left (be sure to stay within the footer pane). When the page number is at approximately the center of the footer pane, release the mouse button.

Dragging a selected page number is a way that you can quickly adjust page number position. Remember that the change affects all page numbers.

14. You can add emphasis to your page number. With the page number still selected, click **B**. The page number now has the bold format.

15. Click ⬇.

The page number on page 3 should also be bold and approximately centered. (If it is not, drag to select the number, drag it to the center of the footer pane, and check page 2 to see if the page number there also changes.)

16. Click **Close** on the Header and Footer Toolbar.

17. Clear the screen without saving.

FIGURE 6.6
Header and Footer
Toolbar and Footer Pane

Headers and Footers

Headers and footers are information and/or graphics that print in the top and bottom margin of each page. Your document can have a header, a footer, or both. Headers and footers can be a single paragraph or multiple paragraphs. Using a header or footer is also an alternate way to add page numbers to a document. The advantages to using the View Header and Footer command rather than the Insert Page Numbers command are that you can include text with the page number, and you can use different headers and footers for odd/even pages.

EXERCISE 6.6
Adding a Header and Footer to a Multiple-Page Document

1. Open the Data Disk file **exercise.doc** and save it in the appropriate place for Student Disk files as **chap6-3**.

2. Choose View Header and Footer.

Word switches temporarily to Page Layout View. The Header and Footer Toolbar and a blank header pane appear, and the document pane is dimmed as shown in Figure 6.7.

FIGURE 6.7
Header and Footer Toolbar and Header Pane

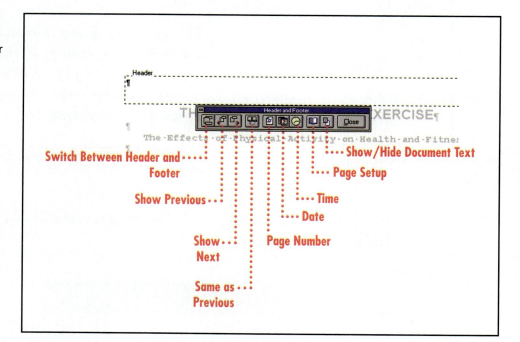

Switch Between Header and Footer

Show Previous

Show Next

Same as Previous

Page Number

Date

Time

Page Setup

Show/Hide Document Text

3. Change the first page setting and change margins:

   a. Click the Page Setup icon on the Header and Footer Toolbar 📖.

   b. If there is no *X* in the Different First Page box, click the check box to select the option, because you generally do not want a header or footer on the first page of a document.

   c. Click the Margins folder tab.

   d. Change the left and right margins to 1.25 inches.

   e. Click [**OK**].

The header pane is now labeled First Page Header. You will leave this pane blank.

4. Click the Show Next icon on the Header and Footer Toolbar 📄. You will create a header beginning on page 2.

5. Key **The Hidden Benefits of Exercise** (this text will print at the left margin at the top of each page but the first).

6. Press **Tab**, key **Page**, space once, and click the Page Number icon on the Header and Footer Toolbar 🔢.

The page number will print centered at the top of each page except the first. Note that in this case you used the page number with text (the word "Page"). Alternatively, you could have used hyphens before and after the number, or you could have used the page number alone with no accompanying text.

7. Click the Show Previous icon on the Header and Footer Toolbar 📄. Notice that the first-page header pane is still blank.

8. Click 📄 to return to the header you created.

In most cases you will not use both a header and a footer in a document. In the following steps, however, you will create a footer for document identification. If you want to, you can add this type of footer to all your documents from now on (but do not turn on Different First Page if you have a one-page document).

9. Click the Switch Between Header and Footer icon on the Header and Footer Toolbar 📄. A blank footer pane is displayed at the bottom of the second page.

10. Key **chap6-3.doc**.

11. Press **Tab** and click the Date icon on the Header and Footer Toolbar 📅.

The current date (at the time of printing) will print at the bottom center of each page except the first.

12. Press **Tab** and click the Time icon on the Header and Footer Toolbar 🕐.

The current time (at the time of printing) will print at the bottom right of each page except the first.

13. Click [**Close**] to return to your document.

14. Click 🔍 to check that you have no header or footer on the first page.

15. Click ⬇ to see that you have both a header and a footer on the second page.

16. Close Print Preview.

17. Scroll through your document. If any heading (such as "Depression and Anxiety") is on a

separate page from its related text, insert a page break at the beginning of the heading.

18. Save and print the document; then clear the screen. (When you clear the screen, you may be prompted to re-save your document, because the Date and Time functions are updated at the time of printing.)

EXERCISE

6.7 Adding a Header to a Multiple-Page Letter

In the following steps you will add a three-line header to a two-page letter. Block-style letters generally use a block-style header rather than one spread across the page like the one you just created.

1. Open your Student Disk file **act3-2a.doc** and save it as **chap6-4**.

2. Choose View Header and Footer.

3. Change the first page setting and the margins:

   a. Click 📖 on the Header and Footer Toolbar.

   b. Turn on Different First Page.

   c. Click the Margins folder tab.

   d. Change all margins except the bottom margin to 1.25 inches.

   e. Click OK .

4. Click 📑 to go to the header pane on the second page.

5. Key **Ms. Shelley Azano,** and press Enter .

6. Key **Page**, space once, click 🔢, and press Enter .

7. Key **March 2, 19—**.

8. Click Close .

9. Scroll through your document. If a heading (for example, "Educational Programs and Workshops") is on a separate page from its related text, insert a page break at the beginning of the heading. (Do not add any unnecessary page breaks.)

10. Click 🔍. Check that there is no header on the first page of the letter. Close Print Preview.

11. Save and print the document; then clear the screen.

to change starting
Page #'s

EXERCISE

6.8

Adding Headers and Footers Within Sections

1. Open your Student Disk file **chap6-1.doc** and save it as **chap6-5**.

Although you could keep the same filename, renaming will allow you to go back to the original **chap6-1.doc** to correct any errors.

2. Choose View Header and Footer.

Because your document is divided into sections for the title page you created earlier, you should see a pane labeled "Header Section 1."

3. Create a header beginning on the third page of the document:

a. Click 📑 to skip the header pane for the title page section (leave it blank).

b. Click 📖.

c. Turn on Different First Page so that you will have no header or footer on the first page of this section.

d. Click ⬚ OK ⬚.

e. Click 📑 to skip the first-page header pane (leave it blank).

Notice that the Same as Previous icon on the Header and Footer Toolbar 📇 is highlighted. Initially, Word connects headers and footers for all sections. Because you want blank headers for the title page and the first page, but headers for this portion of the document, you need to turn off the connection.

f. Click 📇 to turn off the connection to the

blank title-page and first-page header panes. You can now create a different header with text for this portion of the document.

4. Key **Chapter 1**.

5. Press (Tab) and key **Strengthening Your Immune System**.

6. Press (Tab), key **Page**, space once, and click 🔳.

The page number is currently 3. The title page should not be included in the page numbering, however, so this page should actually be page 2.

7. Change the starting page number so that the title page section will not be numbered:

a. Choose Insert Page Numbers and click Format. The dialog box shown in Figure 6.8 appears.

FIGURE 6.8
Page Number Format
Portion of Insert Page Numbers Dialog Box

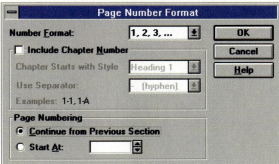

b. Click Start At so the section following the title page will begin with the page number *1*.

c. Click [OK] twice.

Notice that the status bar now shows "Page 1" for your first page of document text. Remember, though, that no page number will print for this page because you turned on Different First Page and left the header pane blank.

8. Click [🖺] to return to the Header Section 2 pane.

Notice that this portion of the document now begins with Page 2 rather than Page 3.

9. Create a footer beginning on your new page 2:

a. Click [🖺] to switch to a footer pane.

b. Click [🖺] to turn off the connection to the blank title-page and first-page footer panes. You can now create a different footer with text for this portion of the document.

10. Key your name, press (Tab), click [🖺], press (Tab), and click [⊘].

11. Click [Close].

12. Change the margins for the entire document:

a. Choose File Page Setup.

b. Click the Margins folder tab.

c. Change the left and right margins to 1.25 inches.

d. Select Whole Document in the Apply to list box.

e. Click [OK].

13. Preview your document:

a. Click [🖺].

b. Check that there is no header or footer on the title page or the following page.

c. Check that there are both a header and a footer on all succeeding pages.

d. Click the arrow next to the Zoom Control box and change to Page Width to enlarge your view.

e. Scroll to see if the header page numbering begins with 2.

f. Change the Zoom Control back to Whole Page; then close Print Preview.

14. Save and print the document but do not clear the screen.

Footnotes

Footnotes are references that give credit to the source of the information or give the reader additional information. These references are generally listed at the bottom of the page on which the information appears. In some cases, all the references may be printed at the end of the section or document (*endnotes*). If the footnote is to appear at the bottom of the page (the default), Word adjusts page breaks to allow space for the footnotes.

E X E R C I S E
6.9
Adding Footnotes

● ●

1. If you closed **chap6-5.doc**, open it from your Student Disk. Save it with a new name, **chap6-6**.

2. Scroll to the third paragraph. Position the insertion point immediately after the period at the end of the second sentence (it begins: "One of the functions . . .").

3. Choose Insert Footnote to open the dialog box shown in Figure 6.9.

In the Footnote and Endnote dialog box, you can create your own custom footnote reference mark (for example, an asterisk). Creating your own reference mark, however, means that if you rearrange your text or move, copy, or delete a footnote, you must manually rearrange the other custom footnotes. When you select AutoNumber, Word inserts a raised (superscript) number as the reference mark and automatically renumbers footnotes and reference marks whenever text or footnotes are rearranged.

4. If they are not already selected, select Footnote and AutoNumber.

5. Click [**OK**].

The window is now split into the document pane and the footnote pane, and a footnote reference mark (the number *1*) appears in both panes (Figure 6.10 on page 136).

6. Key the following footnote: **Maria Gonzales, "Strengthening the Immune**

FIGURE 6.9
Insert Footnote and Endnote Dialog Box

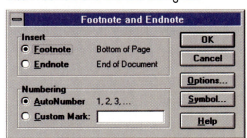

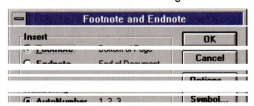

Footnotes

Footnotes are references that give credit to the source of the information or give the reader additional information. These references are generally listed at the bottom of the page on which the information appears. In some cases, all the references may be printed at the end of the section or document (*endnotes*). If the footnote is to appear at the bottom of the page ...

Reference

| All Footnotes | ▼ | Close |

Adding Footnotes

1. If you closed **chap6-5.doc**, open it from your Student Disk. Save it with a new name, **chap6-6**.

2. Set the insertion point at the end of the paragraph that begins "Survey results ..."

9. Insert the following footnote: **Yoshi Ito, "The Aging Process,"** *Today's Health,* **January 1994, pp. 46–47.**

In the Footnote and Endnote dialog box, you can

FIGURE 6.9
Insert Footnote and Endnote Dialog Box

Footnote and Endnote	
Insert	**OK**
○ Footnote Bottom of Page	**Cancel**
○ Endnote End of Document	
	Options...
● AutoNumber 1 2 3	**Symbol...**

Pressing Ctrl + ... is a shortcut to insert an autonumbered ... Endnote dialog box.

create your own custom footnote reference mark (for example, an asterisk). Creating your own reference mark, however, means that if you re-arrange your text or move, copy, or delete a footnote, you must manually rearrange the other ...

HINT: *Press* Ctrl *+* End *; then click at the end of the last paragraph.*

12. Insert the following footnote: **Jenny Gubbels, "Genetics and Health,"**

4. If they are not already selected, select Footnote and AutoNumber.

5. Click OK.

The window is now split into the document pane and the footnote pane, and a footnote reference mark (the number 1) appears in both panes (Figure 6.10 on page 151).

EXERCISE

6.10

Viewing Footnotes

● ●

1. Move the insertion point to the top of the document.

2. Go to a specific footnote reference and open the footnote pane:

   a. Double-click the page number on the status bar.

   b. In the Go to What list box, click Footnote.

   c. Click Next twice; then click [**Close**].

The insertion point is now at the second footnote reference mark.

   d. Double-click the footnote reference mark to open the footnote pane to the second footnote.

TIP

You can view footnotes by choosing View Footnotes.

3. Click an insertion point in each footnote in the footnote pane, and watch how the view in the document pane adjusts to match the new position.

With the footnote pane open, you will be able to go back and forth between the footnote pane and the document pane simply by clicking in the desired pane. You must use the Insert Footnote command, however, to add footnotes.

EXERCISE

Moving around foot notes

Editing Footnotes

● ●

1. Move the insertion point to the first footnote (the document pane now shows the paragraph containing this footnote reference mark).

Notice that the footnotes are in the following order: Maria Gonzales, Yoshi Ito, and Jenny Gubbels.

2. Move a paragraph containing a footnote:

   a. Click in the document pane.

   b. Position the mouse pointer in the selection bar next to the paragraph containing the footnote reference number *1*. Double-click to select the paragraph.

   c. Move the selected paragraph to the end of the document.

HINT: *Click* ✂ *, press* **Ctrl** *+* **End** *, and click* 📋 *.*

Notice that this paragraph now has the reference mark *3* instead of *1*. The footnotes are now in the following order: Yoshi Ito, Jenny Gubbels, and Maria Gonzales.

3. Undo the move.

HINT: *Open the Undo list box and drag to select both Paste and Cut.*

The footnotes are in their original order: Maria Gonzales, Yoshi Ito, and Jenny Gubbels.

4. Click an insertion point in the document pane to deselect the text.

5. Copy a footnote:

a. Scroll if necessary, to the first reference mark in the document pane; then drag to select it.

b. Copy the reference mark to the end of the first sentence in the same paragraph (it begins: "There is one …").

HINT: *Use [icon] and [icon].*

There are now two reference marks in the paragraph and the footnote pane shows four footnotes: Maria Gonzales, Maria Gonzales (an identical footnote except for the number), Yoshi Ito, and Jenny Gubbels.

6. Delete a footnote:

a. Select the first reference mark in the document pane (the one you just pasted).

b. Press (Delete), then adjust the spacing between sentences.

The copied footnote is deleted and the footnotes are again rearranged.

IMPORTANT: Footnotes cannot be deleted by deleting the footnote text in the footnote pane; the paragraph mark and the footnote reference numbers would remain. Footnotes can only be deleted by deleting the footnote reference mark in the document pane.

7. Scroll up to the second paragraph and insert the following footnote at the end of the sentence that begins "As people age …": **Joseph Kolinski, "Immune Systems," Better Health, February 1994, pp. 17–20.**

Notice that the other footnotes in the footnote pane have been automatically renumbered.

8. Click in the document pane.

9. Scroll down to the subheading "Nutrition and Stress." Position the insertion point at the end of the first paragraph (beginning "Proper nutrition can …").

10. Insert the following footnote: **Dennis Burns, "Nutrition Is Important," Health Report, May 1994, pp. 36–40.**

Look at the footnotes in the footnote pane. The footnotes are now in the following order: Joseph Kolinski, Maria Gonzales, Yoshi Ito, Dennis Burns, and Jenny Gubbels.

11. Close the footnote pane.

12. Scroll through your document and delete the three hard page breaks (not the section break for the title page).

13. Save and print the document, then clear the screen.

Computer Activities

ACTIVITY 1

1. Open your Student Disk file **chap6-4.doc** and save it as **act6-1**.

2. Insert a footnote at the end of the first sentence under the heading "References for New Membership." Use an asterisk as the custom reference mark. In the footnote pane, key **The new member must pledge membership for a minimum of one year.**

3. Close the footnote pane and save your changes.

4. Scroll through your document to check your page breaks. Make the adjustments below if needed:

   a. If you have a hard page break and now have a blank page because text moved down when you added the footnote, delete the page break.

   b. If a heading (for example, "Educational Programs and Workshops") is on a separate page from its related text, delete two returns between the letterhead and the date. (Inserting a page break for the heading would cause you to have a third page with just part of the complimentary closing lines of the letter.)

5. Preview your document to check that you have a footnote and a header on the second page; then close Print Preview.

6. Save your document, print it, and clear the screen.

ACTIVITY 2

1. Open the Data Disk file **remedies.doc** and save it in the appropriate place for Student Disk files as **act6-2**.

2. Spell-check the document. (Note that "urushiol" is not an error and should not be changed.)

3. Make the changes indicated in Figure 6.11 on pages 141–144.

4. Insert page numbers to be centered at the bottom of the page; however, a page number should not be included for the first page.

5. Beginning at the top, scroll through your document. If a heading (such as "Insect Bites") is separated from its related paragraphs, insert a page break.

6. Save your document, check it in Print Preview, print a copy, and clear the screen.

FIGURE 6.11
Document with Proofreaders' Marks

(HOME REMEDIES) *14-point, no bold*

Add a blank line.

You do not always have to see a doctor for what ails

you. For years home remedies have been used to treat ~~just~~

~~about~~ everything from athlete's foot to yawning. Some home

remedies are based on scientific fact while others work in

spite of the fact that they have no ~~known~~ *medicinal* merit. Some

doctors will tell you that home remedies often work simply

because of the placebo effect. They essentially offer a

soothing ⌃ solution. *or gratifying*

Probably at one time or another you have used home

remedies to relieve minor ~~ailments~~. *ills* For example, maybe you

drank a cup of hot tea with honey and lemon to soothe a

sore throat. It is likely, too, that ⌃ at least one of those *on*

~~times~~ you claimed that your home remedy was more effective *occasions*

than a doctor's care.

A few household items are used so frequently as home

Continued on next page

remedies that they are frequently called cure-alls. For

instance, baking soda will stop bleeding gums. A wet tea bag

will take the sting out of a fever blister or ease

eyestrain. Ground oatmeal in the bath water will dry up

oozing blisters resulting from chicken pox.

Home remedies make everyday life easier and usually

save you time and money by eliminating trips to the doctor for

medical care. A few home remedies *some of which you may not be aware of* are described below.

You should always use ~~your~~ common sense when applying

these home remedies. If the ailment does not improve

within a day or two, or if the symptoms get worse, you

should contact a doctor immediately for some sound

medical advice.

Insect Bites *underline*

All of us have been bitten by mosquitoes, and we know

they can be quite painful. One of several known home

Continued on next page

remedies to relieve the pain of a mosquito bite is to apply

a drop of household ammonia to the ~~effective~~ *affected* area.

(Poison Ivy/Poison Oak) *underline*

Since youth, we have all learned to stay away from

three-leafed plants that contain a sap called urushiol.

Urushiol causes a bad rash that we commonly know as poison

ivy. *or poison oak* If you come in contact with urushiol, wash your skin

immediately with soap and water. If a rash develops, apply

a baking soda *and water* solution to dry the oozing blisters.

(Congestion) *underline*

Often when you catch a cold, you experience

congestion. *in the throat and lungs* Licorice is a natural ingredient that will

help to discharge the mucus from the respiratory tract.

Lozenges or tea that contain licorice are especially

effective in clearing your throat and lungs.

Continued on next page

<u>Tension Headaches</u> *underline*

      The best cure for a tension headache is to ~~cure~~ *relieve* the

headache at its source by ending the stress. Relaxation

techniques such as a warm bath, a massage, or meditation

can provide comfort. To relieve the pain, drink a cup of

coffee or a soda drink containing caffeine at the first

sign of the symptoms. Caffeine is sometimes found in

over-the-counter pain relievers.

<u>Hiccups</u> *underline*

      No doubt you have heard of placing a paper bag over

your head to get rid of hiccups. It rarely works, though.

Hiccups are caused by nerve impulses in your mouth that

cause your diaphragm to contract. The next time you have

hiccups, try eating a teaspoon of *granulated* sugar. The sugar interferes

with the nerve impulses. Using sugar is especially handy

when treating young children with hiccups.

ACTIVITY 3

1. Open your Student Disk file **act5-1.doc** and save it as **act6-3**.

2. Position the insertion point at the beginning of the first page of the actual document (not the title page) and press **Enter** once. Move the insertion point back up one line and key **ABSTRACT** in all caps.

3. Press **Enter** twice. Turn off the bold format, and turn on justified alignment.

HINT: *Click* ▤ *on the Formatting Toolbar.*

4. Press **Tab** and key the paragraph shown in Figure 6.12. Press **Enter** once at the end of the paragraph.

5. Select the paragraph and spell-check it. Click No when prompted to check the remainder of the document.

6. Save your changes.

7. Position the insertion point at the beginning of the title "EMPLOYEE WELLNESS PROGRAMS" in the document (not on the title page) and insert a Next Page section break so that "EMPLOYEE WELLNESS PROGRAMS" begins on the third page.

8. Insert an appropriate header with page numbers for this section (not the title page or the abstract sections).

HINT: *Be sure to turn on Different First Page in Page Setup; then show the next pane and turn off* ▦ *.*

FIGURE 6.12
Abstract Text

> Businesses have learned that to fulfill their potential, employees must be physically, mentally, and emotionally healthy. Consequently, many mainstream businesses are offering wellness programs. Wellness programs focus on educating employees to make them more health-conscious so they can enhance their health. Although this preventive approach to health care can be expensive, businesses have found that wellness programs pay for themselves because employees stay healthier and have reduced medical bills.

9. Change the format so that page numbering starts in Section 3 rather than on the title page or abstract page.

HINT: *With the insertion point in the header for Section 3, choose Insert Page Numbers.*

10. Check Print Preview to be sure that you have no header or footer on the title page, abstract page, or first page of the document, but that you do have a page number on the last page. Close Print Preview.

11. Change the left and right margins for the entire document to 1.25 inches.

12. Add the following footnote at the end of the first paragraph that begins "Employers value . . ." (you will need to select AutoNumber if you just completed Activity 1): **Sharon Valdez, "The Cost of Sick Leave,"** *Office Technology,* **January 1994, p. 119.**

13. Add a footnote at the end of the last paragraph that begins "Although wellness programs . . .": **Douglas Brown, "The Future of Wellness Programs,"** *Business Today,* **March 1994, p. 14.**

14. Scroll up and add a footnote after the second sentence in the paragraph that begins "Many mainstream businesses . . .": **Maria Sanchez,** *The Cost of Doing Business,* **(New York: Dunn Books, Inc., 1994), p. 8.** (The Douglas Brown footnote is now the third footnote.)

15. Select the first footnote reference and move it up to the end of the third sentence in the same paragraph, which begins "Employers value . . ." Adjust the spacing before and after the footnote reference number if necessary.

16. Insert a footnote at the end of the first sentence in the paragraph that begins "In return for offering . . .": Robert Garcia, **"Health Care Costs,"** *Office Magazine,* **May 1994, pp. 38–39.** (The Douglas Brown footnote is now the fourth footnote.)

17. Close the footnote pane, save your changes, print one copy, and clear the screen.

CREATE YOUR OWN ••••••••••••

Start a course journal by keying a summary of what you have learned in each chapter. The completed summary should describe or explain each of the features and/or concepts presented in that chapter. In addition, the summary should include what you liked and did not like, what you found easy to do and what was challenging for you to complete, and so on.

Double-space the summary. Insert a Next Page section break after completing the description for each chapter so that each chapter description begins on a new page. Beginning at the top of your document, add a footer that indicates the part number, chapter number, and page number. For each place where you have a section break, choose View Header and Footer, switch to the footer, turn off 🖳🖳, and change the chapter number. For Chapter 5 and for the first chapter in each new part of the text, change the part number as well as the chapter number.

As you complete each new chapter in this text, add the chapter summary to your journal. Writing each chapter summary will help you review what you have learned. When you complete the text, this journal will serve as a description of all that you have accomplished in the course.

REVIEW EXERCISES

TRUE / FALSE

Each of the following statements is either true or false. Indicate your answer on the left by circling T if the statement is true or F if the statement is false.

T **F**   **1.** Page numbers are considered to be headers or footers. Changes made to one page number are made throughout the entire document or section.

T **F**   **2.** Headers and footers can only be a single paragraph.

T **F**   **3.** When you rearrange text, the footnotes must always be manually rearranged.

T **F**   **4.** Soft page breaks cannot be deleted.

FILL IN THE BLANKS

Complete the following sentences by writing the correct word or words in the blanks provided.

5. To add page numbers without text, choose the ___Insert, Page #'s___ command.

6. To add a footnote, choose the ___Insert Footnote / View, Header & footer___ command.

MATCHING

Find the key(s) or icon on page 149 that matches the description below and write the appropriate letter in the blank provided.

_I_   **7.** Page Layout   _G_   **10.** Hard page break   _I_   **13.** Show Previous

_C_   **8.** Page Forward   _E_   **11.** Switch Between Header and Footer   _A_   **14.** Show Next

_F_   **9.** Page Back   _B_   **12.** Page Setup   _H_   **15.** Same as Previous

a.	e.	i.
b.	f. ⬆	j.
c. ⬇	g. (Ctrl) + (Enter)	k.
d. (Shift) + (Enter)	h.	

REFERENCE QUESTIONS

Referring to the *Microsoft Word User's Guide*, write the answers to the following questions in the space provided.

1. If you are using endnotes rather than footnotes in your document, how can you start the end-notes on a separate page rather than the last page of the document or section?

   Cut & Paste ?

   _____

   _____

2. How can you use Roman numerals for page numbers?

   default ?

   _____

   _____

TABS, INDENTS, AND MARGINS

OBJECTIVES
Upon completion of this chapter, you will be able to:

- Set and clear custom tabs for left, right, center, and decimal alignment.

- Start new lines without creating new paragraphs.

- Use the Format Painter to repeat formats.

- Select columns of text.

- Add leaders to text.

- Indent all lines of text from the left and/or right margins.

- Indent the first line of text automatically.

- Create hanging indents.

- Create bulleted and numbered lists.

Preparation

1. To complete the chapter activities, you will need to access the Data Disk files ATLANTA.DOC, CASH.DOC, DIRECTOR.DOC, TREAD.DOC, and TEN.DOC and your Student Disk file CHAP6-2.DOC.

2. Remember to save frequently as you work. You will generally not be reminded to save until all work is completed for a document.

3. If you make mistakes as you work with the exercises in the chapter, remember to click ⟲⬇ immediately after completing the action.

4. At the end of each class session, be sure to close Word and Windows properly. If you are using the hard drive to store your completed work, back up your files onto your formatted Student Disk and erase your files from the directory you used on the hard drive. (Do not erase the Data Disk files unless your instructor tells you to do so.)

Using Tabs

Generally, you press (Tab) to begin new paragraphs. Each time you press (Tab), the insertion point moves ½ inch to the right (the default distance between tab stops). For short tables, however, you may want to set your own custom tabs. Word allows you to set four types of custom tab stops: left-aligned, center-aligned, right-aligned, and decimal-aligned.

The ruler shows tick marks every ⅛ inch. Default tab stops are indicated in the shaded area beneath the ruler by small marks every ½ inch. Custom tab stops you set will be shown on the ruler with a capital letter *L* for left-aligned tabs, a backwards capital letter *L* for right-aligned tabs, an upside-down letter *T* for centered tabs, and an upside-down letter *T* with a period for decimal-aligned tabs. Default tab stops to the left of custom tab stops are automatically cleared.

As you work with tabs in this chapter, remember that tabs are a type of paragraph format. If you accidentally delete a paragraph mark and your tab stops are deleted, undo the deletion immediately.

EXERCISE

Setting Custom Tab Stops with the Ruler

Figure 7.1 illustrates the tab stop alignment icons on the ruler. You can set tabs by clicking at the far left end of the ruler until you see the icon for the desired alignment and then clicking on the ruler.

FIGURE 7.1
Tab Stop Alignment Icons

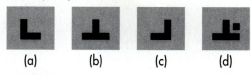

| (a) | (b) | (c) | (d) |

(a) Left-aligned tab icon; (b) Center-aligned tab icon; (c) Right-aligned tab icon; (d) Decimal-aligned tab icon

1. Key the three lines shown below as explained in steps a–c on page 153.

JC212K	5/8#	Ninety-nine	31.985
AE98M	2¼#	Fifty-four	178.55
DA43E	8#	Two hundred	400

a. Use 12-point Times New Roman.

HINT: *To create an entire document with a font or font size other than the default 10-point Times New Roman, select the beginning paragraph mark and make the change.*

b. Press **Tab** once at the beginning of each line and between columns (you will adjust the tab stop positions after keying the table).

c. Press **Shift** + **Enter** twice at the end of the first two lines and press **Enter** once after the last line.

Shift + **Enter** is known as the NEWLINE key. The NEWLINE key forces a line break without starting a new paragraph. All lines ending with the nonprinting NEWLINE character can then be formatted and edited as a single paragraph. ↵

2. Save the document in the appropriate location for Student Disk files as **chap7-1**.

3. Position the insertion point anywhere in the group of lines.

(Remember that paragraph formats can be set with the insertion point anywhere in a paragraph. By using the NEWLINE key, you formatted the entire list as a single paragraph.)

4. Set a left-aligned tab:

a. If the icon at the left end of the ruler is not the left-aligned tab icon ⎣L⎦, click the existing symbol until ⎣L⎦ is displayed.

b. Click the tick mark on the ruler at the ⅝-inch (¾-inch) position (two tick marks before the 1-inch position).

Notice that a marker that looks like the alignment icon is now displayed on the ruler at ¾ inch (Figure 7.2) and the part numbers all start at ¾ inch.

FIGURE 7.2
Left-Aligned Tab Stop

JC212K

AE98M

DA43E

5. Set a right-aligned tab:

a. Click the symbol at the far left end of the ruler until you see the right-aligned tab icon ⎣⅃⎦.

b. Click on the ruler at 1¾ inches.

A right-aligned tab marker is displayed on the ruler at 1¾ inches (Figure 7.3) and the pound symbol (#) in each weight is now at 1¾ inches.

FIGURE 7.3
Right-Aligned Tab Stop

→ 5/8#

→2·1/4#

→ 8#

6. Change to the center-aligned tab icon and set a center-aligned tab at 2½ inches.

A center-aligned tab marker is displayed on the ruler at 2½ inches (Figure 7.4) and each spelled-out quantity is centered under the tab stop (half of each quantity to the left of the tab stop and the other half to the right of the tab stop).

FIGURE 7.4
Center-Aligned Tab Stop

→   Ninety-nine →

→   Fifty-four →

→   Two·hundred→

7. Change to the decimal-aligned tab icon ⊥ and set a decimal-aligned tab at 3¼ inches.

A decimal-aligned tab marker is displayed on the ruler at 3¼ inches (Figure 7.5) and the decimal point for each total aligns with the tab stop. When a number has no decimal point (for example, 400), the last digit of the number is aligned with the tab stop as if there were an imaginary decimal point and zeros following the last digit.

FIGURE 7.5
Decimal-Aligned Tab Stop

3 · ⊥ · | ·
→ 31.985↵

· 178.55↵

→400¶

EXERCISE 7.2

Deleting and Moving Custom Tab Stops
Format

The table would look better with tabs set farther apart, so you will adjust their positions in the following steps.

1. Delete a tab:

a. Position the mouse pointer on the left-aligned tab at ¾ inches.

b. Drag down off the ruler into the document window; then release the mouse button. The tab stop is deleted from the ruler.

The table shifts to the right to start at the new first tab (the old second tab, right-aligned at 1¾ inches). When you want to adjust a table, you can delete the old tabs and set new ones. Moving the tabs is faster and simpler, however.

2. Click ⤺⬚ to restore the tab you deleted.

3. Move the tab stops as follows:

a. Drag the decimal-aligned tab from 3¼ inches to 4¾ inches. The decimal point for each number in the last column now aligns at 4¾ inches.

b. Drag the centered tab from 2½ inches to 3½ inches.

c. Drag the right-aligned tab from 1¾ inches to 2½ inches.

d. Drag the left-aligned tab from ¾ inch to 1 inch.

4. Move the insertion point to the blank paragraph below the list.

Notice that ⊥ is still displayed, although this paragraph has no custom tabs set. When you set a tab stop alignment, Word will use that alignment for all future custom tabs you set until you change the alignment or exit Word.

5. Since most tabs you set will be left-aligned, click to display L so that you will not accidentally set the wrong type of tab in future documents.

6. Save the changes to the document, print one copy, and clear the screen.

EXERCISE

7.3

Selecting a Column of Text

• •

1. Open a new document window and key the text shown in Figure 7.6 as follows:

   a. Use the 12-point Times New Roman font.

   b. Press (Enter) four times after the title.

   c. Press (Tab) once after each city name (you will adjust the tab placement after

   you finish keying the document) and press (Enter) after each date.

   d. Press (Enter) twice after each convention center name.

   e. Press (Enter) once after the last convention center name.

FIGURE 7.6
Unformatted Table

1) Type it in.

```
                HEALTH AND FITNESS EXPO SCHEDULE


COLUMBUS     February 8-10
Ohio Center


DENVER       April 12-14
Colorado Convention Center


LOS ANGELES June 28-30
Los Angeles Convention Center


ATLANTA      September 6-8
World Congress Center


NEW YORK CITY    November 15-17
Javits Convention Center
```

Practice

Note that each line of this table will need to be formatted separately because you are not using the NEWLINE feature (each line will be a separate paragraph).

2. Save the document in the appropriate location for Student Disk files as **chap7-2**.

3. Center the title and format it 18-point Arial bold.

4. Select the first city name ("COLUMBUS") and format it 14-point Courier New bold (do not format the date or convention center name).

5. Repeat multiple formats (in this case, the font, font size, and bold font style):

a. With the city name still selected, double-click the Format Painter icon on the Standard Toolbar 🖌. The icon will be highlighted.

b. Move the mouse pointer (now shaped like the icon, along with the I-beam) to each city name and click on each word of each city to repeat the 14-point Courier New bold format (you can use the scroll bar as needed).

c. Click 🖌 again one time to turn off the feature.

6. Select the entire document.

✗ **HINT:** *To select an entire document* *Triple-click in the selection bar.*

7. Set a left-aligned tab at 4½ inches.

HINT: *With* ⌊L⌋ *displayed at the left end of the ruler, click at 4½ inches.*

Selecting the entire table is faster than setting an individual tab on each line with a date.

8. Save the changes to the document.

9. Select the second column:

a. Position the insertion point immediately to the left of the "F" in "February."

b. Hold down **Alt** and drag to the right and down until all the dates are selected. Then release the mouse button and **Alt**.

10. Click ⌊I⌋. All the dates are italicized.

11. The dates look better without emphasis. Click ⟲⬇.

E X E R C I S E

7.4   Adding Leader Characters to Text

Leader characters guide the reader's eye from one column to the next. They are useful in tables such as financial statements and in tables of contents.

1. Select the entire document.

HINT: *Triple-click in the selection bar.*

2. Choose Format Tabs.

The dialog box shown in Figure 7.7 appears. Note that you can use this dialog box to set tabs at more precise positions than at ⅛-inch increments (for example, 6.35 inches) but generally you will use the ruler to set tabs and use this dialog box only to add leaders.

FIGURE 7.7
Format Tabs Dialog Box

3. If necessary, key **4.5** in the Tab Stop Position box and select Left under Alignment.

4. Click 2 under Leader; then click [**OK**].

5. Click an insertion point to deselect the text so you can see the leaders more clearly.

Each date now begins at 4½ inches, with a row of dots (the leader) preceding the date (see Figure 7.8).

6. Save the changes to the document, print one copy, and clear the screen.

FIGURE 7.8
Table with Leaders

Leaders

COLUMBUS ....→	....................February·8-10¶
Ohio·Center¶	
¶	
DENVER ....→	.........................April·12-14¶
Colorado·Convention·Center¶	
¶	
LOS·ANGELES ....→	..........................June·28-30¶
Los·Angeles·Convention·Center¶	
¶	
ATLANTA ....→	...................September·6-8¶
World·Congress·Center¶	
¶	
NEW·YORK·CITY ....→	.................November·15-17¶
Javits·Convention·Center¶	

Indenting Text

A paragraph *indent* is the distance between paragraph boundaries and the page margins. Indents control the width of the paragraph and the horizontal boundaries of the paragraph. Word has several types of paragraph indents, as illustrated in Figure 7.9 on page 158: standard (no indent), first-line, left, right, left and right combination, and hanging. These indents can be used to set text off from surrounding text.

When you set an indent, the measurement is added to the margin. For example, if the left margin is 1 inch and you set a ½-inch left indent, the paragraph will start 1½ inches from the edge of the paper. Figure 7.10 illustrates the first-line, left, and right indent markers on the ruler. These markers are dragged to set the desired indents.

FIGURE 7.9
Paragraph Indents

This paragraph is keyed with the defaults (no indents). Text begins at the left margin and continues as closely as possible to the right margin on each line.

This paragraph is keyed with a $\frac{1}{4}$-inch first-line indent. All other lines begin at the left margin. A first-line indent can be used as an alternative to pressing TAB to begin each paragraph. First-line indents can use measurements other than the default tab distance of $\frac{1}{2}$-inch. A first-line indent is the distance from the left indent, not the left margin (unless the left indent is 0).

This paragraph is keyed with a $\frac{3}{4}$-inch left indent. When all lines are indented, the text is sometimes called "nested" text.

This paragraph is keyed with a $1\frac{1}{2}$-inch right indent. Although this paragraph has only a right indent, right indents are generally combined with left indents to set off text.

This paragraph is keyed with a 1-inch left and right indent. A combination left and right indent is often used for long quotes in reports.

This is an example of a 1-inch hanging indent. Notice that the first line extends to the left of the other lines. Hanging indents are most often used for enumerated or bulleted items.

FIGURE 7.10
Indent Markers

■ **First-Line Indent**
Marker

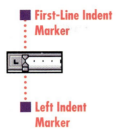

■ **Left Indent**
Marker

Right Indent ■
Marker

Left Portion of Ruler

Right Portion of Ruler

EXERCISE

7.5

Setting Indents with the Ruler

1. Open the Data Disk file **cash.doc** and save the file in the appropriate location for Student Disk files as **chap7-3**.

2. Set a first-line indent:

a. Position the insertion point anywhere in the paragraph that begins "Investment of funds ..."

b. Drag the first-line indent marker ▽ to ½ inch.

The first line of the paragraph is indented ½ inch and the first-line indent marker is at ½ inch.

3. Position the insertion point in the paragraph that begins "Allowable securities ..." and choose Edit Repeat to repeat the indent.

4. Move the insertion point to the end of the

document. Repeat the first-line indent format for the last paragraph that begins "Maturities shall be ..."

5. Move the insertion point to the top of the document. Click an insertion point in the word "Safety" in the list under the first paragraph.

IMPORTANT: To create a left indent, you must move *both* the left indent marker ⌂ and the first-line indent marker ▽. If you drag only the left indent marker, the first line will "hang" to the left of the rest of the paragraph.

6. Set a left indent: point to the small box under the left indent marker ⌂ and drag it to the right to 1 inch.

Notice that the first-line indent marker moves along with the left indent marker.

7. Repeat the format for the following paragraphs:

- Liquidity
- Yield
- Diversification
- U.S. Treasury and Agency Securities
- Commercial Paper
- Banker's Acceptances (BAs)
- Certificates of Deposit (CDs)
- Corporate Bonds and Medium Term Notes (MTNs)
- Money Market Funds
- Tax-Exempt Securities

8. Set a combination left and right indent:

   a. Scroll up and position the insertion point in the paragraph that begins "Rating must be A1/A1+ ..." (under "Commercial Paper").

   b. Set a left indent at 1½ inches.

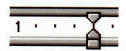

HINT: *Drag the small box.*

The paragraph is now indented 1½ inches on the left. (Remember that the first-line indent marker also moves.)

   c. Drag the right indent marker (Edit) to 4½

inches (1½ inches from the right margin).

The paragraph is now indented 1½ inches on both the left and the right (Figure 7.11).

FIGURE 7.11
Paragraph with Left and Right Indent

Rating·must·be·A1/A1+·by·Standard·&·Poor's·Corporation·(S&P)·and·P1·by·Moody's·Investor·Service,·Inc.·(Moody's).··Dual·rating·required.¶

Because you have set two separate formats using the ruler (a left and a right indent), you must use Format Painter rather than Edit Repeat to repeat the formats.

9. Repeat the multiple paragraph formats:

   a. Select just the paragraph mark at the end of the paragraph that begins "Rating must be ..."

   b. Double-click ✐.

   c. Click in each of the following paragraphs:

- "No new purchases of private ..."
- "If letter of credit ..."
- "The guarantor bank ..."
- "No new purchases of foreign ..."
- "Both demand and time ..."
- "No savings ..."
- "The guarantor bank ..."

- "Rating must be AA/AA ..."

- "Issuer also ..."

- "Managed by ..."

- "Credit quality criteria ..."

- "Must have one ..."

- "No zero coupon ..."

d. Click 🖌 one time to turn off the feature.

10. Add an appropriate header that includes the page number.

HINT: *Choose View Header and Footer. Be sure to click* 📖 *and turn on Different First Page so no header will print on the first page.*

11. Move paragraphs as follows:

HINT: *Use* ① *and* → *. Be sure to include the paragraph mark below the paragraphs being cut.*

a. Select and move the paragraph "U.S. Treasury and Agency Securities" from the first page to become the next-to-last paragraph (just above the paragraph that begins "Maturities shall be ...")

b. Select the paragraph "Commercial Paper" plus the three indented paragraphs below it. Move the four paragraphs below the second occurrence of the paragraph that begins "The guarantor bank ..."

12. Position the insertion point at the end of the word "Diversification" on the first page and insert a footnote: **Measurement of diversification excludes U.S. Government and Agency securities and money market funds.**

13. Position the insertion point at the end of the paragraph "Tax-Exempt Securities" on the last page and insert a footnote: **Demand notes must not require more than 30 days' notice**.

14. Move the insertion point to the top of the document, and scroll through it. Adjust spacing between paragraphs if necessary. If a heading (such as "Commercial Paper") is separated from its related paragraphs, insert a page break at the beginning of the heading.

15. Save the changes, preview the document, print one copy, and clear the screen.

EXERCISE

7.6 Using the Formatting Toolbar to Set Left Indents

1. Open the Data Disk file **director.doc** and save it in the appropriate location for Student Disk files as **chap7-4**.

2. *Nest* (indent) a paragraph to set it off from surrounding paragraphs:

a. Position the insertion point anywhere in the paragraph that reads "Member, Board of Directors."

b. Click the Increase Indent icon on the Formatting Toolbar ⊞.

The paragraph is nested to the first default tab stop (½ inch). Notice that the paragraph "Member, Board of Directors" is now nested between the "Title" and "Purpose" paragraphs. Notice also that the first-line indent marker is at the same position as the left indent marker.

3. Repeat the nest for the following paragraphs:

- "To determine policies . . ."
- "Three years . . ."
- "Regularly"
- "Occasionally NATIONAL FAMILY . . ."
- "Chair, Board of Directors"
- "In writing to . . ."
- All six paragraphs under "Responsibilities and Powers"
- The first and the sixth through tenth paragraphs under "Specific Duties . . ."

4. Set a multiple-level indent:

a. Position the insertion point in the paragraph that begins "Monthly board meetings . . ." on the first page under "Meeting Attendance."

b. Click ⊞ three times to nest the paragraph to the third default tab stop (1½ inches).

5. The paragraph is indented too far. Click the Decrease Indent icon on the Formatting Toolbar ⊞ once to move the paragraph back one tab stop (to 1 inch).

6. Nest the following paragraphs to 1 inch:

HINT: *Click* ⊞ *twice.*

- "Standing Committee . . ."
- "Ad hoc committee . . ."
- "Special events . . ."
- The second through fifth paragraphs under "Specific Duties . . ." (beginning with "Attend regularly . . .")

7. Add an appropriate header that includes a page number.

8. Change the following paragraphs to uppercase:

HINT: *Choose Format Change Case.*

- "Title"
- "Purpose"
- "Term"
- "Meeting Attendance"
- "Responsible To"
- "Resignation"
- "Responsibilities and Powers . . ."
- "Specific Duties . . ."

9. Scroll through your document. If any headings are separated from the text below them, insert a page break. If one or two lines are on a third page, delete returns below the title lines and/or change the left and right margins to 1 inch.

10. Save the changes, preview the document, print one copy, and clear the screen.

Creating Hanging Indents

A *hanging indent* is a special type of indent in which a first-line indent is set to the left of a left indent. All lines but the first "hang" to the right of the first line. Hanging indents are used, for example, for numbered lists, bulleted lists, bibliographies, and terms with the definitions on the right.

E X E R C I S E

7.7 Setting Hanging Indents Using the Ruler

• •

1. Open the Data Disk file **tread.doc** and save it in the appropriate location for Student Disk files as **chap7-5**.

2. Position the insertion point to the left of "For" in the paragraph that begins "For strength training . . ." Key the number **1** and a period and press **Tab**.

3. Position the insertion point to the left of the word "For" in the paragraph beginning "For an upper body workout . . ." Key **2.** and press **Tab**.

4. Position the insertion point to the left of the word "For" in the paragraph beginning "For a lower body workout . . ." Key **3.** and press **Tab**.

5. Position the insertion point to the left of the word "For" in the last paragraph, key **4.**, and press **Tab**.

6. Set a hanging indent:

   a. Position the insertion point in the paragraph numbered 1.

   b. Position the mouse pointer on ⌂ and drag the top portion (the triangle) to ½ inch.

must put cursor arrow only on the Triangle. Otherwise it will move the whole top & Bottom margin icons

163

When you set a hanging indent as you did in Step 6, ♡ does not move.

TIP

A shortcut to create a hanging indent is to press (Ctrl) + (T). To remove a hanging indent, press (Ctrl) + (Shift) + (T).

7. Set ½-inch hanging indents for each of the other numbered paragraphs.

8. Use the spelling and grammar functions to correct the errors in this document (ignore the suggestions for "TREADWALL," "simulate," and "up").

9. Save your changes and print one copy but do not clear the screen.

EXERCISE

7.8 Creating Bulleted Lists Using the Formatting Toolbar

1. Save your file with a new name, **chap7-6**.

2. Select the four numbered paragraphs and the blank lines between them.

HINT: *Drag down the selection bar.*

3. Click the Bullets icon on the Formatting Toolbar.

4. If you see a message about replacing numbers with bullets, click Yes.

A bullet is now inserted for each of the four paragraphs. Word automatically calculates the best distance for the hanging indent for bulleted paragraphs. (In this case, Word used ½ inch because the numbers you replaced were indented ½ inch.) If you need a different indent distance, after adding the bullets, simply drag the markers on the ruler.

5. Save your document, print a copy, and clear the screen.

EXERCISE

Creating Enumerated Lists Using the Formatting Toolbar

1. Open the Data Disk file **ten.doc** and save it in the appropriate location for Student Disk files as **chap7-7**.

2. Select all ten paragraphs that begin with an all-caps title ("ASPARAGUS" through "SWEET POTATOES").

3. Click the Numbering icon on the Formatting Toolbar ▤.

A number is automatically added to each paragraph so the ten paragraphs are now enumerated with the associated text hanging to the right. Word automatically calculates the best distance (in this case, ¼ inch) for the hanging indent for enumerated paragraphs. If you need a different indent distance, after adding the numbers, simply drag the markers on the ruler.

4. Move the paragraph "BRUSSELS SPROUTS" to become the second enumerated paragraph.

HINT: *Use* ① *and* → *. Note that you must position the insertion point on the text rather than the number in order to paste.*

Word automatically renumbers all the enumerated paragraphs when you move, copy, or delete.

5. Open the Undo list box and undo both the paste and the cut.

6. Add an appropriate header with a page number.

7. If your document is now three pages, delete the blank line above the company address at the bottom of the document.

8. Save and print your document; then clear the screen.

Do Practice

COMPUTER ACTIVITIES

ACTIVITY 1

1. Open your Student Disk file **chap6-2.doc** and save it as **act7-1**.

2. Format the first paragraph (beginning "We spent a lot of time …") with a ½-inch first-line indent.

3. Select the next three paragraphs ("You want to know how . . ." "You want to know the latest . . ." and "Most importantly . . .") and set ¾-inch left and right indents (the first-line and left indent markers will be at ¾ inch and the right indent marker will be at 5¼ inches).

4. With the paragraphs still selected, add bullets.

5. Format the paragraph beginning "So that is what . . ." with a ½-inch first-line indent.

6. Format the next three paragraphs ("To that end . . ." "The new program . . ." and "You can still count . . .") with a ½-inch left indent (remember that the first line must also be indented).

7. Select the following 12 paragraphs: begin the selection with "Body Strength . . ." and extend the selection to the end of the paragraph that begins "Informed Choices . . ." (Do not include the blank line below the paragraph that begins "Informed Choices . . .")

8. Enumerate the selected paragraphs.

9. Format the next two paragraphs (beginning "Classes include . . ." and "The classes are . . .") with a 1-inch left and right indent (the right indent marker will be at 5 inches).

10. Format the last two paragraphs (beginning "Getting fit . . ." and "Expect the best . . .") with a ½-inch first-line indent.

11. Position the insertion point at the end of the paragraph "A Variety of Fitness Classes" and key **For example:**

12. Position the insertion point in the paragraph mark below "For example:" and press (Enter) once.

13. Key the text illustrated in Figure 7.12 on page 167. Press (Tab) once at the beginning of each line and between columns (you will adjust the tab positions in Step 13). Press the NEWLINE key once at the end of each line except the last and press (Enter) once after the last line.

14. Position the insertion point anywhere in the group of lines and set a left-aligned tab at ⅜ inch;

FIGURE 7.12
Table to Be Added to Document

Step Aerobics I	Beginners	10:00 - 10:45 a.m.	6:00 - 6:45 p.m.
Step Aerobics II	Intermediate	9:00 - 9:45 a.m.	7:00 - 7:45 p.m.
Step Aerobics III	Advanced	12:00 - 12:45 a.m.	8:00 - 8:45 p.m.
Jazzercise	All Levels	7:00 - 7:45 a.m.	5:30 - 6:15 p.m.
Water Aerobics	Beginners	9:30 - 10:30 a.m.	8:30 - 9:30 p.m.
Floor Exercises	Advanced	8:15 - 9:00 a.m.	6:15 - 7:00 p.m.

a left-aligned tab at $1\frac{7}{8}$ inches; a right-aligned tab at $4\frac{1}{4}$ inches; and a right-aligned tab at $5\frac{5}{8}$ inches.

15. Insert a page break at the beginning of the heading "YOU TOLD US YOU WANT . . ."

16. Scroll down. If Heading 9 (above the table) is separated from any part of the table, insert another page break.

17. Save the changes and print one copy.

ACTIVITY 2

In the following steps you will prepare bibliographies for STRENGTHENING YOUR IMMUNE SYSTEM and EMPLOYEE WELLNESS PROGRAMS, which are documents you worked with in earlier chapters. Figures 7.13 and 7.14 on page 168 contain the information for the bibliographies.

1. Key the documents using the following guidelines:
   - **a.** Use 12-point Courier New.
   - **b.** Press **Enter** four times after the centered heading, "BIBLIOGRAPHY"; then change to left alignment.
   - **c.** Single-space the items with a double space between.
   - **d.** Format each of the paragraphs in the bibliography with a $\frac{1}{2}$-inch hanging indent.
   - **e.** Italicize the titles.

2. Save the bibliography in Figure 7.13 as **act7-2a** and print one copy.

3. Save the bibliography in Figure 7.14 as **act7-2b** and print one copy.

FIGURE 7.13
Bibliography for IMMUNE.DOC

> *Bibliography*
>
> Burns, Dennis. "Nutrition Is Important." Health Report,
> May 1994.
>
> Gonzales, Maria. "Strengthening the Immune System."
> Fit, January 1994.
>
> Gubbels, Jenny. "Genetics and Health." Today's Health,
> March 1994.
>
> Ito, Yoshi. "The Aging Process." Today's Health, January 1994.
>
> Kolinski, Joseph. "Immune Systems." Better Health,
> February 1994.

FIGURE 7.14
Bibliography for WELLNESS.DOC

> *Bibliography*
>
> Brown, Douglas. "The Future of Wellness Programs." Business
> Today, March 1994.
>
> Garcia, Robert. "Health Care Costs." Office Magazine, May 1994.
>
> Sanchez, Maria. The Cost of Doing Business. New York: Dunn
> Books, Inc., 1994.
>
> Valdez, Sharon. "The Cost of Sick Leave." Office Technology,
> January 1994.

ACTIVITY 3

1. Open the Data Disk file **atlanta.doc** and save it in the appropriate location for Student Disk files as **act7-3**.

2. Position the insertion point on the paragraph mark below "Nutrition products and information."

3. Add the four items below. Press the NEWLINE key after the first three items but press **Enter** after the last item.

   Nutrition software programs

   Travel / R&R

   Vitamin and mineral supplements

   Workout videos

4. Position the insertion point somewhere in the list and set a 1-inch left indent (remember that the first-line indent moves also).

5. Position the insertion point somewhere in the list under "A Look at ..." and repeat the format.

6. Position the insertion point somewhere in the list under "Seminars and Films" and repeat the format.

7. Use the spelling function to correct the errors in this document.

8. If your status bar shows that your document is now two pages, delete returns everywhere except below the title lines so that there are only two returns between parts of the document rather than four.

9. Save the changes, print one copy, and clear the screen.

ACTIVITY 4

1. Open a new document. Set approximately 2-inch left and right margins and change to 12-point Times New Roman.

2. Key the centered, bold title **NUTRITION TERMS**. Then press **Enter** four times and change to left alignment.

3. Set a 1-inch hanging indent (the first-line indent marker remains at 0).

4. Key the terms and definitions shown in Figure 7.15 on page 170. In each case, key the term, press **Tab**, key the definition, and press **Enter** twice (press **Enter** only once after the last definition). Each term will "hang" to the left of all lines of its definition.

FIGURE 7.15
Terms to Be Keyed

Calories	The amount of energy a certain food yields when it is completely used by the body.
Cholesterol	One of the major fatty substances in the blood used for energy or stored for later use.
Fat	One of three main classes of nutrients that provides energy to the body.
Protein	Supplies the body with amino acids that are absorbed in the body and used for growth and repair of cells.
Sodium	A mineral that regulates the body's water balance, maintains a normal heart rhythm, and is responsible for the conduction of nerve impulses and the contraction of muscles.

5. Select each term and format it italics.

6. Spell-check and proofread your document.

7. Save the document as **act7-4**, print one copy, and clear the screen.

CREATE YOUR OWN

In your own words, create a list of numbered steps describing how to create a subdirectory and save files in that subdirectory. If you are not familiar with how to create subdirectories, research the topic first. Assume that you are writing these steps for someone who has very little computer experience. Therefore, each step must be complete and written very clearly.

Format each step with a hanging indent so that all lines but the first "hang" to the right of the first line. Save the file (you choose the filename) and print one copy. Keep this list of steps for future reference.

REVIEW EXERCISES

FILL IN THE BLANKS

Complete the following sentences by writing the correct word or words in the blanks provided.

1. To select a column with the mouse, point to one corner of the text, hold down _____alt_____ & _____mouse_____, and drag to the opposite corner.

2. To add leaders to existing text, choose the _____Format, tabs, Leader_____ command.

3. A type of indent in which the first-line indent is set to the left of a left indent is called a _____hanging_____ indent.

MATCHING

Find the key(s) or icon on the right that matches the description on the left, and write the appropriate letter in the blank provided at the left margin.

H 4. Format Painter

M 5. Center-aligned tab

O 6. Left-aligned tab

G 7. Right-aligned tab

I 8. NEWLINE

A 9. Left indent

J 10. Right indent

E 11. First-line indent

C 12. Increase Indent

K 13. Decrease Indent

D 14. Bullets

L 15. Numbering

a. ⬠ *Left indent*

b. 🗐

c. 📑

d. 📋

e. ▽ *first-line*

f. (Ctrl) + (Shift) + (Enter)

g. ↵

h. 🖌

i. (Shift) + (Enter)

j. ⬠

k. 📑

l. 📋 1 2 3

m. ⊥

n. ⊥

o. L

REFERENCE QUESTIONS

Referring to the *Microsoft Word User's Guide*, write the answers to the following questions in the space provided.

1. How do you change the default setting for the distance between tab stops without setting custom tab stops?

   _____

   _____

   _____

2. What are two fast ways to remove all formats in a paragraph at one time?

   _____

   _____

   _____

P A R T

3

EDITING, TABLES, AND MAIL MERGE

REVISION MARKS, ANNOTATIONS, SEARCH AND REPLACE

OBJECTIVES
Upon completion of this chapter, you will be able to:

- Use revision marks to mark edited text.

- Search for revision marks and accept or undo marked edits.

- Add annotations (notes) to a document.

- Format, edit, and remove annotations.

- Print annotations.

- Search for text and formats.

- Automatically search for and replace text and formats.

Preparation

1. To complete the chapter activities, you will need to access the Data Disk files MINUTES.DOC, NEWMEM.DOC, LEASE.DOC, and WILL.DOC.

2. Remember to save frequently as you work. You will generally not be reminded to save until all work is completed for a document.

3. If you make mistakes as you work with the exercises in the chapter, remember to click ⟲ ⊡ immediately after completing the action.

4. At the end of each class session, be sure to close Word and Windows properly. If you are using the hard drive to store your completed work, back up your files onto your formatted Student Disk, and erase your files from the directory you used on the hard drive. (Do not erase the Data Disk files unless your instructor tells you to do so.)

Marking Revisions

In many organizations, work groups are formed for special projects such as preparing technical manuals. When more than one person works on a document, it is important to be able to keep track of changes so that each person in the group can review and comment before the final document is printed. Usually, when you edit your documents, you have no way to keep track of the changes you have made. Word, however, provides a feature called revision marking (or *redlining*) that allows you to mark your changes. Word will mark all points at which you insert, delete, and move characters, including special characters. Word will not, however, mark most format changes (such as character formats and paragraph formats). After marking your revisions, you can search one by one for revisions and accept or undo the changes, or you can automatically accept or undo all changes.

EXERCISE

8.1 Turning On Revision Marks

1. Key the document shown in Figure 8.1 on page 178, using 12-point Times New Roman, and double space between paragraphs. Save it as **chap8-1**.

2. Turn on *revision marks* before you begin editing: *"Tools" "Revision"*

   a. Double-click MRK on the status bar. The dialog box shown in Figure 8.2 will appear.

   Down at Bottom of Screen

   b. Turn on Mark Revisions While Editing.

   c. If necessary, turn on Show Revisions on Screen and Show Revisions in Printed Document.

   d. Click OK . MRK is now highlighted on the status bar.

3. In the first sentence, position the insertion point at the beginning of the word "starches" and key **complex carbohydrates**.

   As you revise your text with revision marks turned on, note that you will not be able to use OVERTYPE; you will only be able to insert or delete text.

FIGURE 8.2
Tools Revisions Dialog Box

Revisions
Document Revisions
☐ **Mark Revisions While Editing**
☒ **Show Revisions on Screen**
☒ **Show Revisions in Printed Document**
Review...	Accept All	Reject All
Compare Versions...	Merge Revisions...	Options...

Buttons: OK, Cancel, Help

FIGURE 8.1
Paragraphs To Be Keyed and Edited

It is a common myth that starches make you fat. Foods like potatoes, rice, breads, and pasta are all starches, and they are a primary source of energy for the body. Many people who are trying to lose weight think that carbohydrates will cause them to gain weight.

Fat is stored in the body more easily than carbohydrates, and only a small percentage of carbohydrates is actually converted to fat in the body. As a result, experts advocate that as much as 50 percent of our diet be composed of carbohydrates.

Each gram of carbohydrates contains 4 calories. Each gram of fat has 9 more calories.

Therefore, if you want to diet, your diet should be low in fat and high in complex carbohydrates.

4. Without spacing, delete the word "starches" (do not delete the space).

5. Make the same correction in the second sentence (key **complex carbohydrates** and delete "starches" but do not delete the comma).

Notice that the word "starches" is shown with the strikethrough format and the words "complex carbohydrates" are underlined. Additionally, a revision bar (also known as a *change bar*) appears at the left edge of the screen (Figure 8.3).

6. In the third sentence of the first paragraph, add the word **eating** and a space between the words "that carbohydrates." The word "eating" is underlined.

that·eating·carbohydrates·

7. At the end of the same sentence, add a space and the phrase **instead of losing weight**.

8. Move the second paragraph to make it the next-to-last paragraph.

FIGURE 8.3
Revised Text and
Revision Bar

→ It·is·a·common·myth·that·complex·carbohydratesstarches·make·you·fat.··Foods· like·potatoes,·rice,·breads,·and·pasta·are·all·complex·carbohydratesstarches,·and·they·are·a· primary·source·of·energy·for·the·body.··Many·people·who·are·trying·to·lose·weight·think· that·carbohydrates·will·cause·them·to·gain·weight.¶

Revision Bar

FIGURE 8.4
Paragraph Moved to
New Location

Old Location ■

New Location ■

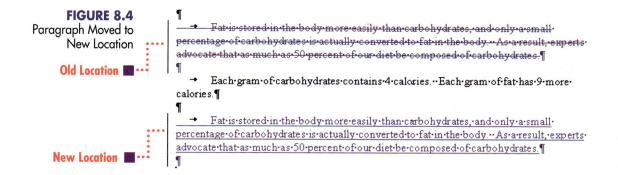

HINT: *Cut the second paragraph plus the paragraph mark below the paragraph and paste to the left of the tab for "Therefore..."*

In the paragraph's original location, the text is shown with the strikethrough format; in the new location, the text is underlined (Figure 8.4).

9. In the paragraph that begins "Each gram..." change the second sentence so that it reads "On the other hand, each gram...."

10. In the same sentence delete the word "more" and the space that follows.

11. In the following paragraph (the new location for the paragraph you moved), change "advocate" to **recommend**.

recommend that

Notice that when you delete text that has been moved, it is actually deleted, not formatted with the strikethrough format.

12. In the second sentence of the same paragraph, change "50" to **60**.

13. In the last paragraph, position the insertion point on "Therefore" and use Tools Thesaurus to replace "Therefore" with a synonym of your choice.

Notice that the synonym is underlined and the original word is shown with the strikethrough format. With revision marking turned on, Word marks all changes made when you use the Thesaurus, grammar checker, or spelling checker.

14. In the same paragraph change "want to diet" to **want to lose weight**.

15. Double-click MRK on the status bar, turn off Mark Revisions While Editing, and click OK.

16. Save the document and print one copy, but do not clear the screen.

EXERCISE 8.2

Reviewing Revisions and Accepting or Undoing Changes

After you have marked revisions in your document, you can review them and decide to keep the changes or discard (undo) them. You can review each revision individually and decide to accept or undo each change separately, or you can accept or undo all changes at one time. You can also select a portion of the document and accept or undo changes.

1. Save your file with a new name, **chap8-2**, to prevent accidental changes to your marked document as you perform the following steps.

IMPORTANT: Do not save this document again until instructed to do so in Step 10.

2. Review revisions and accept, reject, or skip changes:

    a. Position the insertion point at the beginning of the document and double-click MRK on the status bar.

    b. Click Review. The Review Revisions dialog box (Figure 8.5) appears. Do not close

the dialog box until instructed to do so in Step 3.

    c. Turn on the Find Next After Accept/Reject check box so you will not have to click Find for all occurrences.

    d. To find the first revision in the document, click the Find Next button Find ⇨. The first text you marked ("complex carbohydrates" and "starches") is highlighted.

    ·complex·carbohydratesstarches·

    e. Click Accept.

    ·complex·carbohydrates·make·

The new words ("complex carbohydrates") are inserted, the underline format is removed, and the old word ("starches") with the strikethrough format is deleted. The next marked text in the paragraph is automatically highlighted (the second occurrence of "starches" and "complex carbohydrates").

    f. Click Accept to change "starches" to "complex carbohydrates."

    g. Temporarily skip over the next highlighted change (adding the word "eating") by clicking Find ⇨.

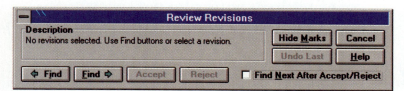

FIGURE 8.5
Tools Review Revisions Dialog Box

Word jumps to the next marked text, "instead of losing weight ..." The word "eating" remains marked.

h. Click Reject to restore the original text.

·cause·them·to·gain·weight.¶

The text added with the underline format ("instead of losing weight ...") is removed at the end of the sentence.

3. Click [Close] to exit the dialog box.

⚠ IMPORTANT: Do not save your document.

4. If necessary, move the insertion point to the beginning of the document. Double-click MRK on the status bar.

5. Click Reject All. Click Yes when the prompt

"Do you want to reject all revisions in CHAP8-2.DOC?" appears (Figure 8.6).

All remaining revisions are removed and the original text for those revisions is restored.

6. Close the dialog box. Clear the screen but do not save the changes.

7. Open **chap8-2.doc** again.

8. Double-click MRK on the status bar. This time, click Accept All. Click Yes when the prompt "Do you want to accept all revisions in CHAP8-2.DOC?" appears.

9. Close the dialog box. If necessary, correct any spacing errors between words.

10. Save the document, print one copy, and clear the screen.

FIGURE 8.6
Prompt to Reject All Revisions

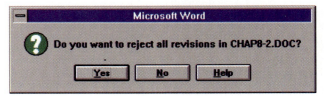

Annotating a Document

Frequent revisions and reprinting can be costly, especially with expensive laser toner cartridges and paper. Word provides a tool called *annotations* to reduce the need for printing draft copies. Annotations are notes (comments) that are added within a document by the author and reviewers. They are similar to footnotes except that they are formatted as *hidden text*. These annotations can be printed. Authors and reviewers can exchange comments until they are satisfied. The final changes can then be made to the document and a final copy printed.

EXERCISE 8.3

Inserting Annotations

1. Open the Data Disk file **minutes.doc** and save the file in the appropriate location for Student Disk files as **chap8-3.**

2. If ¶ is highlighted on the Standard Toolbar, click it to turn off the display of all nonprinting characters temporarily.

3. Set options to use your initials and display tab, space, and paragraph characters:

a. Choose Tools Options.

b. In the Options dialog box, click the User Info folder tab.

c. If necessary, key your initials. (The initials in the User Info category are used for the annotation mark when you insert annotations.) You do not need to change the Name or Address boxes.

d. In the Options dialog box, click the View folder tab.

Notice that no check boxes are selected under Nonprinting Characters because you turned off Show/Hide.

e. Turn on Tab Characters, Spaces, and Paragraph Marks (Figure 8.7) so you will still be able to see these nonprinting characters but will not see annotation marks, which are formatted as hidden text.

```
Nonprinting Characters
  [X] Tab Characters
  [X] Spaces
  [X] Paragraph Marks
  [ ] Optional Hyphens
  [ ] Hidden Text
  [ ] All
```

FIGURE 8.7
Turning On Special Nonprinting Characters

f. Click OK.

Notice that ¶ is not highlighted. Remember that clicking the icon toggles on and off the display of *all* nonprinting characters, so you needed to use the dialog box to specify those nonprinting characters to be displayed.

4. Add an annotation:

a. Select the word "ATTENDANCE" and choose Insert Annotation.

An annotation *pane* (Figure 8.8) opens. Your initials and the number *1* appear in both the annotation pane and the document pane.

b. With the insertion point positioned after the annotation mark in the annotation pane, key **These centered headings may look better left aligned and bold with a larger font size.**

c. Click Close . Notice that the annotation reference in your document is now hidden.

FIGURE 8.8
Annotation Pane
Opened and
Annotation Mark
Inserted in Both
Panes

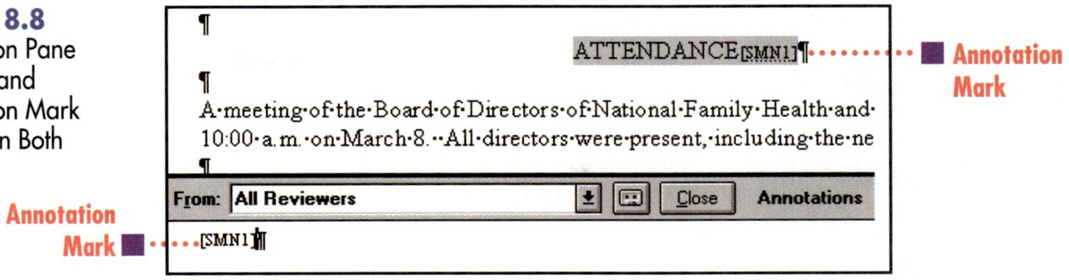

¶

¶   ATTENDANCE[SMN1]¶ •••••••• ■ **Annotation**
                                                                                                      Mark

A·meeting·of·the·Board·of·Directors·of·National·Family·Health·and·
10:00·a.m.·on·March·8.··All·directors·were·present,·including·the·ne

¶

Annotation
Mark ■ •••• [SMN1]⟨⟩¶

From: All Reviewers   ⬍ ⊡ Close   Annotations

TIP

If you have a sound board and a microphone, you can insert voice annotations. For Step 4b, click the Insert Sound Object icon in the annotation *pane* ⊡ ; then record the sentence. Click Yes if asked to update the object.

5. Choose Tools Options. Click the User Info folder tab and change the initials to JCK (for a different reviewer, Joan C. Kestella); then click ▢ **OK** ▢ .

6. Scroll down and select the name "Donald Goldstein" in the "Membership" paragraph.

7. Choose Insert Annotation.

[SMN1]These·
[JCK2]¶

Notice that the annotation reference mark now has the initials "JCK" rather than your initials, and it has been assigned the next available annotation number (2).

8. Key **Donald Goldstein decided not to accept our offer for employment. Please change this name to Matthew Wang.**

9. Close the annotation pane.

10. Choose Tools Options and change the initials in User Info back to your own initials; then click ▢ **OK** ▢ .

11. Scroll up two paragraphs and select the paragraph heading "Finance." (drag to select because you must include the period in your selection).

12. Choose Insert Annotation.

[SMN1]These·ce
[SMN2]¶
[JCK3]Donald·G
Wang.¶

Notice that this becomes the second annotation, and the JCK annotation is automatically renumbered as the third annotation. Annotations, like footnotes, are automatically rearranged when you insert, delete, move, or copy them.

13. Key **These paragraph headings should either be underlined or set off as separate paragraphs.**

14. Close the annotation pane.

EXERCISE

Viewing and Editing Annotations

1. Move the insertion point to the top of the document.

2. Because you now want to work with your annotations, click ¶ to display all nonprinting characters, including the annotation marks.

3. Go to a specific annotation mark and open the annotation pane:

a. Double-click the page number on the status bar.

b. In the Go to What list box, click Annotation.

c. Click Next twice; then click Close. The insertion point moves to the second annotation mark.

d. Double-click the annotation mark to open the annotation pane to the second annotation.

With the annotation pane open, you will be able to go back and forth between the annotation pane and the document pane by simply clicking in the desired pane. Remember, though, that only the Insert Annotation command can be used to add annotations.

4. Click an insertion point in each annotation in the annotation pane.

Notice that, each time, Word scrolls to the related annotation mark in the document pane and highlights the annotated text.

TIP

You can also view annotations by choosing View Annotations. If you have a sound board, you can listen to voice annotations by double-clicking the sound icon next to the annotation mark.

5. Change the annotation text for the second annotation to read **These paragraph headings should be bold and underlined.** Delete the remainder of the text for the second annotation.

6. Move the insertion point to the third annotation in the annotation pane; then click in the document pane.

7. Drag to select the third annotation mark in the document pane, and press Delete.

The annotation mark is removed, and the annotation mark and text in the annotation pane are also removed.

IMPORTANT: Deleting all the text in the annotation pane does not remove the annotation mark in the document pane. You must delete the annotation mark in the document *pane* to remove an annotation.

PART 3: EDITING, TABLES, AND MAIL MERGE

8. Undo this change; then close the annotation pane and deselect the annotation mark.

9. Add a header to the document and change the margins:

   a. Choose View Header and Footer and click 📖.

   b. Turn on Different First Page; then click the Margins folder tab.

   c. Change the left and right margins to 1.25 inches; then click [**OK**].

   d. Click [icon], key an appropriate header with a page number, and close the header pane.

10. Spell-check the document.

11. Save the document, but do not clear the screen.

EXERCISE 8.5

Printing a Document with Annotations

• •

1. Print a copy of the document with the annotations:

   a. Choose File Print (do not click 🖨 this time).

   b. In the Print dialog box, click Options. The Print category of the Tools Options dialog box is displayed.

   c. Turn on Annotations under Include with Document.

Notice, as shown in Figure 8.9, that Hidden Text is also turned on automatically.

   d. Click [**OK**] twice.

The document with annotation marks and a separate page at the end containing the annotation text are printed.

2. For final copy, you will not print the document with annotations. Choose Tools Options, click the Print folder tab, turn off both Annotations and Hidden Text, and click [**OK**].

3. If you want to, click 🖨 to print another copy of your document (this time, it will print without annotation marks or the annotation page).

4. Save your changes, but do not clear the screen.

Include with Document
- ☐ <u>S</u>ummary Info
- ☐ <u>F</u>ield Codes
- ☒ <u>A</u>nnotations
- ☒ Hi<u>d</u>den Text
- ☒ Dra<u>w</u>ing Objects

FIGURE 8.9
Annotations and Hidden Text Turned On in Print Category of Tools Options Dialog Box

Searching For and Replacing Text

Scrolling through a long document to locate a specific section of text, as you have discovered, is time-consuming and not very efficient. The Word Find and Replace commands (in the Edit menu) make searching for and replacing text much quicker.

EXERCISE 8.6

Searching for Text

1. Save the document you have been working on with a new name, **chap8-4**.

2. Although you can begin a search anywhere in a document, for consistent directions for this exercise, begin by moving the insertion point (if necessary) to the top of the document.

3. Search for the word "be":

   a. Choose Edit Find.

   The Find dialog box (Figure 8.10) is displayed. Note that your dialog box may contain an entry in the Find What box; it may have a format below the Find What box; it may have a different Search option selected; or it may have check boxes turned

on. Each time you use the Find or Replace features, the settings from the previous search and/or replace are displayed. Be sure to check each option before clicking Find Next.

   b. In the Find What box, key **be** (deleting the current entry, if any).

   c. If a format shows below the Find What box, click No Formatting.

   d. If necessary, change to the default settings: Search should be All, and all check boxes should be off.

   e. Click Find Next to begin the search.

Word stops at the first occurrence of "be" in the sentence "The new total is estimated to be ..."

FIGURE 8.10
Edit Find Dialog Box

f. Click Find Next to search for the next occurrence.

Word highlights "Membership" because "be" is contained in the word "Membership."

g. You do not want to search for words other than "be," so turn on Find Whole Words Only. Then click Find Next.

h. As Word finds each occurrence of "be" (including the one in the annotation pane), click Find Next.

i. Click [**OK**] when you see the prompt "Word has finished searching the document."

4. Search for "A":

a. If necessary, click No Formatting to clear any formats listed under Find What, and change Search to All.

b. Key **A** in the Find What box.

c. Turn off Find Whole Words Only and turn on Match Case (to search only for words beginning with the capital letter A).

d. Click Find Next. Word locates the first A (in "BOARD").

e. Click Find Next to continue the search. Word locates the second A (in "NATIONAL").

f. This time, turn on Find Whole Words Only (leave Match Case on as well) and click Find Next so Word will look only for the word "A" and not all words containing the capital letter A.

g. Each time Word locates one of the three occurrences of the word "A," click Find Next.

h. Click [**OK**] when you see the prompt "Word has finished searching the document."

5. Search for text and change it in the document:

a. If necessary, click No Formatting to clear any formats listed under Find What, and change Search to All.

b. In the Find What box, replace the current entry with **Ms. Kotovet**.

c. Turn off Match Case.

d. Click Find Next.

The first occurrence of "Ms. Kotovet" is in the sentence that begins "The first order of business . . ." You do not need to make a change here.

e. Click Find Next to locate the next occurrence.

The next occurrence of "Ms. Kotovet" is in the following sentence. This is the occurrence you want.

f. Click in the document pane and key **Tatyana** to change "Ms. Kotovet" to "Tatyana."

Ms.·Kotovet.··Tatyana·has·

g. Click Find Next to search for the next occurrence of "Ms. Kotovet," in the "Finance" paragraph.

h. Click in the document pane, change "Ms. Kotovet" to **Tatyana**, and click Find Next.

Word begins the search again from the top of the document and highlights the occurrence you skipped earlier.

i. Click │Cancel│ to exit the dialog box; then click an insertion point to deselect the text.

IMPORTANT: Always be sure to deselect all text before you begin or repeat a search. With text selected, Word will search only the selected text. If you see a message that Word has checked the selection but could not find the search item, click Yes to search the remainder of the document.

6. Repeat a search for text specified earlier:

a. Choose Edit Find.

b. If necessary, click No Formatting to clear any formats listed under Find What, change Search to All, and turn off all check boxes.

c. Click the arrow next to the Find What box. Word allows you to select from the last four entries for which you have searched.

d. Click "be"; then click Find Next.

7. Click │Cancel│ to exit the dialog box.

TIP

You can also use (Shift) + (F4) to repeat a search.

8. Search for text and add formats:

a. Choose Edit Find.

b. If necessary, click No Formatting to clear any formats listed under Find What, change Search to All, and turn off all check boxes.

c. Key **Finance.** (including the period) in the Find What Box; then click Find Next.

d. When Word locates "Finance." click in the document pane, then click │*I*│ on the Formatting Toolbar to italicize the word "Finance" and the period following it.

9. Click │Cancel│ to exit the dialog box.

10. Scroll or search for "Training." (including the period) and italicize it.

11. Scroll or search for "Membership." (This time, include the period and turn on Match Case so Word will stop only at the beginning of a sentence.) Add italics.

12. In the same paragraph, change "Donald Goldstein" to **Matthew Wang**; then, if necessary, cancel the dialog box.

EXERCISE

8.7 Searching for Formats

Word also allows you to search for character and paragraph formats.

1. Move the insertion point to the top of the document.

2. Change the two lines of the title to 16-point Arial bold.

3. Search for character formats:

   a. Choose Edit Find.

   b. If necessary, click No Formatting to clear any formats listed under Find What, change Search to All, and turn off all check boxes.

An entry is in the Find What box. Although you can search for a combination of text and formats, you will search only for formats this time.

   c. Delete the entry in the Find What box.

   d. Click I on the Formatting Toolbar.

You can click more than one icon when you need to search for combined formats like bold and italic.

Notice that, in the Find dialog box, "Format: Italic" now appears under the Find What box (Figure 8.11).

   e. Click Find Next. The first italicized text, "Finance." is highlighted.

4. Click the Format button in the dialog box to display the pop-up menu shown in Figure 8.12.

5. Click Font.

Notice all the formats that can be searched for (and replaced). You will use this dialog box in Activity 2. For now, click Cancel twice to exit to the document.

6. Search for paragraph formats:

   a. Choose Edit Find.

FIGURE 8.11
Searching for the Italic Character Format

FIGURE 8.12
Format Pop-Up Menu in
Edit Find Dialog Box

b. If necessary, change Search to All, turn off all check boxes, and delete any entry in the Find What box.

c. With the insertion point in the Find What box, click No Formatting to clear the previous format search.

d. Click ▤ on the Formatting Toolbar. The dialog box should now show "Format: Centered."

e. Click Find Next to find the first occurrence of the centered format after the insertion point.

7. Click the Format button in the dialog box; then click Paragraph.

Notice the types of formats that you can search for and replace. You will not use this dialog box in this chapter, but take note of it for future reference.

8. Click ⎡Cancel⎤ twice to exit to your document.

9. Search for a combination of paragraph and character formats:

a. Choose Edit Find.

b. If necessary, change Search to All, turn off all check boxes, and delete any entry in the Find What box.

c. With the insertion point in the Find What box, click No Formatting to clear the previous format search.

d. On the Formatting Toolbar, click ▤, click Arial in the Font box (the second box on the Toolbar), click 16 in the Font Size box (the third box on the Toolbar), and click ⎡B⎤.

e. When the dialog box looks like Figure 8.13, click Find Next. Word highlights the first line of the title.

10. Click ⎡Cancel⎤.

FIGURE 8.13
Searching for Multiple Formats

EXERCISE

Automatically Replacing Text and Formats

When you need to replace multiple occurrences of the same text or format, you can use the Edit Replace command to replace each occurrence auto-matically. Any combination of search and replace can be used. For example, you can key text in the Find What box and key no text in the Replace With box. You can then select a format, so that the text you search for will be formatted automatically. You can leave both the Find What box and the Replace With box blank and search for and replace formats only. You can even leave the Replace With box blank (and select no format), in which case the text you specify in the Find What box will be deleted automatically. Do not, however, select a format under Find What and leave both the Replace With box and the format area below it blank, because the formatted text—not just the format—will be deleted.

IMPORTANT: Before you begin to search for and replace text, be sure no text is selected, or Word will search only the selected text.

1. If necessary, move the insertion point to the top of the document.

2. To search for and replace text:

a. Choose Edit Replace.

The Replace dialog box will be displayed, with settings from the previous search (if this is not the first). You can also open the Replace dialog box by clicking Replace in the Find dialog box.

b. If necessary, change Search to All and turn off all check boxes.

c. Key **March** in the Find What box.

d. Click No Formatting to clear the formats from the previous search (if any).

e. Key **April** in the Replace With box.

f. If necessary, click No Formatting to delete any formats under Replace With.

g. When the dialog box looks like Figure 8.14, click Find Next. Word highlights the first occurrence of "March" after the insertion point.

h. Click Replace. "March" is replaced with "April" and the next occurrence of "March" is highlighted.

i. This time, click Replace All to replace all other occurrences of "March" with "April."

Word indicates that three replacements were made (after you clicked Replace All; this number does not include the replacement you made with the Replace button).

j. Click [**OK**].

3. Replace all instances of **February** with **March**. When Word indicates that two replacements were made, click [**OK**].

FIGURE 8.14
Replacing "March" with "April"

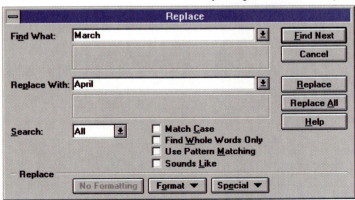

4. Replace a character format with other character formats:

a. If necessary, change Search to All and turn off all check boxes.

b. Delete any text in the Find What box because you will be replacing only formats. If necessary, click No Formatting to clear any formats.

c. With the insertion point in the Find What box, click I on the Formatting Toolbar. "Format: Italic" is displayed below the Find What box.

d. Delete any text in the Replace With box. If necessary, click No Formatting to clear any formats listed under Replace With.

e. With the insertion point in the Replace With box, click B and U on the Formatting Toolbar. "Format: Bold, Underline" is displayed below the Replace With box.

f. With the insertion point still in the Replace With box, click I twice so that "Format: Bold, Not Italic, Underline" is displayed below the Replace With box.

IMPORTANT: When you want to replace character formats rather than just add to the existing character formats, you must click the icon twice, until you see "Not" or "No" with the format name that is to be replaced.

g. When the dialog box looks like Figure 8.15, click Replace All to replace all occurrences of italic with the bold and underline formats.

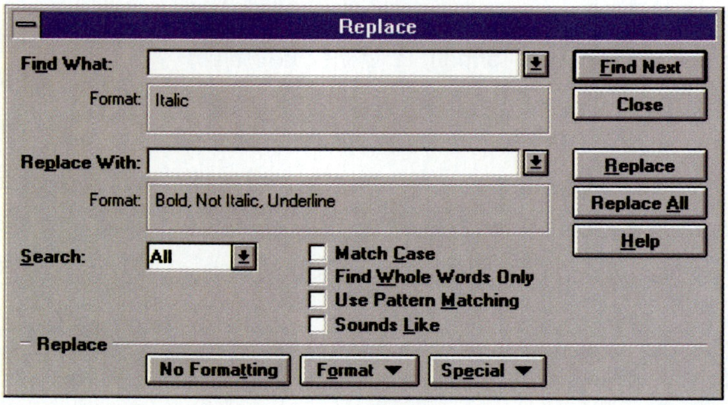

FIGURE 8.15
Replacing Italic with the Bold and Underline Formats

h. Click OK when Word indicates that three replacements were made.

5. Replace a paragraph format with another paragraph format:

a. If necessary, change Search to All and turn off all check boxes.

b. If necessary, delete any text in the Find What box. Click No Formatting to clear any formats.

c. Click on the Formatting Toolbar. "Format: Flush left" should be displayed below the Find What box.

d. If necessary, delete any text in the Replace With box. Click No Formatting to delete any formats listed under Replace With.

e. On the Formatting Toolbar, click. "Format: Justified" should be displayed below the Replace With box.

f. When the dialog box looks like Figure 8.16, click Replace All.

g. When Word indicates that the replacements were made, click ☐ **OK** ☐.

6. Replace a paragraph format with another paragraph format plus character formats:

a. If necessary, change Search to All and turn off all check boxes.

b. If necessary, delete any text in the Find What box. Click No Formatting to clear any formats.

c. Click ▤ on the Formatting Toolbar. "Format: Centered" should be displayed below the Find What box.

d. If necessary, delete any text in the Replace With box. Click No Formatting to delete any formats listed under Replace With.

e. On the Formatting Toolbar, click ▤ and **B**.

f. Click the arrow next to the Font Size box (the third one on the Toolbar) and click 14.

FIGURE 8.16
Replacing Left-Aligned Text with Justified Text

The dialog box should now look like Figure 8.17. Do not make any replacements yet.

In the following steps, you will replace some centered items, and some you will not. Be very cautious about clicking Replace All. It is sometimes better to click Find Next and Replace for each individual occurrence rather than to click Replace All. If necessary, as you search for and replace text, drag the title bar for the dialog box to see more of the highlighted text.

g. Click Find Next.

h. For the two lines of the title ("MINUTES OF THE BOARD OF DIRECTORS" and "NATIONAL FAMILY HEALTH AND FITNESS CLUB"), click Find Next to skip to the next occurrence without making any changes. For "ATTENDANCE," "OLD BUSINESS," NEW BUSINESS," and "ADJOURNMENT," click Replace.

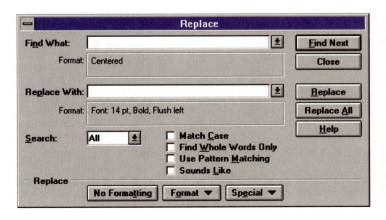

FIGURE 8.17
Replacing Centered Text with Left-Aligned, 14-Point Bold Text

7. If you see a message indicating that the search is completed, click ⬚ **OK** ⬚.

8. Click ⬚ **Close** ⬚ and save your changes, but do not clear the screen.

Searching for and Replacing Special Characters

To delete annotation marks

In addition to searching for text and formats, you can search for and/or replace special characters such as tabs, hard (manual) page breaks, footnote reference marks, and annotation marks.

1. Choose Edit Replace.

2. If necessary, change Search to All and turn off all check boxes.

3. If necessary, delete any text in the Find What box. Click No Formatting to clear any formats.

4. With the insertion point in the Find What box, click the Special button in the dialog box. The menu shown in Figure 8.18 appears.

⬚ Spe**c**ial ▼ ⬚

5. Click Annotation Mark. The code for annotation marks (^a) appears in the Find What box.

6. If necessary, delete any text in the Replace With box. Click No Formatting to delete any formats below Replace With.

Both the Replace With box and its format box must be left blank if you want to search for and delete the annotation marks automatically.

7. Click Replace All. When Word indicates that three replacements were made, click ⬚ **OK** ⬚; then click ⬚ **Close** ⬚.

8. Click View in the menu bar. Notice that Annotations is dimmed, meaning that this document has no annotations.

9. Click View again to close the menu.

10. Save the changes to the document, print one copy, and clear the screen.

Paragraph Mark
Tab Character
Annotation Mark
Any **C**haracter
Any **D**igit
An**y** Letter
Ca**r**et Character
Column Break
E**m** Dash
E**n** Dash
Endnote Mark
Fiel**d**
Footnote Mark
Grap**h**ic
Manual **L**ine Break
Manual Page Brea**k**
Nonbreaking **H**yphen
Nonbreaking **S**pace
Optional Hyphen
Section **B**reak
White Space

FIGURE 8.18
Special Characters Menu in Find and Replace Dialog Boxes

COMPUTER ACTIVITIES

ACTIVITY 1

1. Open the Data Disk file **newmem.doc** and save it in the appropriate location for Student Disk files as **act8-1**.

2. Review the revisions. Accept each revision except where 300 is changed to 350. In that instance, click Reject to restore the original text.

3. Add your initials at the bottom of the memo.

4. Save the changes, print one copy, and clear the screen.

ACTIVITY 2

1. Open the Data Disk file **lease.doc** and save it in the appropriate location for Student Disk files as **act8-2a.doc**.

2. Replace all instances of the underline format with all caps without the underline format.

HINT: *Find What should show "Format: Underline." Replace With should show "Format: No Underline, Not Small Caps, All Caps." To set the Replace With formats, click Format, then click Font. Be sure the Underline box shows "none." Not Small Caps is selected automatically when you select All Caps.*

3. Turn on revision marking.

4. Replace all occurrences of "Property Owner" with **Landlord**, then replace all occurrences of "Renter" with **Tenant** (be sure to clear all formats).

5. Search for "premises" and change to **single-family home** for the first, third, fourth, and sixth occurrences, then close the dialog box.

HINT: *Drag the title bar for the dialog box to see text as needed.*

6. In the first paragraph, make the following revisions.
   a. Change the date to the 9th day of September.
   b. Change "Jim" to "James R."
   c. Add **Lynn** after "Jennifer."

7. In the third paragraph, change "July 1" to "October 1."

8. In the fourth paragraph, delete the preceding comma and the words, "keep the common grounds safe, care for the lawn, and keep the premises neat and clean" (do not delete the period).

9. In the fifth paragraph, delete the words "water and."

10. In the tenth paragraph, add **, water,** (include the commas) after "electric."

11. In the eleventh paragraph, add **except for a bird** after "no pets."

12. In the sixteenth paragraph, change "first day" to "fifth day."

13. In the eighteenth paragraph, change the amount to fifteen dollars (including the amount in parentheses).

14. Turn off revision marking, save the changes, and print one copy with the revisions.

15. Accept all revisions, then change the year in the first and third paragraphs. Save the document as **act8-2b**, print one copy, and clear the screen.

ACTIVITY 3

1. Open the Data Disk file **will.doc** and save it in the appropriate location for Student Disk files as **act8-3a**.

2. Turn on revision marks.

3. Replace the initial and period in each name with the middle name listed at the top of Figure 8.19 (for example, replace "William J." with "William James" and "MaryJane V." with "MaryJane Valarde").

4. Close the dialog box and edit the remainder of the document as indicated by the proofreaders' marks in Figure 8.19, on pages 197–200.

HINT: *To make editing easier, click the arrow next to the Zoom Control box on the Standard Toolbar and click Page Width.*

5. Turn off revision marking and save the changes to the document.

6. Add annotations to the document as follows:
   a. In Paragraph 3, select the sentence you added and, using your own initials, add this annotation: **The family has already been informed about the burial arrangements.**

Activity 3 continues on page 201

FIGURE 8.19
Revisions to Will

Please spell out the names of the individuals as follows:

William James Valarde	Daniel Roger Valarde
LaDonna Becker Valarde	MaryJane Valarde Torres
Linda Valarde Lewis	John Andrew Torres
Laura Suzanne Valarde	Russell Anthony Valarde

LAST WILL AND TESTAMENT

1.   I, William J. Valarde, a resident

of the State of Ohio, declare and publish this as my

Will and revoke all previous Wills and Codicils.

2.   I am married. My wife's name is

LaDonna B. Valarde. I have two daughters, Linda V.

Lewis and Laura S. Valarde, and ~~one~~ *two* son*s*, Russell A.

Valarde *and Phillip Michael Valarde*.

3.   I want a simple and inexpensive

burial with a graveside service. *I want my body to be buried in Rosewood Cemetery in Centerville, Ohio, where I have already purchased a burial plot.*

4.   I want any debts, taxes, and

expenses of my estate to be paid out of my estate

before any property is distributed to anyone under

Continued on next page

this Will ○ ~~except that if the land still has a~~ ℮

~~mortgage on it at the time of my death, my son,~~ ℮

~~Russell A. Valarde, should be solely responsible for~~ ℮

~~that mortgage.~~ ℮

     5.   I want my interest in my house

located at ~~554 East Fifth~~ [1074 Fairfield] ℮ Street, Centerville, Ohio

45458-0931, excluding any of the personal property

in the home, to go to my [two] son [s] Russell A. Valarde [and Phillip Michael Valarde]

~~If he dies before me~~ ℮ [If one of them dies before me,] it should go to each of my [it should go to the surviving son. In the event that both sons die before me,]

daughters, Linda V. Lewis and Laura S. Valarde, to

be divided equally. In addition, I give all the

personal property in the home to my children to be

divided equally. I give [fifty] ~~fifteen~~ thousand dollars

($1[50],000) to each of my children. If one of my

children dies before me and said child does not have

Continued on next page

any children surviving at the time of my death, my

deceased child's share of my estate shall be divided

equally among my surviving children at the time of

my death. "Children" does not include stepchildren^, but does include children born or adopted after I write this will⊙

6.   I appoint my wife, LaDonna B.

Valarde, as executrix of my estate. If she cannot

serve as executrix, I appoint my brother, Daniel R.

Valarde, as executor. I give them the power to sell

or not sell and to deal with my property in any way

they feel is in the best interest of my estate. I wish them to serve without bond⊙

7.   If my wife, LaDonna B. Valarde,

dies before me, I appoint my sister, MaryJane V.

Torres, and her husband, John A. Torres, as

guardians of my minor children and their property. I wish them to serve without bond⊙

Continued on next page

8.   Dated this 11th day of April, 19— *~6* *March*

_____
Testator

The above Will was signed, declared, and published as his Will by William J. Valarde in our presence, and at his request we have signed our names to this Will as witnesses, this 11th day of *~6* April, 19—. *March*

Witness   _____

Residing _____

          _____

Witness   _____

Residing _____

   b. In Paragraph 5, select the last sentence ("'Children' does not include . . ."), change the initials to "AEM" in the Tools Options User Info category, and add this annotation: **No mention was made about William Valarde's mother, Janice Henson Valarde, who resides in West Palm Beach, Florida. If this was not an oversight, a sentence should be added specifying that nothing is being left to her.**

   c. In Paragraph 6, select the second sentence (beginning "If she cannot serve . . ."), change back to your own initials, and add this annotation: **Has Daniel Valarde been informed that he is the alternate executor of this will?**

7. Save the changes to the document and print one copy with the annotations and revisions. Then turn off Annotations and Hidden Text.

8. Before searching for and accepting revisions, save the document with a new name, **act8-3b**.

9. Space twice after the annotation mark at the end of Paragraph 5 and add the following sentence: **Because my mother, Janice Henson Valarde, is financially stable and is well provided for, I am intentionally omitting her from this will.**

10. Move the insertion point to the top of the document. Accept all revisions.

11. Search for and delete the annotations.

12. If necessary, change the Zoom Control box back to 100 percent.

13. Save the document again, print one copy, and clear the screen.

▼ CREATE YOUR OWN • • • • • • • • • •

Everyone has her or his own writing style. Now you will have an opportunity to revise one of the documents you worked with in this text.

Open the Data Disk file **remedies.doc** again, and save the document under an appropriate filename that you choose. Turn on revision marks and edit the paragraphs as you wish to fit your own writing style. For example, you may choose to move a sentence or even an entire paragraph and then edit that text to fit your own writing style. If you want to, add sentences to describe your own home remedies for the ailments listed. You can also add to the list of ailments if you know of additional home remedies that you can describe.

After all revisions are completed, print a copy with the revision marks and ask a friend to review your edits. After discussing the changes with your friend, accept the revisions you want to keep, reject those that you do not plan to keep, and print a revised copy of the document. Consider sharing your home remedies with other members of your class. Everyone will enjoy hearing about some of your own home cures.

REVIEW EXERCISES

TRUE / FALSE

Each of the following statements is either true or false. Indicate your answer on the left by circling T if the statement is true or F if the statement is false.

T **(F)** **1.** Annotation marks are displayed in the document at all times.

T **F** **2.** OVERTYPE can still be used when Mark Revisions is turned on.

T **(F)** **3.** Deleting the annotation text in the annotation pane also removes the annotation mark from the document pane.

T **F** **4.** Annotations are always formatted as hidden text.

T **F** **5.** When searching for a character or paragraph format, you must also specify the text.

T **F** **6.** Once revisions are made in a document, all the changes must be either accepted or undone at one time.

FILL IN THE BLANKS

Complete the following sentences by writing the correct word or words in the blanks provided.

7. To add an annotation to a document, choose the _____ command.

8. To discard all revisions, click _____ in the Review Revisions dialog box.

9. To search and replace automatically, choose the _____ command.

10. To search for particular text or formats, choose the _____ command.

REFERENCE QUESTIONS

Referring to the *Microsoft Word User's Guide*, write the answers to the following questions in the space provided.

1. How can you combine all annotations and revisions from multiple reviewers in the original document?

    _____

    _____

    _____

2. How do you protect a document to enable reviewers to read the document and add and read annotations but prohibit them from editing the document?

    _____

    _____

    _____

WORKING WITH TABLES

OBJECTIVES
Upon completion of this chapter, you will be able to:

- Insert a blank table grid and key text in a table.

- Adjust column widths and center a table horizontally.

- Select and edit text in individual cells.

- Move, insert, and delete rows and columns.

- Add a title above a table.

- Set tabs and indents for table columns.

- Add printable borders to tables.

- Create a heading that spans several columns.

- Convert text with tabs into a table.

- Use the Word Table feature to create side-by-side paragraphs.

Preparation

1. To complete the chapter activities, you will key data presented in tables within the chapter. You will also need the Data Disk file JUICES.DOC.

2. Remember to save frequently as you work. You will generally not be reminded to save until all work is completed for a document.

3. At the end of each class session, be sure to close Word and Windows properly. If you are using the hard drive to store your completed work, back up your files onto your formatted Student Disk, and erase your files from the directory you used on the hard drive.

Introduction to Tables

Setting up tables by calculating tab-stop positions as you did in Chapter 7 can be complicated. Editing changes such as moving columns can be even more difficult when you set up tables with tab stops. Word has simplified working with tables by providing a Table menu and the Insert Table icon on the Standard Toolbar.

Figure 9.1 identifies the parts of a table using the Word Table feature. A table consists of rows and columns of boxes (*cells*) to which you add text or graphics. Rows are cells going across the page. Columns are cells going down the page. Each cell is surrounded by nonprinting dotted lines called *gridlines*. These gridlines help you to see the cell, row, and column in which you are working more clearly.

FIGURE 9.1
Parts of a Table

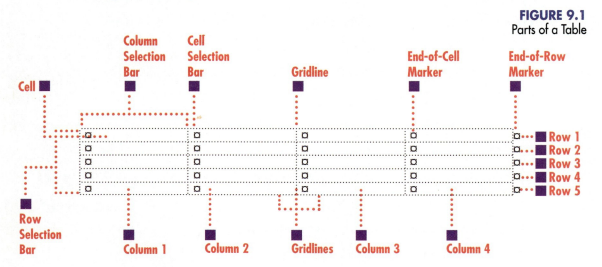

Creating Tables

EXERCISE

9.1

Using the Toolbar to Create a Table

1. Before you set up a table, check to be sure that gridlines and cell and row markers will be displayed.

a. Click Table on the menu bar to open the Table menu. If a check mark appears next to Gridlines (Figure 9.2), click Table again

Insert Table...
Delete Cells...
Merge Cells
Split Cells...

Select Row
Select Column
Select Table   Alt+Num 5

Table AutoFormat...
Cell Height and Width...
Headings

Convert Text to Table...
Sort Text...
Formula...
Split Table
✓ **Gridlines**

FIGURE 9.2
Table Gridlines
Turned On

to cancel the menu. If a check mark does not appear next to Gridlines, click Gridlines to select the command.

b. Cell and row markers are nonprinting characters. If ¶ on the Standard Toolbar is not highlighted, click it now to turn on the display of nonprinting characters.

2. Select the paragraph mark and change to the 12-point font size. Then click in the document window to deselect the paragraph mark.

IMPORTANT: If you change the font size without selecting the paragraph mark, the table you insert will revert to the default 10-point size. If you do not deselect the paragraph mark after changing the font size, a dialog box will appear rather than a sample table grid when you click the Insert Table icon.

3. Insert a blank table *grid:*

a. Click the Insert Table icon on the Standard Toolbar ▦. The sample table grid (Figure 9.3) will appear.

FIGURE 9.3
Sample Table Grid

b. Drag down the sample grid until five rows of cells are displayed; then drag across until the bottom of the sample grid reads "5 x 4 Table" (Figure 9.4). Release the mouse button.

gives the end row icon

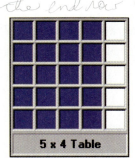

FIGURE 9.4
Completed Sample Table Grid

4. Key the table shown in Figure 9.5 on page 208:

a. Key the first row. Press **Tab** to move from cell to cell.

b. Click an insertion point in the first cell in the third row (the second row is to be blank).

c. Key the next three rows shown in Figure 9.5, again pressing **Tab** to move from cell to cell.

FIGURE 9.5
First Part of Table

Name	Title	Location	Date Hired
Gordon Redmondson	Fitness Trainer	Reynoldsburg	3-4-90
Terry Curran	Administrative Assistant	Hilliard	5-31-85
Pat Swearingen	Manager	Worthington	6-15-71

Notice that text in cells automatically wraps to a new line when the end of the cell is reached (for example, for "Gordon Redmondson"). Notice also that when you reach the end of a row and press **Tab**, the insertion point moves to the next row.

d. After keying the third date (6-15-71), press **Tab**. A blank row has been inserted.

e. Complete the table as shown in Figure 9.6.

f. After keying the last date, click an insertion point below the table to end the table.

5. Save the table as **chap9-1** in the appropriate location for Student Disk files.

FIGURE 9.6
Second Part of Table

Brian David	Manager	Hilliard	10-15-89
Juanita Crisanti	Director	Worthington	6-15-71
Mildred Rush	Sales Representative	Worthington	2-7-91
Anne Swartz	Fitness Trainer	Hilliard	5-14-92
Roger Lee	Manager	Reynoldsburg	4-5-82

6. With the insertion point positioned on the blank line below the table, press (Enter) four times to leave space for a second table.

7. Insert a blank table grid with 10 rows and 4 columns (10 x 4).

8. Click the down scroll bar arrow until the blank table grid is at the top of the screen.

9. Key the table shown in Figure 9.7. Leave the second row blank. Leave the ZIP cell blank in each row (simply press (Tab) to move to the next column).

10. Click below the table. Then save again, but do not print or clear the screen.

FIGURE 9.7
Second Table for the Document

Name	Address	ZIP	Employee #
Matthew Wang	199 Rita Ct.		27815
Tanya Kotovet	580 E. Rich St.		28875
Chris Dickerson	401 Pierce Ave.		24133
Karen Mercier	793 S. Yearling Rd.		23714
Ike Gibson	399 N. James Rd.		26421
Barbara Schaper	105 Patricia Ln.		26019
Agnes Tuttle	305 Parsons Ave.		22877
David Barry	2805 Briarwood Dr.		23001

Adjusting Column Widths and Centering the Table

When you create tables, Word inserts the number of columns specified but makes all the columns approximately the same width. You can adjust the width of each column manually (either widening or narrowing) or you can adjust all columns automatically. You can also center a table horizontally (the default is left-aligned). If you adjust a column and are not satisfied with the results, you can click ⟨↶⟩⟨⊡⟩.

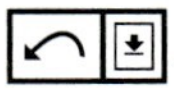

9.2

Adjusting Column Width Manually

● ●

 IMPORTANT: Do not save your work in this exercise.

1. Move the insertion point to the top of the document.

2. Widen the first column using the vertical gridline:

   a. Position the mouse pointer at the border (the vertical gridline) between the first and second columns until you see the gridline pointer +||+.

Name□	Title□
□	□
Gordon·Redmondson□ ←||→	Fitness·Trainer□
Terry·Curran□	Administrative·Assistant□

   b. Drag the border about ½ inch to the right.

   All columns to the right of the first column adjust proportionally (the overall table width remains the same).

3. Widen the second column using the ruler:

   a. Position the mouse pointer on the ruler at the column marker (the box) between the second and third columns.

   b. When you see the two-headed arrow, drag the marker about ½ inch to the right.

TIP

You can double-click +||+ on the right border of a column to resize a column quickly to the size of the longest entry. In some tables, however, you may have to narrow one or more columns before you can double-click to widen another.

Again, all columns to the right adjust proportionally (the overall table width remains the same).

4. Open the Undo list box and drag to undo both "Column Width" edits.

Generally, when you need to adjust a column, you can simply drag as explained in Steps 2 and 3. In the following steps, however, you will experiment with some techniques that give you more control over how the other columns adjust. If you want to see column measurements as you drag on the ruler, hold down (Alt) as well as the keys listed in Steps 5 to 7. Be sure you release the mouse button before all other keys in the following steps, or your results may differ.

5. Using either +||+ or the column marker on the ruler, hold down (Shift) and drag to widen the second column slightly.

Notice that this time only the second column and *one* column to the right adjust (the overall table width remains the same).

6. Hold down **Ctrl** and drag to widen the first column slightly.

Notice that all columns to the right are now equal size (the overall table width remains the same).

7. Hold down both **Ctrl** and **Shift** and drag to widen the second column.

Notice as you drag that the ruler shifts, rather than just the markers. After you release, notice that *no other* columns adjust. Instead, the entire table is now wider.

8. Clear the screen. *Do not save your changes.*

EXERCISE

Centering Horizontally and Adjusting Table Column Width Automatically

1. Open **chap9-1.doc**.

To center the table and adjust the width of all columns in the table at one time, you must first select the table.

2. Choose Table Select Table.

3. Center the table horizontally and adjust column width:

a. Choose Table Cell Height and Width.

b. If necessary, click the Row folder tab to highlight it. A dialog box similar to the one shown in Figure 9.8 should be displayed.

c. Click Center under Alignment.

d. Click the Column folder tab. The dialog box shown in Figure 9.9 should appear (your measurements may vary from those shown).

e. Click AutoFit.

Word closes the dialog box and adjusts all column widths as needed and centers the table horizontally.

FIGURE 9.8
Row Category of Table Cell
Height and Width Dialog Box

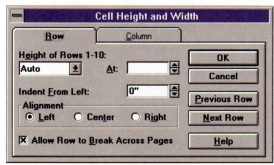

FIGURE 9.9
Column Category of Table Cell
Height and Width Dialog Box

4. Save your work, but do not print or clear the screen yet (you will adjust the second table later).

Editing Table Text and Moving Rows and Columns

Editing table text is similar to editing other document text. You select individual words; cells, rows, or columns; or even the entire table. Then you can insert, delete, copy, or move text. You can also adjust the width of all columns and the horizontal centering for the table. If you make an error as you edit, remember to click ⟲⬆.

EXERCISE

Selecting and Editing Individual Cells

1. Click the down scroll bar arrow until the second table is at the top of the screen.

2. Click an insertion point in the ZIP cell for Matthew Wang and key **43213-1145**.

3. Select the cell:

   a. Position the mouse pointer slightly to the right of the left border for the cell (the *cell selection bar*).

   b. When the cell selection pointer (a diagonal arrowhead) appears, click the left mouse button.

   ⟋43213-1145⊐

4. Copy the ZIP Code in this cell to the ZIP cell in the next row.

HINT: *Use*  *and* 🗒.

5. Move the insertion point down to the next ZIP cell and paste again.

(Remember that information stays in the Clipboard until it is replaced with new information, so you can paste in more than one location.)

6. Continue pasting until all the ZIP cells are completed.

7. Select the ZIP cell for Tanya Kotovet and press [Delete].

8. Select the ZIP cells for Ike Gibson and Agnes Tuttle and delete the ZIP Codes.

9. Move the insertion point to the ZIP cell for Tanya Kotovet and key **43215-2219**.

10. Move the insertion point to the ZIP cells for Ike Gibson and Agnes Tuttle and repeat this change.

HINT: *Choose Edit Repeat.*

11. Change the ZIP extensions (the last four digits) as follows:

2045, 3941, 4564, 2909, 3778, 2112, 1942, 4091

HINT: *Use* [OVR].

12. Center and *"autofit"* the table.

HINT: *Select the table and choose Table Cell Height and Width.*

13. Save and print the document; then clear the screen. Note that the printed tables do not contain gridlines.

EXERCISE

9.5 Selecting and Moving Rows and Columns

● ●

1. In a new document window, use the 12-point font size and insert a blank table grid with six columns and six rows.

2. Key the table shown in Figure 9.10 on page 214, leaving the second row blank (some of your lines may wrap). Do not be concerned about the appearance of your table; you will make adjustments later.

3. Save the table as **chap9-2**.

4. Select a row:

a. Position the mouse pointer in the *row selection bar* (slightly left of the first column's left border) next to the third row (beginning with "55677761").

go into
Border

FIGURE 9.10
Order Form Table

Item #	Description	Quantity	Total Price	Unit Price	Ship Date
55677761	golf pencils	3,500	140.00	0.04	11/05
55673214	ruled legal pads	500	275.00	0.55	11/05
55678009	calculators	50	1,228.00	24.56	12/9
55679001	roller pens, red	450	94.50	0.21	12/17

b. When you see the row selection pointer (a diagonal arrowhead), click the left mouse button to select the row.

a. Position the mouse pointer on the top column border (the *column selection bar*) above the fourth column ("Total Price").

b. When you see the thick, dark column selection pointer, click the left mouse button.

5. Move the row to become the fourth row.

HINT: Use ✂ and 📋.

"Item 55673214" should be in the third row, and "item 55677761" should be in the fourth row.

6. Select a column:

7. Move the column to become the fifth column. The "Unit Price" column should become the fourth column, and the "Total Price" column should become the fifth column.

8. Save the changes to the table, but do not print or clear the screen.

Formatting Tables

You can select and format individual cells, rows, or columns in a table. Some of the formats you will add or change in your tables include:

- character formats (such as underlines)
- paragraph formats (such as centering and right alignment)
- tabs and indents
- printable borders
- titles above the table

EXERCISE

9.6

Adding a Title, Character and Paragraph Formats, and New Tabs

1. Position the insertion point at the beginning of the first cell in the table and press **Enter**. A blank line (paragraph mark) appears above the table.

2. Key **ORDER FORM** and press **Enter** three times to separate the title from the table.

3. Center the title and format it in 16-point Arial bold.

4. Select the row containing the column titles and add the center and underline formats.

TIP

If text already exists above a table, click above the table and press **Enter**.

HINT: *To select the row, position the mouse pointer on the row selection bar to the left of the row and click.*

5. Center and *"autofit"* the table.

HINT: *Select the table and choose Table Cell Height and Width.*

IMPORTANT: Always adjust column widths before you set tabs.

6. Set a right-aligned tab for the quantities:

a. Drag down to select just the amounts (not the column title) in the "Quantity" column.

b. Click at the left end of the ruler until you see ⌐.

c. Click at approximately the ⅝-inch tick mark for the column (one tick mark past the ½-inch tick mark).

Notice that although you have set a custom tab, the quantities are not yet aligned.

d. Click an insertion point before each quantity and press (Ctrl) + (Tab). ((Ctrl) + (Tab) is a special key combination for tables; pressing (Tab) would move the insertion point to the next cell and highlight it.)

Tab characters are added, and the last digit in each quantity should now be aligned (Figure 9.11).

7. Set a decimal-aligned tab for the unit prices:

a. Drag down to select just the amounts in the "Unit Price" column.

b. Click at the left end of the ruler until you see ⊥ .

c. Click on the ruler approximately halfway across the "Unit Price" column.

When you set a decimal tab in tables, the numbers automatically align at the decimal point (Figure 9.12); you do not have to press (Ctrl) + (Tab) to insert tab characters. In the future you may also want to use a decimal tab for columns of numbers like those in the "Quantity" column. When numbers have no decimal points, Word aligns the numbers as if there were a decimal point. You will use this procedure in Activity 3.

TIP

If the columns do not align correctly after setting a tab (because of printer differences), drag the tab on the ruler slightly to the right or left.

8. Set a decimal-aligned tab for the amounts in the "Total Price" column approximately halfway across the column.

9. Save the document, but do not print or clear the screen.

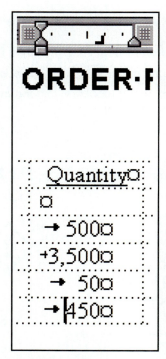

FIGURE 9.11
Column with Right-Aligned Tab

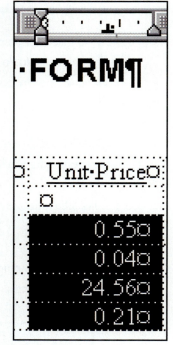

FIGURE 9.12
Column with Decimal Tab

EXERCISE 9.7

Adding Printable Table Borders and Shading

In most cases tables do not need printed borders. Setting off the column titles by underlining them is usually enough to make a readable table. When the table is a form, however, it often looks better with a printed border surrounding it.

1. Select the table.

HINT: *Choose Table Select Table.*

2. Add a printable border manually:

  a. If the Borders Toolbar (Figure 9.13) is not displayed, click the Borders icon on the Formatting Toolbar ⊞.

  b. Click the underlined arrow next to the Line Style box on the Borders Toolbar (currently showing ¾ pt) and click 1½ pt.

  c. Click the Inside Border icon ⊞.

  d. Click the Outside Border icon ▣.

3. Add *shading* to the row with the column titles manually:

  a. Select the row with the column titles.

  b. Click the underlined arrow next to the Shading box (currently showing Clear) and click 10%. Then deselect the row so you can see the format. A light shade has been added to the row with the column titles.

4. Click the underlined arrow for the Undo list box. Drag down the list to undo the shading and the two borders.

5. Add borders and shading automatically:

  a. With the insertion point anywhere in the table, choose Table Table AutoFormat. The dialog box shown in Figure 9.14, on page 218, appears.

  b. Turn off First Column because you do not need a special format for the first column of this table.

  c. If necessary, turn on Borders, Shading, Font, AutoFit, and Heading Rows.

Notice the Preview box. This box shows approximately how your table will be formatted with the current selections in the dialog box.

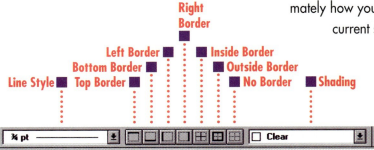

FIGURE 9.13
Borders Toolbar

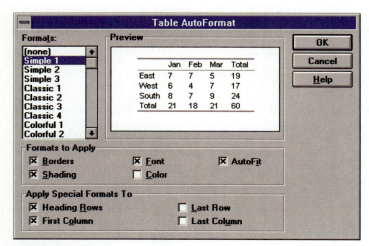

FIGURE 9.14
Table AutoFormat Dialog Box

OK to return to your table with the new formats.

f. If you are not satisfied with the appearance of your table, undo the changes and repeat Steps a–e. You can also experiment with the Borders Toolbar and format individual cells or rows or the entire table.

d. Click Simple 2 in the Formats list box and notice the change to the Preview box.

e. Experiment by clicking once on different choices in the Formats list box. When you are satisfied with the appearance of the sample shown in the Preview box, click

6. Select the row with the column titles and click U to remove the underline format.

7. Click ⊞ on the Formatting Toolbar to turn off the display of the Borders Toolbar.

8. Save the table, print one copy, and clear the screen.

Inserting and Deleting Rows and Columns

As you key text for your tables, you simply press **Tab** to insert new rows at the end of a table. Word also allows you to insert and delete rows and columns easily within a table.

EXERCISE

Changing the Number of Rows and Columns in a Table

1. In a new document window, use the 12-point font size and insert a blank table grid with five rows and two columns.

2. Key the table shown in Figure 9.15 (leaving the cell next to "Lee Rupert" blank, as shown). Tab to add additional rows to the table as needed.

3. Save the table as **chap9-3**.

4. Insert two rows within the table as follows:

    a. Select the rows for "Lee Rupert" and "Suzanne Michaels."

HINT: *Drag the row selection pointer down the row selection bar.*

    b. Click the Insert Rows icon (same as the Insert Table icon) on the Standard Toolbar 📰.

Because you selected two rows, two rows are added, *above* the selected rows.

5. Add the following two names and sales figures: **Rita Homminga, 73,583** and **William Josephs, 60,921**.

6. Add three rows above the first row: select the first three rows and click 📰.

7. In the new top row, key **FOURTH QUARTER SALES** (you will adjust the placement of this heading later).

8. In the second column of the next row, key **October**.

FIGURE 9.15
Sales Figures Table

Al Jankins	64,316
Amy Miller	66,243
Chris Parkerville	70,108
Lee Rupert	
Suzanne Michaels	62,063
Jean Murphy-Lewis	72,478
Valerie Weston	71,575

9. Add columns at the end of the table:

   a. Select the end-of-row markers as a column (Figure 9.16).

HINT: *Position the mouse pointer just above the first end-of-row marker and click when you see the column selection pointer.*

FIGURE 9.16
End-of-Row Markers Selected as a Column

   b. Click the Insert Columns icon (same as the Insert Table icon) on the Standard Toolbar [icon].

One column is added to the left of the end-of-row markers.

   c. Click [icon] two more times to add two more columns.

10. Scroll to the right. In the third column of the second row, key **November**; in the fourth column, key **December**; and in the last column, key **Total**.

11. Complete the "November" column of the table using the numbers shown in Figure 9.17 (leave the cell below the cell containing "60,744" blank).

> **TIP**
>
> To insert columns inside a table—rather than at the far right end of the table— select the column or columns to the right of where the new columns are to be added and click [icon].

12. Lee Rupert no longer works for the company. Delete the row:

   a. Scroll left and select the "Lee Rupert" row.

   b. Choose Table Delete Rows.

> **TIP**
>
> When you need to delete columns, select the columns and choose Table Delete Columns.

Before adjusting the column widths, you must key an entry under "Total" to allow for proper spacing for the numbers that you will add in Chapter 10. The "December" column heading is wider than the entries to be added in Chapter 10 so no entry is needed to adjust this column.

13. Key **X** nine times in the second row below "Total."

14. Center and *"autofit"* the table.

15. Underline each column heading but do not underline "FOURTH QUARTER SALES."

16. Delete the **X**'s for "Total." Then save the table, but do not print or clear the screen.

November
66,152
67,075
69,927
74,116
60,744
61,565
73,889
72,097

FIGURE 9.17
November Entries

EXERCISE 9.9

Merging Table Cells

The top row of the table would look better spread across several columns rather than just the first column. Creating a heading that spans several columns is called *merging cells.*

1. Merge the cells in the top row:

   a. Select the top row.

   b. Choose Table Merge Cells.

2. Center the heading and change it to 16-point Arial bold. The top row should now look like Figure 9.18.

3. Save the table, print one copy, and clear the screen.

FIGURE 9.18
Merged Cells

FOURTH·QUARTER·SALES¶				
¤				
¤	October¤	November¤	December¤	Total¤

Converting Text to Tables

Word can quickly convert text separated by paragraph marks, commas, or tab characters into a table with cells.

EXERCISE 9.10

Converting Text to a Table

1. Open the Data Disk file **juices.doc** and save it as **chap9-4**.

2. Convert text with tabs to table form:

   a. Select the entire document except for the ending paragraph mark.

   b. Choose Table Convert Text to Table. The dialog box shown in Figure 9.19, on page 222, appears.

   c. If necessary, click Tabs under Separate Text At; then click [**OK**].

3. Center and *"autofit"* the table.

FIGURE 9.19
Table Convert Text to Table Dialog Box

4. Right-align each entry in the third and fourth columns.

HINT: *Click* .

5. If you want to, add additional formats:

    a. Add blank lines (not blank rows) above the top row and key a centered title for this analysis of calories and protein for juices (with an appropriate font and font size).

    b. Use Table Table AutoFormat and select an appropriate format for the table (turning off Heading Rows and First Column).

6. Save the table, print one copy, and clear the screen.

Working with Side-by-Side Paragraphs

Some documents require keying text that has corresponding text aligned in a column to the right. These *side-by-side paragraphs* can be quickly set up using the Word Table feature.

EXERCISE

9.11 Keying Side-by-Side Paragraphs

● ●

1. In a new document window, use the 12-point font size and insert a blank table grid with one row and two columns (1 x 2).

2. Drag the column marker on the ruler between the first and second columns back to approximately 2½ inches. (AutoFit will not make a large enough adjustment for the second column in this table.)

3. Key the table shown in Figure 9.20 with the following guidelines:

    a. Key the first course title; then press **Tab** and key the course description.

b. Press ⬭Enter⬭ twice, key **Prerequisite:**, press ⬭Ctrl⬭ + ⬭Tab⬭, and key the information for the prerequisite.

c. Press ⬭Tab⬭ three times to leave a blank row.

d. Repeat Steps a–c until you complete the table.

FIGURE 9.20
Side-by-Side Paragraphs

SPRING QUARTER CLASS OFFERINGS

HPR 301 Kinesiology

An analysis of the principles of mechanics as they relate to fundamental and complex motor skills in physical education activities. Analysis includes the muscular interrelationships in basic body movements.

Prerequisite: BIO 208 and 209, and HPR 101 and 410

HPR 405 Applied Exercise Physiology

Practical applications in exercise physiology including methods of conditioning, training, implementation, and other special considerations.

Prerequisite: HPR 400

HPR 505 Principles of Physical Fitness

Instruction concerning the principles of physical fitness including aerobic and muscular fitness.

Prerequisite: None

HPR 555 Total Fitness Lifestyle

Discussion of lifestyle variables and their effects on total fitness. Includes emphasis on body composition, blood lipids, cardiovascular fitness, and strength.

Prerequisite: HPR 505

4. Spell-check and proofread the document; then save the table as **chap9-5**.

5. Create a hanging indent for the prerequisites:

    a. Position the insertion point in the second column on the line with the first prerequisite.

    b. Position the mouse pointer on ⌂ on the ruler and drag the bottom half (the small box) to approximately 4 inches (▽ also moves).

    c. Drag ▽ back to approximately 3 inches on the ruler.

    d. Set the same hanging indent for the remaining prerequisites.

6. Add a blank line above the top row, key **SPRING QUARTER CLASS OFFERINGS**, and press **Enter** three times.

7. Change the heading to 16-point Arial bold and center it.

8. Save the table, print one copy, and clear the screen.

COMPUTER ACTIVITIES

ACTIVITY 1

1. Open a new document window. In Print Preview, change the left and right margins to approximately 2 inches; then close Print Preview.

HINT: *Hold down (Alt) as you drag on the horizontal ruler.*

2. Using the 12-point font size, create a table with 7 rows and 2 columns.

3. Key the schedule illustrated in Figure 9.21.

4. Move the second column to become the first column.

5. Insert three rows above "Friday, June 24."

6. Add the days and dates for June 21–June 23 (use "11 a.m. – 8 p.m." for the times).

7. Center the table and, if necessary, adjust the width of the columns.

8. Add four blank lines above the first row.

9. On the first line, center and key **EXHIBIT HOURS** using 16-point Arial bold.

10. Save the document as **act9-1**, print one copy, and clear the screen.

FIGURE 9.21
Schedule

10 a.m. – 9 p.m.	Friday, June 17
10 a.m. – 9 p.m.	Saturday, June 18
10 a.m. – 6 p.m.	Sunday, June 19
11 a.m. – 8 p.m.	Monday, June 20
10 a.m. – 9 p.m.	Friday, June 24
10 a.m. – 9 p.m.	Saturday, June 25
10 a.m. – 6 p.m.	Sunday, June 26

ACTIVITY 2

1. Create the table shown in Figure 9.22, using 1-inch margins and the 12-point font size.

2. Insert a third column at the end of the table.

3. Key the column title **Corporation** and the following list of company names:

   Life Fitness, Inc.
   Fitness Innovations
   South-West Trainers
   National Fitness Corporation
   Voiers Manufacturing
   The Equipment Company

4. Center the table and adjust the width of the columns for a more attractive layout.

5. Add two new rows above the column headings. In the first row, key the title **FITNESS ALLIANCE OFFICERS**.

6. Merge the cells in the title row. Center the heading and change it to 16-point Arial bold.

7. Center and underline the column headings.

8. Save the document as **act9-2**, print one copy, and clear the screen.

FIGURE 9.22
List of Officers

Name	Title
Magdalena Lugo	President
Daniel George	President-Elect
Sara Osvaldo	Past President
Clark Forrest	Secretary
Laurie Miesen	Treasurer
Paul Landry	Board Member (1994-1996)

ACTIVITY 3

1. Create the income statement shown in Figure 9.23:

FIGURE 9.23
Income Statement

FITNESS INNOVATIONS
Income Statement
For the year Ending December 31, 19--

Revenue from Sales

Sales			1,112,656
Less Sales Returns and Allowances	1,990		
Sales Discount	5,789	7,779	
Net Sales			1,104,877

Cost of Goods Sold

Finished Goods Inventory, January 1	76,551	
Cost of Goods Manufactured	410,883	
Cost of Goods Available for Sale	487,434	
Less Finished Goods Inventory, December 31	129,460	
Cost of Goods Sold		357,974

Gross Margin 746,903

Selling and Administrative Expenses

Administrative Salaries Expense	357,045
Advertising Expense	20,000
Depreciation Expense--Office Equipment	10,800
Insurance Expense	5,433
Miscellaneous Expense	991
Sales Commissions and Salaries Expense	144,506
Total Selling and Administrative Expenses	538,775

Net Income 208,128

a. Set 1-inch margins, choose the 12-point font size, and insert a table grid.

b. Key the table text (you will add formats and the title lines after you finish).

c. Drag the first column marker right to approximately 3¾ inches (the other columns will automatically adjust).

d. Set ¼-inch left indents for "Sales" and all other second-level rows (the next second-level row is "Finished Goods Inventory, January 1").

e. Set ½-inch left indents for "Less Sales Returns and Allowances" and all other third-level rows (the next two third-level rows are "Sales Discount" and "Cost of Goods Available for Sale").

f. Set ¾-inch left indents for "Net Sales" and "Cost of Goods Sold" (under "Less Finished Goods Inventory, December 31").

g. Set a decimal-aligned tab for all amounts at approximately the right border for the column.

h. Add underlining as shown (for the double Underline, select Double in the Underline list box in the Format Font dialog box).

i. Add the centered title lines above the table using appropriate fonts and font sizes, then deselect.

j. Center the document vertically.

HINT: *Click Layout in the File Page Setup dialog box.*

2. Check the document in Print Preview.

3. Save the document as **act9-3**, print one copy, and clear the screen.

ACTIVITY 4

1. Key the document shown in Figure 9.24, using 1-inch margins and the 12-point font size.

HINT: *Insert and key the side-by-side paragraphs in table form first; then add the title and text above and below the table using appropriate fonts and font sizes.*

2. Add a printable border to the entire table (you do not need a special format for the heading row or first column).

3. Spell-check and proofread. Save the document as **act9-4**, print one copy, and clear the screen.

FIGURE 9.24
Document with Side-by-Side Paragraphs

HIGH PERFORMANCE FOODS

Antioxidant vitamins that help prevent diseases are getting a lot of attention these days. Below are descriptions of Beta Carotene, Vitamin C, Vitamin E, and Vitamin D including an explanation of the foods that provide these vitamins.

Beta Carotene is one of the key components in many fruits and vegetables. It is an antioxidant that helps fight disease and is essential to good health, good vision, and good-looking skin.	Foods that provide high amounts of Beta Carotene include apricots, broccoli, spinach, carrots, chard, kale, peaches, cantaloupes, squashes, and sweet potatoes.
Vitamin C is effective in keeping teeth, blood vessels, and bones healthy; however, it does much more than prevent and cure scurvy. It is now believed that Vitamin C also helps prevent heart disease, prevents or delays the onset of some cancers, and keeps people healthy longer.	Foods that provide high amounts of Vitamin C content include broccoli, cantaloupes, oranges, grapefruits, and cranberries.
Vitamin D is essential for developing strong teeth and bones. It increases the absorption of calcium and phosphorus into bones. Vitamin D is formed in the skin by exposure to sunlight or ultraviolet rays.	Foods that provide high amounts of Vitamin D include milk and milk products like yogurt and cheese, egg yolk, and fish-liver oils.

Continued on next page

Vitamin E is one of the most important antioxidants in the body. It helps to form healthy red blood cells, muscles, and other tissues. It protects cells, and as a result, it has been linked to the aging process.	Foods that provide high amounts of Vitamin E include vegetable oil, margarine, nuts, and leafy greens such as spinach and kale.

Beta Carotene and Vitamin E are the most potent antioxidants.

CREATE YOUR OWN

Create a table listing each course in which you are currently enrolled. For each course include the course name, the instructor's name, the room number or location, and the day and time that the class meets. When you complete the document, save the file (choose an appropriate filename) and print one copy.

For example:

Course Name	Instructor	Location	Day	Time
Introduction to Business	Hisako	HH 214	M, W, F	9–10 a.m.

On a separate page, write a paragraph about each course and describe what you are learning in the course. Explain also how what you are learning in the course will help you in your current work experience or will help you prepare for a career.

Save the table so that you can revise and update it next term when your course schedule changes.

REVIEW EXERCISES

TRUE/FALSE

Each of the following statements is either true or false. Indicate your answer on the left by circling T if the statement is true or F if the statement is false.

T F 1. When Word creates a table, it makes all the columns approximately the same width.

T F 2. The gridlines surrounding the table cells will print as displayed on the screen.

T F 3. When column widths are being adjusted, the insertion point must be positioned in the first line of the table.

T F 4. Custom tabs and indents cannot be set for table columns.

T F 5. New rows are added above selected rows and new columns are added to the left of selected columns.

FILL IN THE BLANKS

Complete the following sentences by writing the correct word or words in the blanks provided.

6. The Table feature can also be used to create _____ paragraphs, in which text on the left aligns with corresponding text in a column to the right.

7. To display gridlines as you work with tables, choose the _____ command.

8. To adjust column width automatically, choose the Table Cell Height and Width command, click Column, and click _____.

9. To delete rows, choose the _____ command.

10. To insert a tab character in a cell, press _____.

11. To change text keyed with tabs into a table with cells, choose the _____ command.

12. Press _____ at the end of the last cell to add a new row automatically.

13. To center a table horizontally, choose the _____ command, and select Center under Alignment.

14. To create a heading that spans several columns, choose the _____ command.

15. To add a title above a table, position the insertion point in the first cell and press _____.

MATCHING

Find the icon on the right that matches the description on the left and write the appropriate letter in the blank provided at the left margin.

___ **16.** Gridline pointer

___ **17.** Insert Table

___ **18.** Column selection pointer

___ **19.** Row/cell selection pointer

___ **20.** Borders

a.   ↗

b.   ⊞

c.   ▦

d.   ⬭*

e.   ↓

REFERENCE QUESTIONS

Referring to the *Microsoft Word User's Guide*, write the answers to the following questions in the space provided.

1. What is the maximum number of columns you can have in a table?

_____

_____

_____

2. If you wanted to divide a table to insert ordinary text (for example, to add a note between the "Gross Margin" and the "Selling and Administrative Expenses" in Figure 9.23), what would you do?

_____

_____

_____

SORT AND CALCULATE

CHAPTER

10

OBJECTIVES
Upon completion of this chapter, you will be able to:

- Sort a one-column list.
- Sort a multiple-column list created with tabs.
- Sort a table.
- Sort paragraphs.
- Calculate totals in tables.

Preparation

1. To complete the chapter activities, you will need to access the Data Disk files PRODUCTS.DOC and PAYROLL.DOC and your Student Disk files CHAP7-1.DOC, CHAP9-1.DOC, and CHAP9-3.DOC.

2. Before sorting, always be sure to save your work.

3. Remember to save frequently as you work. You will generally not be reminded to save until all work is completed for a document.

4. If you make mistakes as you work with the exercises in the chapter, remember to click [⟲⊞] immediately after completing the action.

5. At the end of each class session, be sure to close Word and Windows properly. If you are using the hard drive to store your completed work, back up your files onto your formatted Student Disk, and erase your files from the directory you used on the hard drive. (Do not erase the Data Disk files unless your instructor tells you to do so.)

Sorting Text

Word allows you to rearrange your text *alphanumerically* (numbers first, then letters), by numbers only, or by date. You can sort tables, paragraphs, or lists created with commas, tabs, spaces, or other separators. You can sort in either ascending or descending order. *Ascending order* is from A to Z, from 1 to 10, or from the earliest date to the latest date; *descending order* is from Z to A, from 10 to 1, or from the latest date to the earliest date. You can turn on *Case Sensitive* so words beginning with the same letter will be sorted with uppercase before lowercase letters. You can sort by as many as three criteria at a time.

 IMPORTANT: Each time you sort during a Word session, the previous sort settings are retained. Be sure to check all settings before you click ⎡ OK ⎤ .

EXERCISE 10.1

Sorting Single-Column Lists

If a document you are creating contains a list of items in a column and you want the items arranged in a certain order, you can enter the items out of order and sort them later.

1. Key the document shown in Figure 10.1:

   a. Use the 12-point font size.

   b. Press **Enter** at the end of each line rather than the NEWLINE key (**Shift** + **Enter**). Word cannot sort entries in a list that are separated with the NEWLINE key.

   c. Leave a blank line between each list.

   d. Use 📋 for each list of names.

   Don't take the paragraph symbol

2. Save the document as **chap10-1**.

3. Sort the list of numbers in ascending order:

   a. Select the list of five-digit numbers at the bottom of the document (do not select the paragraph mark below the list).

   b. Choose Table Sort Text. A dialog box similar to the one in Figure 10.2 appears (your settings may vary).

```
1.   Greene, Nancy
2.   Macneil, Kyle
3.   Green, William
4.   Lund-Matthews, Anna
5.   Yukimura, Elizabeth
6.   Chu, Yuan
7.   Lund, Anna K.
8.   Dunn, Lawrence
9.   MacNeil, Kyle
10.  Lund, A.
11.  Nozaki, Eizaburo
12.  Schuck, James
13.  Nieves, Tomas
14.  Lund, Anna

1.   Robert C. Jackson
2.   Donna Leon
3.   Robert Jackson
4.   Donna Kelly
5.   Robert Leon Jackson
6.   Kelly C. Jackson
7.   Robert Carl Jackson

78254
49862
96411
20537
85109
13268
62043
38876
51380
```

FIGURE 10.1
Lists of Numbers and Names
To Be Sorted

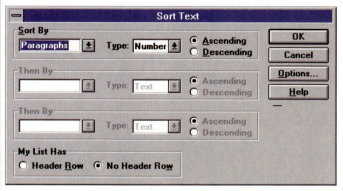

FIGURE 10.2
Table Sort Text
Dialog Box

c. Click Options.

d. In the Sort Options dialog box (Figure 10.3), if necessary, reset the defaults: select Tabs (under Separate *Fields* At) and turn off Case Sensitive.

e. Click   OK   .

FIGURE 10.3
Sort Options Dialog Box

e. Click   OK   .

f. In the Sort Text dialog box, make any necessary changes until the dialog box shows: Paragraphs (under Sort By), Number (under Type), Ascending, and No Header Row (under My List Has); then click   OK   .

The list should now be sorted from the lowest to the highest number. (Figure 10.4, page 236)

FIGURE 10.4
List Sorted in Ascending
Numeric Order

13268¶
20537¶
38876¶
49862¶
51380¶
62043¶
78254¶
85109¶
96411¶

4. Undo the sort.

5. With the list of numbers selected, choose Table Sort Text again and change to Descending; then click ⬚ **OK** ⬚.

The list is now sorted from the highest to the lowest number.

6. Sort the first list of names in descending order:

 a. Select the first list of names. (Do not select the paragraph mark above or below the list.) Note that the numbers you inserted with the Numbering icon are not highlighted but are actually selected with the names.

 b. Choose Table Sort Text.

 c. Click Options.

 d. This time, select Commas under Separate Fields At since your fields (last name and first name) are divided by commas.

 e. Click ⬚ **OK** ⬚.

 f. In the Sort Text dialog box make any necessary changes until the dialog box shows: Paragraphs (under Sort By), Text (under Type), Descending, and No Header Row (under My List Has); then click ⬚ **OK** ⬚.

The list should now be sorted from names at the end of the alphabet to names at the beginning of the alphabet. Notice that Word automatically renumbered the list as it sorted (Figure 10.5).

1. Yukimura, Elizabeth¶
2. Schuck, James¶
3. Nozaki, Eizaburo¶
4. Nieves, Tomas¶
5. Macneil, Kyle¶
6. MacNeil, Kyle¶
7. Lund-Matthews, Anna¶
8. Lund, Anna K.¶
9. Lund, Anna¶
10. Lund, A.¶
11. Greene, Nancy¶
12. Green, William¶
13. Dunn, Lawrence¶
14. Chu, Yuan¶

FIGURE 10.5
Names Sorted in Descending Order and Renumbered

7. Undo this sort (do not undo the previous sort).

8. Sort again in ascending order.

The list is now sorted from names at the beginning of the alphabet to names at the end of the alphabet. Again, Word automatically renumbered the list.

9. Sort the second list of names:

 a. Select the second set of names (do not include paragraph marks above or below the list).

 b. Choose Table Sort Text; then click Options.

c. If necessary, turn off Case Sensitive.

d. If necessary, click Other under Separate Fields At.

e. Click in the text box, delete the entry in the box (if any), and press (Space Bar) (indicating that you want the separator to be a space).

f. Click [OK].

g. In the Sort Text dialog box, open the Sort By box and click Word 3 (indicating that you want the third word in each item in the list to be sorted). Make sure Text shows for Type and Ascending is selected; then click [OK].

Word sorts the list and automatically renumbers it. The list is not sorted properly, however (Figure 10.6), because some items in the list do not have a third word.

1. Donna·Leon¶
2. Robert·Jackson¶
3. Donna·Kelly¶
4. Robert·C.·Jackson¶
5. Robert·Leon·Jackson¶
6. Kelly·C.·Jackson¶
7. Robert·Carl·Jackson¶

FIGURE 10.6
Incorrectly Sorted List of Names

10. Undo this sort.

Although you could rekey the list with last name first and then sort as you did for the first list of names, another way to sort is to make each item in the list three parts.

11. Correctly sort the second list of names:

a. For Donna Leon, Robert Jackson, and Donna Kelly, add an additional space between the first and last names. (Word will consider the blank spaces a second word when you sort.)

b. Select the list again and Choose Table Sort Text. Do not click Options this time because these settings should remain the same.

c. In the Sort Text dialog box, if necessary, open the Sort By list box and click Word 3 to indicate again that the last name is to be sorted first.

d. Open the first Then By list box and click Word 1 to indicate that when last names are the same, the first name is to be used as the sort criteria.

e. Open the second Then By list box and click Word 2 to indicate that the middle name (or space left for a middle name or initial) is to be used when the first and second criteria are the same.

f. Click [OK].

The list is now sorted and numbered properly (Figure 10.7).

1. Kelly·C.·Jackson¶
2. Robert··Jackson¶
3. Robert·C.·Jackson¶
4. Robert·Carl·Jackson¶
5. Robert·Leon·Jackson¶
6. Donna··Kelly¶
7. Donna··Leon¶

FIGURE 10.7
Correctly Sorted List of Names

g. Delete the spaces you added.

12. Save the document, print one copy, and clear the screen.

Sorting Multiple-Column Lists Created with Tabs

To sort a multiple-column list created with tabs, follow the same procedures as for a single-column list, but be sure to specify Tabs for the Separate Fields At option and select the desired column (field number) in the Sort By box. If you want to sort a single column without rearranging the rows for the entire list, select only the one column and turn on Sort Column Only.

1. Open **chap7-1.doc** from your Student Disk and save it with a new name, **chap10-2**.

2. Replace all NEWLINE characters with a regular paragraph mark.

   HINT: *Use Special in Edit Replace and select Manual Line Break and Paragraph Mark.*

3. Sort based on the second column (the first column is a blank column of tab symbols):

   a. Select the list (do not include any paragraph marks below the list); then choose Table Sort Text.

   b. Click Options. If necessary, click Tabs and turn off Case Sensitive. Click [OK].

   c. In the Sort By box, click Field 2. If necessary, select Text (for Type) and Ascending.

   d. Click [OK] to perform the sort.

When the sort based on the second column is completed, the rows should be rearranged as shown in Figure 10.8.

Any blank paragraph marks you have inserted between paragraphs in your document will automatically be moved to the top or bottom of the selection during the sort. You could delete the blank lines between paragraphs before sorting; or, after you sort, you could delete any unnecessary blank lines. Then you could reinsert blank lines between paragraphs or lines in your list or table as needed.

4. Delete the two paragraph marks at the top of the selection; then add a blank line between the lines in the list.

5. Save the changes and print one copy.

6. Sort in descending order based on the fifth column (remember that the first column is blank):

   a. Select the list again and choose Table Sort Text.

FIGURE 10.8
Tabular List Sorted Based on Field 2 (First Column After First Tab)

b. Click Options, click Tabs (if necessary), and click [OK].

c. Select Field 5 for Sort By, select Number for the Type, select Descending, and click [OK].

The list is sorted numerically from highest to lowest number based on the last column (Figure 10.9).

7. Delete the last two paragraph marks below the list; then add blank lines between the lines in the list.

8. Save the changes as **chap10-3** and print one copy.

9. Sort just the last column:

a. Delete the blank lines between the rows in the list (you will be sorting a single column rather than rearranging the entire list and will get an error message if you leave the blank lines).

b. Select the last column.

HINT: *Hold down* **Alt** *and drag down and across the column.*

c. Choose Table Sort Text and click Options. If necessary, select Tabs for Separate Fields At. Turn on Sort Column Only and click [OK].

d. If necessary, change Sort By to Paragraphs. Select Number (for Type) and Ascending, and click [OK].

Notice that only the last column is sorted because you turned on Sort Column Only. Compare your current list (Figure 10.10) with Figure 10.9.

10. Add blank lines between the lines of your list.

11. Save the changes as **chap10-4**, print one copy, and clear the screen.

→	DA43E	→	8#	→	Two-hundred	→	400¶
→	AE98M	→	2-1/4#	→	Fifty-four	→	178.55¶
→	JC212K	→	5/8#	→	Ninety-nine	→	31.985¶

FIGURE 10.9
Tabular List Sorted in Descending Numeric Order Based on Field 5 (Column Following Fourth Tab)

FIGURE 10.10
Tabular List with Only Last Column Sorted

→	DA43E	→	8#	→	Two-hundred	→	31.985¶
→	AE98M	→	2-1/4#	→	Fifty-four	→	178.55¶
→	JC212K	→	5/8#	→	Ninety-nine	→	400¶

EXERCISE 10.3 Sorting Tables

1. Open **chap9-1.doc** from your Student Disk and save it with a new name, **chap10-5**.

2. Sort **only** the fourth column of the first table by date:

   a. Select the fourth column in the first table.

HINT: *Position the mouse pointer above the column, and click when you see the column selection pointer.*

FIGURE 10.11
Table with Only Last Column Sorted Incorrectly by Date

Note before you sort that the "Date Hired" entry for Gordon Redmondson is 3-4-90.

   b. Choose Table Sort and click Options.

   c. Turn on Sort Column Only (if necessary); then click [OK].

   d. If necessary, change Sort By to Column 4 and click Ascending. Select Date as the Type and click [OK].

You sorted only the fourth column; the other columns remain unchanged. Notice that the "Date Hired" entry for Gordon Redmondson is now 6-15-71 rather than 3-4-90 (Figure 10.11).

3. Undo the sort.

4. Sort the entire table by date based on the fourth column:

   a. Select the first table.

HINT: *Choose Table Select Table.*

   b. Choose Table Sort.

   c. Select Column 4 (for Sort By), Date (for Type), and Ascending.

   d. Click [OK]. The table should now look like Figure 10.12.

5. Click the down scroll bar arrow until the second table is at the top of the screen.

6. Sort numerically based on the fourth column of the second table:

FIGURE 10.12
Table Correctly Sorted by Date, Based on Fourth Column

Name	Title	Location	Date Hired
Pat Swearingen	Manager	Worthington	6-15-71
Juanita Crisanti	Director	Worthington	6-15-71
Roger Lee	Manager	Reynoldsburg	4-5-82
Terry Curran	Administrative Assistant	Hilliard	5-31-85
Brian David	Manager	Hilliard	10-15-89
Gordon Redmondson	Fitness Trainer	Reynoldsburg	3-4-90
Mildred Rush	Sales Representative	Worthington	2-7-91
Anne Swartz	Fitness Trainer	Hilliard	5-14-92

IMPORTANT: If your table contains column titles and blank rows, select all rows of the table except the blank rows and the title row so that they are not rearranged with the rows you want to sort.

a. Select only the third through the tenth rows of the second table.

HINT: *Drag the row selection pointer down to the tenth row.*

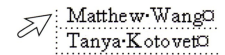

b. Choose Table Sort. Select Column 4 (for Sort By), Number (for Type), and Descending; then click [**OK**].

The table should be rearranged by employee number, with the highest number first.

7. Save the changes, print one copy, and clear the screen.

EXERCISE

Sorting Paragraphs

● ●

Word sorts paragraphs the same way it sorts lists and tables. Word sorts by the first word in each paragraph. If you want to specify a different *field* number (for example, the second word in each paragraph), the text must be separated by commas or tabs.

1. Open the Data Disk file **products.doc** and save the file as **chap10-6**.

Note that PRODUCTS.DOC contains NEWLINE characters. The NEWLINE characters are used here to keep parts of a paragraph together—the product number and the description—and are not used to separate paragraphs. The NEWLINE characters will not affect the sorting because paragraph marks are used to separate the actual items to be sorted—the product numbers only.

2. Drag to select from "HPR 900" down to the end of the "TR-65" description (do not include the paragraph mark below the last paragraph).

3. Choose Table Sort Text. If necessary, select Paragraphs (for Sort By), Text (for Type), and Ascending.

4. Click [**OK**]. The paragraphs are rearranged in the following order:

AB 120
HPR 900
JJTY 200
SS 50/50 R
TR-65
WW 550
YEF 10-20

5. Delete six of the nine paragraph marks above "AB 120," and add a blank line above each product number beginning with "HPR 900."

6. If the document is two pages, do one of the following:

- Change all margins to .75 inch.

- In Print Preview, click the Shrink to Fit icon [icon]. (The font size may be changed for the descriptions.)

7. Save the document, print one copy, and clear the screen.

will make text fit onto 1 page

Performing Math Calculations

With Word, you can perform math calculations in tables such as adding, subtracting, multiplying, dividing, averaging, and calculating a percentage. For calculations, Word assigns letters and numbers to cells. For example, A2 would be the intersection of the first column and second row, B3 would the intersection of the second column and third row, and so on. To perform a calculation, position the insertion point in the cell where the total (result) is to appear, choose Table Formula, either key a *formula* or accept the proposed formula, and click [**OK**].

EXERCISE 10.5

Calculating in Tables

1. Open **chap9-3.doc** from your Student Disk and save it with a new name, **chap10-7**.

2. Key the December figures:

Jankins	**65,202**	Josephs	**61,007**
Miller	**66,947**	Michaels	**62,418**
Parkerville	**71,326**	Murphy-Lewis	**73,601**
Homminga	**73,835**	Weston	**72,352**

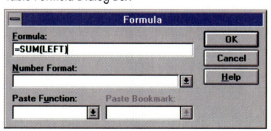

3. To calculate the total for the "Al Jankins" row:

a. Position the insertion point in the last cell in the "Al Jankins" row.

b. Choose Table Formula. The dialog box shown in Figure 10.13 appears, with the proposed formula =SUM(LEFT). *above*

c. Click **OK** to accept the proposed formula. The result (total) of 195,670 is automatically inserted.

4. Repeat the calculation process for the totals in the other rows.

FIGURE 10.13
Table Formula Dialog Box

HINT: *Choose Edit Repeat.*

5. Insert rows at the bottom of the table without pressing (Tab):

a. Position the insertion point on the paragraph mark immediately below the table and click 📅.

b. In the Insert Rows dialog box (Figure 10.14), key **2**; then click **OK**. Two new rows are added.

FIGURE 10.14
Table Insert Rows Dialog Box

6. Key **Total Sales** in the first cell of the last new row.

7. Calculate the total of the "October" column:

a. Position the insertion point in the last cell in the "October" column.

b. Choose Table Formula. Word proposes =SUM(ABOVE).

c. Click **OK**. The total of 541,287 is automatically inserted.

8. Repeat the calculation process for the other three columns. The "Total Sales" row should now look like Figure 10.15 on page 244.

243

FIGURE 10.15
Total Sales Row Completed with Totals Inserted

Total·Sales¤		541,287¤	545,565¤	546,688¤	1,633,540¤	¤

9. Position the insertion point in the "October" column. Drag the first column marker to the left to approximately 2 inches to widen the amount columns slightly.

10. Drag to select just the numbers in the "October" column.

11. Click at the left end of the ruler to display [⊥]. Click on the ruler at approximately the ½-inch mark for the column.

Remember that decimal tabs assume an invisible ".00" when there is no decimal point. Using a decimal tab setting allows you to align the entire column without having to insert tab characters. The commas should all be aligned in the "October" column. If the commas are not aligned correctly, select the numbers again (if necessary) and drag the tab stop to the right. Adjust all tab stops in this chapter as needed for proper alignment.

12. Set decimal tabs for numbers in the "November," "December," and "Total" columns. Drag the tabs as necessary to align the commas properly.

13. Center the column headings.

14. Underline each amount in the "Valerie Weston" row.

15. Select the "October" total of 541,287. Choose Format Font, select Double in the Underline list box, and click [OK].

> **TIP**
>
> A shortcut for the double underline format is Ctrl + Shift + D.

16. Repeat the double underline format for the other totals.

17. Save the changes to the table and print one copy, but do not clear the screen.

EXERCISE

10.6

Updating Tables

After creating a table and calculating totals, you may discover that you need to change amounts. Word provides a shortcut that enables you to recalculate an entire table quickly, rather than recalculating each individual total in each column and row. When you use the Table Formula command, Word inserts hidden fields for each total. To change the totals, you simply select the table and update the fields.

1. Save **chap10-7.doc** with a new name, **chap10-8**.

2. Double-click OVR on the status bar. Then change the December amounts to the following:

Jankins	**65,207**	Josephs	**61,104**
Miller	**67,647**	Michaels	**62,467**
Parkerville	**70,926**	Murphy-Lewis	**73,589**
Homminga	**73,901**	Weston	**72,368**

3. Double-click OVR to turn off OVERTYPE.

4. Select the table.

HINT: *Choose Table Select Table.*

5. Press the Update Field key, F9. All amounts are automatically recalculated. Figure 10.16 illustrates the revised table after deselecting.

6. Save the changes, print one copy, and clear the screen.

FIGURE 10.16
Totals in Table Automatically Recalculated

FOURTH·QUARTER·SALES¶				
¤	October¤	November¤	December¤	Total¤
¤				
Al·Jankins¤	64,316¤	66,152¤	65,207¤	195,675¤
Amy·Miller¤	66,243¤	67,075¤	67,647¤	200,965¤
Chris·Parkerville¤	70,108¤	69,927¤	70,926¤	210,961¤
Rita·Homminga¤	73,583¤	74,116¤	73,901¤	221,600¤
William·Josephs¤	60,921¤	60,744¤	61,104¤	182,769¤
Suzanne·Michaels¤	62,063¤	61,565¤	62,467¤	186,095¤
Jean·Murphy-Lewis¤	72,478¤	73,889¤	73,589¤	219,956¤
Valerie·Weston¤	71,575¤	72,097¤	72,368¤	216,040¤
¤				
Total·Sales¤	541,287¤	545,565¤	547,209¤	1,634,061¤

Computer Activities

ACTIVITY 1

1. Open a new document. Change to the 12-point font size and key the accounts receivable report illustrated in Figure 10.17 in table form.

HINT: *Insert the table grid and key the table. Then add blank lines above the table and add the title in an appropriate font and font size.*

2. Center the table and adjust column widths.

HINT: *Choose Table Cell Height and Width.*

3. Set a decimal-aligned tab for the amounts in the "Account Balance" column.

4. Center and underline the column headings.

5. Save the table as **act10-1a**.

6. Sort the table so that the customers are listed in ascending alphabetical order by last name.

7. Save the changes and print one copy.

FIGURE 10.17
Accounts Receivable Report

ACCOUNTS RECEIVABLE REPORT

Last Name	First Name	Account Balance
Pinion	Louie	$89.32
Blanco	Joaquin	$1,004.21
Puter	Mary	$373.22
Hori	Reiko	$1,025.55
Archer	Ron	$495.19
Pleasant	Karen	$108.55
Heppes	Sharon	$256.47

8. Save a new copy of the document as **act10-1b**.

9. Sort the table so that the customers are ranked by account balances, with the highest balance listed first.

10. Save the changes, print one copy, and clear the screen.

ACTIVITY 2

1. In a new document window, use 1-inch margins and the 12-point font size and key the expense report illustrated in Figure 10.18 in table form. (Remember to add the title line after you complete the table.) Do not format the table until Step 3.

2. Calculate the total for the July column; then repeat the process for the other two columns.

3. Center the table and adjust the width of the columns for a more attractive layout.

FIGURE 10.18
Expense Report

THIRD QUARTER EXPENSE REPORT

Expense	July	August	September
Advertising	1,685.22	2,545.59	1,962.84
Delivery	578.55	403.66	665.74
Insurance	350.00	350.00	350.00
Interest	2,596.43	2,029.55	2,311.89
Maintenance	1,166.98	1,880.78	1,479.24
Miscellaneous	344.21	734.87	591.48
Salaries	42,445.93	45,875.63	49,877.35
Supplies	1,006.66	1,132.45	1,345.56
Taxes	12,878.04	15,886.95	14,459.72
Utilities	2,819.77	2,877.74	2,643.39
Total			

4. Add decimal tabs for the amounts in each column.

5. Center and underline the column headings.

6. Underline the amounts in the "Utilities" row and double-underline the totals.

7. Save the document as **act10-2**, print one copy, and clear the screen.

ACTIVITY 3

1. In a new document window, key the table illustrated in Figure 10.19 using the 12-point font size. Do not add the title or format the table yet.

2. Save the table as **act10-3a**.

FIGURE 10.19
Customer Names/Balances/Dates Due

Company	Balance	Date Due
Southern Equipment Co.	1,436.54	10-06-95
Children's Fitness Gear	4,557.97	10-05-95
French Company	689.04	10-11-95
FF Supply	2,989.94	10-17-95
S & L Equipment	2,945.89	10-24-95
Total Fitness	1,304.37	10-06-95
Kessler Distributors	1,434.56	10-03-95
Powers Manufacturing, Inc.	435.28	10-21-95
Warren Peters, Inc.	454.65	10-10-95
A-1 Fitness and Training	2,435.99	10-14-95
Allen Health Specialists	1,667.54	10-11-95
ADCO Fitness Company	432.66	10-12-95
R & P Nutrition Experts	2,712.31	10-07-95
Wickerson, Inc.	1,308.56	10-13-95
Corbin Fitness Products	4,030.98	10-30-95
Total		

3. Calculate the total for the second column.

4. Sort in ascending order based on the names column.

5. Add a title above the table in an appropriate font and font size.

6. Center the table and adjust column widths.

7. Set a decimal tab for the amounts in the second column.

8. Center and underline each column heading.

9. Underline the amount for the last company in the list and double-underline the total.

10. Save the changes and print one copy.

11. Save the table again with a new name, **act10-3b**.

12. Remove the underline from the amount for the last company.

13. Sort in ascending order based on the date column.

14. Underline the amount for the last company in the list.

15. Save the changes, print one copy, and clear the screen.

ACTIVITY 4

As mentioned earlier, when you need to calculate totals in tables, you can either accept Word's proposed formula for a cell or key your own formula. In the following activity, you will change formulas as needed to complete calculations. To assist you, Figure 10.20 on page 250 shows labels for columns and rows that will help you to identify cells. Additionally, to save time, the formulas in Rows 4-7 have already been inserted so the correct amounts show.

1. Open the Data Disk file **PAYROLL.DOC** and save the file as **act10-4**.

2. Position the insertion point in Cell E3 (the "Total Hours" cell for L. Benitez) and choose Table Formula.

Word proposes =SUM(LEFT). If you accepted this formula, Word would add the hourly rate to the Week 1 and Week 2 hours.

3. Delete the proposed formula. Then key **=c3+d3** and click OK. Word inserts the total for Cell C3 (Week 1 hours) and Cell D3 (Week 2 hours).

4. In Cell F3, use the formula **=e3*b3** to multiply the total hours by the hourly rate.

5. In Cell H3, use the formula **=f3-g3** to subtract the employee investment from the earnings.

6. In Cell C9, (the cell for the total of the "Week 1 Hours" column), click ⬚ **OK** ⬚ to accept Word's proposed formula, **=SUM(ABOVE)**.

7. In Cells D9, E9, F9, G9, and H9, change the formula if necessary to **=SUM(ABOVE)**; then click ⬚ **OK** ⬚.

8. Save the changes, print one copy, and clear the screen.

IMPORTANT: Although you could add trailing zeros where they are not displayed for "Earnings" and "Gross Pay" entries, the zeros would not be included in the hidden *field* and later updates would not be accurate.

FIGURE 10.20
Payroll Report

NATIONAL FAMILY HEALTH AND FITNESS CLUB
BI-WEEKLY PAYROLL RECORD

■ Cell E3

For the payroll period ending: June 10, 19—

	A	B	C	D	E	F	G	H
1	Employee	Hourly Rate	Week 1 Hours	Week 2 Hours	Total Hours	Earnings	Employee Investment	Gross Pay
2								
3	Benitez, L.	14.36	40	40			20	
4	Daniel, K.	15.14	36.25	32	68.25	1033.31	30	1003.31
5	Huang, M.	11.85	32	40	72	853.2	20	833.2
6	O'Neil, A.	13.11	40	36.5	76.5	1002.92	0	1002.92
7	Parker, N.	16.62	40	40	80	1329.6	20	1309.6
8								
9	Total							

CREATE YOUR OWN •••••••••

Create a table to list employment bureaus and agencies that you would consider contacting to gather information in a job search. For example, a school placement office, a state-operated employment bureau, and a private employment agency are all good sources of job information. You can find information about state and private employment agencies in a telephone directory. You can also learn about job openings through the *Occupational Outlook Handbook,* which is distributed by the United States Department of Labor. Be sure to include the names of instructors, friends, and relatives if you think they can aid you in a job search.

The table should include enough columns so you can list the name of the source, the complete address, and a telephone number. Enter each source in a separate row in the table. When you have entered all sources in your table, sort the table by name and print one copy. Keep this list updated; it will be valuable when you are seeking employment.

REVIEW EXERCISES

TRUE / FALSE

Each of the following statements is either true or false. Indicate your answer on the left by circling T if the statement is true or F if the statement is false.

T   F   **1.**   When a column is selected to be sorted with Text or Number as the type, the column titles should be included in the selection.

T   F   **2.**   An alphanumeric sort places letters before numbers.

T   F   **3.**   Word can sort only by the first word in each paragraph, unless the text is separated by commas or tabs.

T   F   **4.**   After calculating a total, you must paste it into your document.

FILL IN THE BLANKS

Complete the following sentences by writing the correct word or words in the blanks provided.

5.   If you have selected an entire table but do not want the table to be sorted based on the first column, you can specify a different Column number in the _____ list box of the Sort dialog box.

6.   To sort a single column and leave the rest of the table or list unchanged, select the column and turn on _____ in the Sort Options dialog box.

7.   To sort from the beginning of the alphabet, the lowest number, or the earliest date, select _____ in the Sort dialog box.

8.   To perform a calculation, choose the _____ command.

9. To sort from the end of the alphabet or to count from the highest number to the lowest, select _____ in the Sort dialog box.

10. If you change numbers in a table for which you have already calculated totals, select the table and press _____ (the Update Field key).

REFERENCE QUESTIONS

Referring to the *Microsoft Word User's Guide,* write the answers to the following questions in the space provided.

1. Suppose you want to average cells in a table. How do you indicate a range of cells (for example, Cells A2 through C2)?

_____

_____

_____

2. How can you mark text so Word can perform calculations on numbers located throughout a document?

_____

_____

_____

MERGING FORM DOCUMENTS AND MAILING LABELS

OBJECTIVES
Upon completion of this chapter, you will be able to:

- Prepare a main document.

- Indicate the field names to be used in the data source.

- Key data records for the data source.

- Preview the merged documents.

- Merge the main document and data source to a printer.

- Sort the data source.

- Select filter criteria for merging documents.

- Prepare mailing labels.

Preparation

1. To complete the chapter activities, you will need to access the Data Disk file DATALBL1.DOC.

2. Remember to save frequently as you work. You will generally not be reminded to save until all work is completed for a document.

3. If you make mistakes as you work with the exercises in the chapter, remember to click 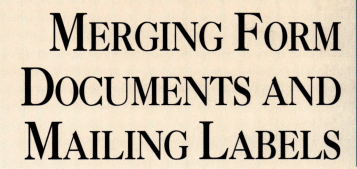 immediately after completing the action.

4. At the end of each class session, be sure to close Word and Windows properly. If you are using the hard drive to store your completed work, back up your files onto your formatted Student Disk, and erase your files from the directory you used on the hard drive. (Do not erase the Data Disk files unless your instructor tells you to do so.)

Creating Form Documents

Form documents are documents with boilerplate text (text that remains constant) and variable text (text that is individualized from document to document). The *main document* contains the boilerplate text, with *merge fields* at the locations where variable text is to be inserted. The *data source* (also known as a database) is the document containing the variable text to be merged into the main document. Examples of form documents include letters, memos, forms, and legal documents.

EXERCISE

11.1

Creating the Main Document

IMPORTANT: Exercises 11.1 to 11.5 should be completed in a single class session. You will need approximately 20 minutes.

1. Key the document illustrated in Figure 11.1 as follows:

   a. Key the centered letterhead using 16-point Times New Roman bold. Use NEW-LINE (**Shift** + **Enter**) at the end of the first two lines.

   b. At the end of the third line of the letterhead, turn off the bold format and change to 12-point. Then press **Enter** four times.

   c. Change to left alignment and key **November 10, 19—**.

   d. Press **Enter** four times and key the remainder of the letter (substitute your initials for "smn"). Be sure to key the letters *xx;* they indicate locations where you will insert merge fields later.

2. Spell-check and proofread your document.

3. Save the document as **mainltr1** in the appropriate location for Student Disk files.

4. Indicate the current letter as the main document to be used for the form letters:

   a. Choose Tools Mail Merge. The dialog box shown in Figure 11.2 appears.

FIGURE 11.2
Mail Merge Helper Dialog Box

FIGURE 11.1
Text for Main Document

FITNESS INNOVATIONS
6651 East 30th Street
Indianapolis, IN 46206-8966

November 10, 19—

xx
xx
xx
xx
xx
xx

Dear xx:

Presently our books reflect a past-due balance in the amount of $xx. This amount includes the total purchases represented on invoice number xx, dated xx.

Our terms are net 30, and we must have your remittance by return mail as soon as possible. We value your patronage and want to continue serving your needs for fitness equipment. Prompt payment will ensure that all future orders will be processed without delay.

Sincerely,

xx
Credit and Collections

smn

b. Under Main Document, click Create; then click Form Letters.

c. When the prompt shown in Figure 11.3 appears, click Active Window.

IMPORTANT: Leave the Mail Merge Helper dialog box displayed for Exercise 11.2.

FIGURE 11.3
Prompt To Create Form Letters

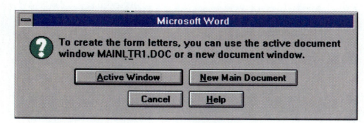

Creating a Data Source

To create a merge document, you can either open an existing data source or create a new data source. Later in the chapter you will open an existing data source to create mailing labels. In Exercises 11.2 and 11.3, you will create a new data source.

IMPORTANT: All the merged form documents will share the same data source. Some of the form documents will use more fields than others. (For example, for this

1. In the Mail Merge Helper dialog box, click Get Data under Data Source.

2. Click Create Data Source.

Word displays the dialog box shown in Figure 11.4. Your first step in creating a data source is to identify each field name to be used in the main document. Word displays common field names in the Field Names in Header Row list box. You can use these field names, delete those you do not need, and add different field names.

FIGURE 11.4
Create Data Source Dialog Box

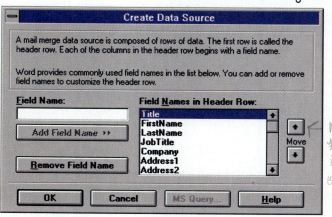

moves field names in to the order you want them

exercise, some letters will have departments and others will not.) You must be sure to include all fields in this dialog box that will be used for any one of the form documents.

3. Remove a field name you do not need:

    a. Click on the field name "Job Title" in the Field Names in Header Row list box.

    b. Click Remove Field Name.

4. Click the down arrow on the scroll bar (not the down arrow under Move). Click on and remove the field names "Country," "Home-Phone," and "WorkPhone."

5. Add a new field name:

    a. Key **Middle** in the Field Name box.

    b. Click Add Field Name.

6. Add the following field names. Do not space between words; key them as shown (for example, "InvoiceAmount").

    Department
    InvoiceAmount
    InvoiceNumber
    InvoiceDate
    Officer

Although it is not necessary for field names to be in a particular order in the data source, it is often more convenient to rearrange the list so that the field names are in the order in which they will appear in the main document.

7. Move a field name up in the list:

    a. Click on the field name "Middle."

    b. Click the Move Up arrow ⬆ to the right of the list box.

    c. Continue to click ⬆ until "Middle" is immediately above the field name "LastName." (If you accidentally move the field name up too far, click the Move Down arrow ⬇.)

8. Move the field name "Department" immediately above "Company."

9. Click [OK].

Your list of field names is complete. The Save Data Source dialog box (Figure 11.5) appears for you to name your data source file.

10. If necessary, change the drive and directory to the same location as the main document (the location for your Student Disk files). Key **dataltr1** in the File Name box; then click [OK].

FIGURE 11.5
Save Data Source Dialog Box

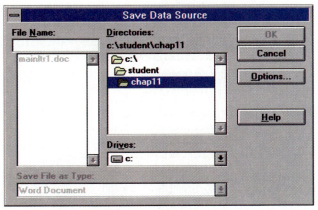

11. When the prompt to edit the data source or the main document appears (Figure 11.6), click Edit Data Source to indicate that you want to work with the data source.

FIGURE 11.6
Prompt To Edit Data Source or Main Document

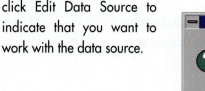

Microsoft Word

The data source you just created contains no data records. You can add new records to your data source by choosing the Edit Data Source button, or add merge fields to your main document by choosing the Edit Main Document button.

[Edit Data Source]   [Edit Main Document]
[Cancel]   [Help]

EXERCISE

11.3

Completing the Data Source

The Data Form dialog box (Figure 11.7) should be displayed on your screen. At the far left are the field names you saved. A blank box (*field*) follows each field name, for variable information you are to key for individual letters. Each data form you complete becomes a *data record*. Each data record will be merged with the main document to create an individualized form letter. Notice the record number at the bottom of the dialog box. This number will change each time you add a new data record.

Figure 11.8 on pages 261–262 lists the information you will key for each data record. Each of the record columns contains the information for a single record. Leave field boxes blank where shown in Figure 11.8.

IMPORTANT: Do not key dollar signs ($) for amounts in the data source—dollar signs should be included in the main document. When you want Word to print only records containing certain amounts, the selection process will not work if you have included dollar signs in the data source.

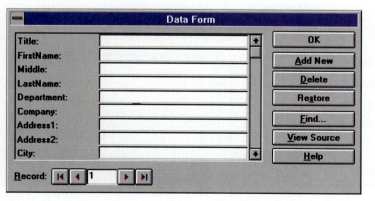

Data Form

Title:
FirstName:
Middle:
LastName:
Department:
Company:
Address1:
Address2:
City:

[OK]
[Add New]
[Delete]
[Restore]
[Find...]
[View Source]
[Help]

Record: [|◀] [◀] 1 [▶] [▶|]

FIGURE 11.7
Data Form Dialog Box

FIGURE 11.8
Variable Information

■ **Field Names**   ■ **Record 1**   ■ **Record 2**   ■ **Record 3**

Title	Mr.	Ms.	Mr.
FirstName	Pablo	Susan	Gene
Middle	R.	L.	A.
LastName	Espino	Reiman	Morris
Department	Accounts Payable	Accounting Department	
Company	Danton Fitness Center	Laredo Training, Inc.	Fitness One
Address1	7007 North Main Street	155 Churchill Drive	2245 West Roosevelt
Address2			
City	Niles	Simi Valley	Jackson
State	IL	CA	MS
PostalCode	60648-3008	93065-1997	39215-0901
InvoiceAmount	1,344.37	4,328.11	563.28
InvoiceNumber	283460	284191	283169
InvoiceDate	July 15,19--	September 6, 19—	June 28, 19—
Officer	John Bjorkquist	MaryAnne Lilly	Dora Wisely

Continued on next page

1. Key the information for the first data record:

   a. Key **Mr.** for "Title."

   b. Press (**Tab**), and key **Pablo** for "FirstName."

   c. Continue to tab and key the information shown in the second column of Figure 11.8. (Note that after you key the street address for "Address1," you will need to press (**Tab**) twice to leave the "Address2" field blank as shown.)

2. After keying the officer's name ("John Bjorkquist"), click Add New.

   A blank data form appears, and the record number at the bottom of the dialog box changes to 2.

3. Key the information shown in the third column of Figure 11.8 (for Ms. Reiman); then click Add New.

Title	Mr.	Ms.
FirstName	Jason	I-chen
Middle	W.	
LastName	Hartford	Kuo
Department		
Company		Madison Iron Works
Address1	165 Kempton Drive	424 Collins Avenue
Address2	Suite 3004	
City	Chicago	Karlstad
State	IL	MN
PostalCode	60650-1241	56732-2069
InvoiceAmount	3,764.98	1,104.29
InvoiceNumber	284143	283868
InvoiceDate	September 1, 19—	August 5, 19—
Officer	Debi Penington	John Bjorkquist

4. Continue to key the information for the next three records.

5. After keying the information for the last column shown in Figure 11.8, click View Source to view the completed data source.

The completed data source appears in table form as shown in Figure 11.9. The first row of your data source (known as the *header row*) contains the field names you will use to merge the main document with the data source. Each remaining row is a data record. Do not be concerned about the appearance of the table. Although text wrapped as needed to fit the table boundaries, you do not need to adjust the table column widths; the information will print appropriately on the merged letters.

A new toolbar, the Database Toolbar (Figure 11.10), also appears.

6. Add a new record to your database:

   a. Click the Add New Record icon on the Database Toolbar 🖳.

FIGURE 11.9
Portion of Completed Data
Source in Table Form

Header Row ▪ ·····

Data Records ▪ ·····

Title¤	FirstName¤	Middle¤	LastName¤	Department¤	Company¤	Address 1¤	Address 2¤	City¤	State¤	Postal Code¤
Mr.¤	Pablo¤	R.¤	Espino¤	Accounts Payable¤	Danton Fitness Center¤	7007 North Main Street¤	¤	Niles¤	IL¤	60641 3008¤
Ms.¤	Susan¤	L.¤	Reiman¤	Accounting Department¤	Laredo Training, Inc.¤	155 Churchill Drive¤	¤	Simi Valley¤	CA¤	9306 1997¤
Mr.¤	Gene¤	A.¤	Morris¤	¤	Fitness One¤	2245 West Roosevelt¤	¤	Jackson¤	MS¤	3921 0901¤
Mr.¤	Jason¤	W.¤	Hartford¤	¤	¤	165 Kempton Drive¤	Suite 3004¤	Chicago¤	IL¤	60650 1241¤
Ms.¤	I-chen¤	¤	Kuo¤	¤	Madison¤	424	¤	Karls	MN¤	5673

b. In the new row that appears, key the following information, pressing ⌨Tab to move from cell to cell:

Ms.

Jean

S.

Graham

Accounts Payable

Delta Fitness

1800 Six Mile Road, N.W.

Suite 602

Livonia

MI

48154-3882

563.28

283004

June 18, 19—

MaryAnne Lilly

7. Click 🖫 to save your completed data source.

FIGURE 11.10
The Database Toolbar

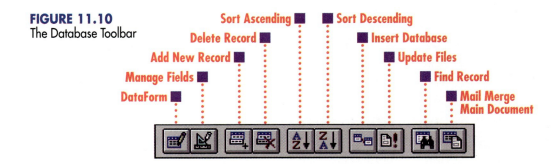

Sort Ascending ▪   ▪ Sort Descending

Delete Record ▪   ▪ Insert Database

Add New Record ▪   ▪ Update Files

Manage Fields ▪   ▪ Find Record

DataForm ▪   ▪ Mail Merge Main Document

EXERCISE

11.4 Completing the Main Document

To complete the main document, you need to substitute field names for the letters *xx* throughout the document.

1. Click the Mail Merge Main Document icon on the Database Toolbar to switch from the data source to the main document.

Notice that you have another new toolbar, the Mail Merge Toolbar (Figure 11.11).

2. Insert a merge field:

   a. Scroll toward the top of the letter.

   b. Delete the first occurrence of the letters *xx*, but do not delete the paragraph mark.

   c. Click | Insert Merge Field | on the Mail Merge Toolbar.

A drop-down menu appears, with a list of the field names from the data source (Figure 11.12).

   d. Click the first field to be inserted ("Title").

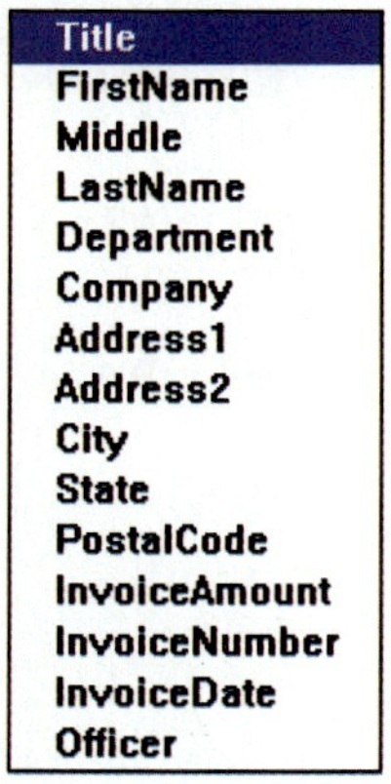

(handwritten note in margin: must look right o will print all on line)

Title
FirstName
Middle
LastName
Department
Company
Address1
Address2
City
State
PostalCode
InvoiceAmount
InvoiceNumber
InvoiceDate
Officer

FIGURE 11.12
Merge Field Drop-Down Menu

"Title" is inserted as a merge field surrounded by chevrons (« »).

3. Press (**Space Bar**), click | Insert Merge Field |, and click "FirstName."

4. Press (**Space Bar**), click | Insert Merge Field |, and click "Middle."

5. Press (**Space Bar**), click | Insert Merge Field |, and click "LastName."

FIGURE 11.11
The Mail Merge Toolbar

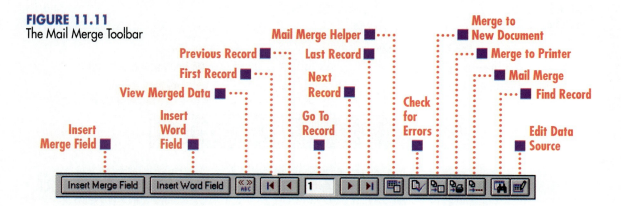

6. On the next four lines, delete the *xx* and insert the fields "Department," "Company," "Address1," and "Address2."

7. On the last line for the address, delete the *xx* and insert the field "City."

8. Key a comma, press (**Space Bar**), and insert the field "State."

9. Press (**Space Bar**) twice, and insert the field "PostalCode."

10. Delete the *xx* in the salutation (do not delete the colon) and insert the fields "Title" and "LastName," with a space between the fields.

Your inside address and salutation lines should now look like Figure 11.13.

11. Delete the first *xx* in the body of the letter (do not delete the dollar sign or the period); then insert the field "InvoiceAmount."

12. Replace the next two *xx*'s with the fields "InvoiceNumber" and "InvoiceDate."

Your first paragraph should now look similar to Figure 11.14.

13. Scroll down and replace the *xx* in the closing lines with the field "Officer."

14. Save the completed main document.

Some or all of the fields from one data source can be used for multiple main documents. For example, you could use the same data source for both a letter main document and a mailing label main document. The mailing label main document would use only the title, name, and address fields from the data source.

FIGURE 11.13
Inside Address and
Salutation with Merge Fields

«Title»·«FirstName»·«Middle»·«LastName»¶
«Department»¶
«Company»¶
«Address1»¶
«Address2»¶
«City»,·«State»··«PostalCode»¶
¶
Dear·«Title»·«LastName»:¶

FIGURE 11.14
First Paragraph with
Merge Fields

Presently·our·books·reflect·a·past-due·balance·in·the·amount·of·$«InvoiceAmount».··This·amount·includes·the·total·purchases·represented·on·invoice·number·«InvoiceNumber»,·dated·«InvoiceDate».¶

11.5

Previewing, Merging, and Printing the Form Documents

Although it is not necessary to preview before you merge and print your form documents, you may find it useful to preview one or two form documents before you print the entire set.

1. Move the insertion point to the top of the document.

2. Preview the first two form documents:

a. With the number *1* displayed in the Go to Record box, click the View Merged Data icon on the Mail Merge Toolbar [«»/ABC]. The icon will be highlighted.

b. Scroll through the displayed letter and notice that the merge fields have been replaced with the variable information from Mr. Espino's data record.

c. With [«»/ABC] still highlighted, click the Next Record icon [▶].

d. Scroll through the displayed letter and notice that the merge fields have been replaced with the variable information from Ms. Reiman's data record.

3. Click the Previous Record icon [◀].

4. Click [«»/ABC].

The field names (rather than the variable information) are again displayed, and the icon is no longer highlighted.

IMPORTANT: In the exercises in this text, instructions are given for merging to a printer. If a printer is not available, click the Merge to New Document icon [⬚] on the Mail Merge Toolbar. Then save the merged document with an appropriate filename. When a printer is available, open the saved, merged file and click [⬚] on the Standard Toolbar.

5. Merge and print all data records:

a. Click the Merge to Printer icon on the Mail Merge Toolbar [⬚].

b. Click [**OK**] in the Print dialog box.

Sorting and Filtering Data Sources

In Exercise 11.5 you printed **all** the merged form letters according to the order in which data records appeared in the data source. To print in a different order or to print only letters with data records meeting a certain criteria, Word allows you to sort and *filter* (select specific records).

EXERCISE

11.6 Sorting the Data Source

Merged form documents print in the order in which data records are arranged in the data source. You can, however, sort the data source and then print all or some of the merged data records in the new order. (For example, after you do an alphabetical sort of a long data source, you could print only those data records beginning with the letter A. Or you could sort by postal code and then print only those data records that have the lowest-numbered postal codes.) You can sort by from one to three fields.

1. If necessary, open **mainltr1.doc**.

2. In the main document, click the Edit Data Source icon on the Mail Merge Toolbar.

3. In the Data Form dialog box, click View Source.

4. Sort by a single data field:

    a. Click anywhere in the "LastName" column.

    b. Click the Sort Ascending icon on the Database Toolbar.

The data source should be rearranged with the last names in ascending (A–Z) alphabetical order. Note that you can also sort in descending (Z–A) alphabetical order by clicking the Sort Descending icon. Numbers (such as postal codes) can also be sorted in ascending or descending order.

5. Undo the sort.

6. Sort the data source by more than one field:

    a. Click Mail Merge Main Document icon on the Database Toolbar to switch to the main document.

    b. Click the Mail Merge Helper icon on the Mail Merge Toolbar.

Notice, at the bottom of the dialog box, Options in Effect. The two default settings are shown (Figure 11.15).

FIGURE 11.15
Options in Effect Portion of Mail Merge Helper Dialog Box

Options in Effect:
Suppress Blank Lines in Addresses
Merge to New Document

IMPORTANT: Changing the sort order adds a new setting to Options in Effect. This setting remains in effect for the document until you change it.

 c. Click Query Options.

 d. Click the Sort Records folder tab.

Notice that you can sort by up to three fields. In the following steps you will sort by two fields.

 e. Click the arrow for the Sort By list box to open the list box. Scroll down and click "State." If necessary, click the Ascending button next to the list box.

 f. Open the first Then By list box. Scroll down and click "City." If necessary, click the Ascending button next to the list box. Do not select anything for the second Then By list box.

 g. When the dialog box looks like Figure 11.16, click [OK] to return to the Mail Merge Helper dialog box.

Notice that Options in Effect now shows "Query Options have been set."

 h. Click [Close] to return to your main document.

 i. Click [icon]; then click View Source.

Your data source should now be sorted with Ms. Reiman's record first (CA). Notice there are two IL records (Mr. Hartford's and Mr. Espino's), so Word then sorted by city (first Chicago, then Niles).

7. Save the sorted data source as **dtasort1**.

HINT: *Choose File Save As. Do not click* [icon].

8. Click Mail Merge Main Document icon.

9. Merge and print only the sorted IL records (now the second and third records):

 a. Click the Mail Merge icon on the Mail Merge Toolbar . The Merge dialog box appears.

IMPORTANT: All settings in this dialog box, like the sort settings, become part of Options in Effect and remain in effect for the document until you change them.

FIGURE 11.16
Sort Criteria Selected in Sort Records Category of Query Options Dialog Box

b. Open the Merge To list box and click Printer.

c. Under Records to Be Merged, key **2** in the From box and key **3** in the To box.

d. When the dialog box looks like Figure 11.17, click Merge; then click OK in the Print dialog box.

10. Change the Options in Effect so future printings can include all records:

a. Click 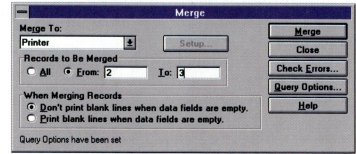.

b. Click All under Records to Be Merged.

c. Click Close .

FIGURE 11.17
Merge Dialog Box with Change to Merge to Printer

Filtering the Data Source for Specific Criteria

In Exercise 11.6 you sorted your data source and merged and printed specific data records. In this exercise you will filter records (specify criteria in your fields that must be met in order for a data record to be merged and printed). Filtering is a useful tool for large databases because only records matching the filters are merged; you do not have to scroll through a sorted database to decide which records to print. The criteria you can use include: Equal to, Not Equal to, Less than, Greater than, Less than or Equal, Greater than or Equal, is Blank, and is Not Blank.

 IMPORTANT: Filter settings, like sort settings and merge settings, become part of Options in Effect and remain in effect for the document until you change them.

1. Select data records meeting certain criteria to be merged and printed:

a. With the main document (**mainltr1.doc**) still displayed, click.

b. Click Query Options.

c. If necessary, click the Filter Records folder tab to display the Filter Records dialog box.

d. Open the first Field list box, scroll down, and click InvoiceAmount.

e. Open the Comparison list box and click Greater than.

f. In the Compare To box, key **1,500.00** (do not key a dollar sign).

Note that you can select additional criteria by selecting "And" or "Or" for the next five rows of list boxes and clicking or keying the desired fields and comparisons. In this case, however, you will use only one filter.

g. When the dialog box looks like Figure 11.18, click [OK] to return to the Mail Merge Helper dialog box.

h. Click Merge.

i. If necessary, click Printer in the Merge To list box.

j. If necessary, click All under Records to Be Merged.

In this case, when you click All, you are not telling Word to merge and print all records. Rather, you are telling Word to merge and print all records that match the filter you have requested.

k. Click Merge; then click [OK] in the Print dialog box.

2. Clear the screen (close both the main and the data source documents). Click Yes when prompted to save the documents.

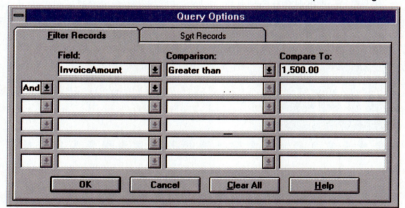

FIGURE 11.18
Criteria Selected in Filter Records Category of Query Options Dialog Box

Preparing Mailing Labels

Before beginning the following exercises, you need to know the type of printer you will be using (a laser printer or a dot-matrix printer). You also need to know the Avery label number. (In the following two exercises, you will be given instructions for the 4146 label on a dot-matrix printer and the 5162 label on a laser printer, but your instructor may ask you to substitute another label.) It is not necessary to use the actual mailing labels for these exercises; you can print on regular paper. Whether or not you have mailing labels available, you should always print a sample on plain paper and hold the sample up on your labels to see if you need to position the labels differently in the printer or if you need to adjust your main document settings (such as margins, page length, and column width).

EXERCISE
11.8

Preparing Mailing Labels from an Existing Data Source

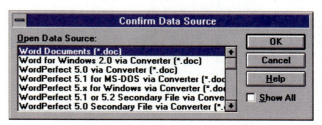

1. In a new document window, choose Tools Mail Merge.

2. Create the main document for the mailing labels:

   a. Under Main Document, click Create; then click Mailing Labels.

   b. When the prompt appears, click Active Window to indicate that this is to be the main document (you will leave it blank for now and complete it later).

3. Attach (open) the existing data source for the mailing labels:

   a. Under Data Source, click Get Data.

   b. Click Open Data Source.

   c. Change the drive and/or directory to the location of your Data Disk file **data-lbl1.doc** (insert the appropriate floppy disk, if necessary).

   d. Click **datalbl1.doc**; then click ⬜ OK.

   e. If a dialog box appears to confirm the data source (Figure 11.19), click ⬜ OK.

FIGURE 11.19
Confirm Data Source Dialog Box

4. Set up (complete) the main document:

   a. At the prompt (Figure 11.20), click Set Up Main Document.

   b. In the Label Options dialog box (Figure 11.21 on page 272), select the type of printer.

   c. If necessary, change the Tray (label feed) selection.

   d. For the exercises in this text, use Avery Standard for the Label Products list box.

   e. For the exercises in this text, under Product Number, click 5162 for a laser printer or 4146 for a dot-matrix printer.

   f. Click ⬜ OK.

FIGURE 11.20
Prompt To Set Up the Main Document

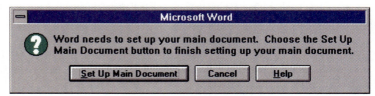

FIGURE 11.21
Label Options Dialog Box

FIGURE 11.21
Label Options Dialog Box

FIGURE 11.22
Create Labels Dialog Box

The Create Labels dialog box (Figure 11.22) appears, with a Sample Label section. You will insert your merge fields here.

g. Click Insert Merge Field and click "name."

h. Press (Enter) and insert the merge field "title."

i. Press (Enter) and insert the merge field "company."

j. Press (Enter) and insert the merge field "street."

k. Press (Enter) and insert the merge field "city."(Do not key a comma after the city field for mailing labels.)

l. Press (Space Bar) and insert the merge field "state."

m. Press (Space Bar) twice and insert the merge field "ZIP"; then press (Enter).

IMPORTANT: If your printer cannot print graphics or if your label height is less than 1.25 inches and you have addresses with more than four lines as you will for this exercise, **skip Steps n to q below and go to Step r.**

n. Click Insert Postal Bar Code.

The Insert Postal Bar Code dialog box appears for you to identify the delivery address for the POST-NET bar code. Using the POSTNET bar code speeds mail delivery.

o. In the Merge Field with ZIP Code box, click "ZIP."

p. In the Merge Field with Street Address box, click "street."

q. When the dialog box looks like Figure 11.23, click OK to return to the

Create Labels dialog box. Your completed sample label should now look like Figure 11.24.

FIGURE 11.23
Insert Postal Bar Code Dialog Box

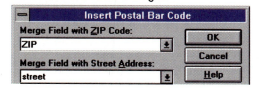

r. Click [OK] to return to the Mail Merge Helper dialog box.

5. Merge and print the labels:

   a. In the Mail Merge Helper dialog box, click Merge.

Delivery point bar code will print here!
«name»
«title»
«company»
«street»
«city» «state» «ZIP»

FIGURE 11.24
Completed Sample Label

b. Click Printer in the Merge To list box.

c. If necessary, click All under Records to Be Merged.

d. Click Merge; then click [OK] in the Print dialog box.

6. After the labels are printed, save your main document in the appropriate location for Student Disk files as **mainlbl1**. Then clear the screen.

EXERCISE 11.9

Preparing a New Data Source for Mailing Labels

1. In a new document window, choose Tools Mail Merge.

2. Create the main document for the mailing labels:

   a. Under Main Document, click Create; then click Mailing Labels.

   b. When the prompt appears, click Active Window to indicate that this is to be the main document (you will leave it blank for now and complete it later).

3. Create the data source for the mailing labels:

   a. Under Data Source, click Get Data.

   b. Click Create Data Source.

   c. Click Remove Field Name for "Country," "HomePhone," and "WorkPhone."

   d. In the Field Name box, key **Middle**. Then click Add Field Name.

   e. Click Move Up until "Middle" is immediately above "LastName."

   f. Click [OK].

g. Save your data source in the appropriate location for Student Disk files with the name **datalbl2** and click | OK |.

h. At the prompt, click Edit Data Source to display the first data form.

i. Key the six records shown in Figure 11.25, clicking Add New after each record except the last. Leave fields blank where appropriate.

j. After completing the last record, click View Source; then click 💾 on the Standard Toolbar.

4. Complete the main document:

a. Click the Mail Merge Main Document icon to switch to the main document.

b. Click 📧.

c. Under Main Document, click Setup.

d. In the Label Options dialog box, select the type of printer.

e. If necessary, change the Tray (label feed) selection.

f. Use Avery Standard for the Label Products list box.

g. Under Product Number, click 5162 for a laser printer or 4146 for a dot-matrix printer.

FIGURE 11.25
Records for Labels Data Source

```
MS DONNA LOUISE BRAKKE          MR CALVIN DOUGLAS
KNAPP FITNESS TRAINERS INC      CONTROLLER
1424 FIFTH AVENUE               RAHALLIS CUSTOM EQUIPMENT
SUITE 1687                      27 WEST MONTEREY ROAD
SEATTLE WA  98101-0467          FONTANA WI  53125-3886


MS HELEN MEEK                   MS AI LIEN YI
VICE PRESIDENT                  ACCOUNTS MANAGER
BUCKEYE FITNESS PRODUCTS        FRANZ TRAINING SYSTEMS
330 WEST STATE STREET           6872 MILLIKEN ROAD
DUBLIN OH  43017-2981           PORTLAND OR  97223-1927


MR THOMAS GORDON CASS           MR EDUARDO C CABRERO
TWIN LAKES FITNESS EQUIPMENT    CABRERO COMPANY
9906 SPRING STREET              2665 MADERA
SACRAMENTO CA  95841-4264       BOX 275
                                SAN MARCOS TX  78666-0275
```

h. Click ［ OK ］.

i. Use the Insert Merge Field button to insert "Title," "FirstName," "Middle," and "LastName," leaving a space between each field name.

j. Press ⟨Enter⟩ and insert the merge field "JobTitle."

k. Press ⟨Enter⟩ and insert the merge field "Company."

l. Press ⟨Enter⟩ and insert the merge field "Address1."

m. Press ⟨Enter⟩ and insert the merge field "Address2."

n. Press ⟨Enter⟩ and insert the merge field "City." (Do not key a comma after the city field for mailing labels.)

o. Press ⟨Space Bar⟩ and insert the merge field "State."

p. Press ⟨Space Bar⟩ twice and insert the merge field "PostalCode"; then press ⟨Enter⟩.

IMPORTANT: If your printer cannot print graphics or if your label height is less than 1.25 inch and you have addresses with more than four lines as you will for this exercise, skip Steps q to t below and go to Step u.

q. Click Insert Postal Bar Code.

r. In the Merge Field with ZIP Code box, click "PostalCode."

s. In the Merge Field with Street Address box, click "Address1."

t. Click ［ OK ］ to return to the Create Labels dialog box.

u. Click ［ OK ］ to return to the Mail Merge Helper dialog box.

5. Merge and print the labels:

a. In the Mail Merge Helper dialog box, click Merge.

b. Click Printer in the Merge To list box.

c. If necessary, click All under Records to Be Merged.

d. Click Merge; then click ［ OK ］ in the Print dialog box.

6. After the labels are printed, save your main document as **mainlbl2**; then clear the screen.

COMPUTER ACTIVITIES

ACTIVITY 1

1. In a new document window, change the margins to 1 inch.

HINT: *Choose File Page Setup.*

2. Using the 12-point font size, key the letter shown in Figure 11.26 on pages 277–278 with the indicated changes. (Be sure to add your initials above "Enclosures.") If space allows, add one or two blank lines below the date, but do not allow the letter to wrap to a second page.

3. Spell-check and proofread your letter. Then save it in the appropriate location for Student Disk files as **act11-1m**.

4. Begin the merge process, indicating the active window as the main document.

5. Create the data source with the following field names: "Title," "FirstName," "LastName," "Address1," "City," "State," and "PostalCode."

6. Save the data source in the appropriate location for Student Disk files as **act11-1d**.

7. Complete the data records using the information in Figure 11.27.

FIGURE 11.27
Data Records Information for Form Letter

```
Mr. Carl Stakenas               Dr. Jane Zapata
P.O. Box 11567                  3947 Broadway
Lahaina, HI  96761-1567         Grove City, OH  43123-2332


Ms. Sally Rollman               Mrs. Geraldine Hanlon
684 Fifth Avenue                P.O. Box C-320
New York, NY  10022-2245        Richmond, VA  23261-0320


Dr. Patrick Coppess
41121 Laiolo Road
Fremont, CA  94538-7786
```

FIGURE 11.26
Main Document for Form Letter

NATIONAL FAMILY HEALTH AND FITNESS CLUB } *Bold*
6000 Lakeview Plaza Boulevard
Worthington, OH 43085-1152

Current Date

xx
xx
xx

Dear xx:

You already know that exercise and nutrition are important

factors you can control for your own well-being. We know

that keeping your budget in check is important, too.

That is   *we are*   *special*
~~That's~~ why ~~we're~~ making this ~~unique~~ offer to you. Right

now you can join (National Family Health and Fitness Club) *bold*

as little as
for ~~only~~ a dollar a day. With this exceptionally low

membership rate, you can begin exercising and improving

You are   *today*
your health immediately. ~~You're~~ invited to join ~~now~~ and

become part of a healthy relationship.

bold (National Family Health and Fitness Club) offers a variety

of services that fit into your life:

Add bullets
Contemporary fitness and training equipment

Professional interaction with fitness trainers

Nutrition education programs

And much, much more!

Continued on next page

Become a member of **National Family Health and Fitness Club**
now. ~~You'll~~ You will be able to begin exercising and learning
about proper nutrition immediately. Joining is easy!
Indicate your membership ~~preference~~ choice on the enclosed card
and return it in the envelope provided. Or call our
Fitness Hotline at 1-800-555-JOIN or 614-555-0186, Monday
through Friday, 8 a.m. to 7 p.m. ~~Eastern time.~~ EDT

~~Cordially,~~ Sincerely

K. B. Laramie
~~CEO~~ Chief Executive Officer

smn

Enclosures

8. View and save the completed data source.

9. Switch to the main document and insert the appropriate fields for the inside address and the salutation.

10. Preview the first two records; then turn off the preview feature.

11. Save the main document.

12. Merge and print the letters; then clear the screen.

ACTIVITY 2

1. Key the document illustrated in Figure 11.28 on page 280. Use 16-point Times New Roman bold for the letterhead and 12-point for the rest of the letter. Be sure to add your initials at the bottom of the letter.

2. Spell check and proofread your document.

3. Save the document as **act11-2m** in the appropriate location for Student Disk files.

4. Begin the merge process for form letters, indicating the active window as the main document.

5. Create the data source with the following field names: "Title," "FirstName," "LastName," "JobTitle," "Company," "Address1," "City," "State," "PostalCode," "Quantity," "Product," "RepFirst," "RepLast," and "DateofCall."

6. Save the data source as **act11-2d**.

7. Key the data record information in Figure 11.29 on page 281. Key the entire first column before keying the second column. (Note that the information in parentheses is not to be keyed.)

8. View and save the completed data source.

9. Switch to the main document and insert merge fields as follows:
   a. Replace the first five lines showing *xx* with the appropriate data for the inside address. (Be sure to include spaces where needed and to include a comma after "City.")
   b. Replace the *xx* in the salutation with "Title" and "LastName" (include a space).
   c. In the first paragraph, replace the first *xx* with "Quantity" and "Product" (leave a space in between).
   d. Replace the next *xx* in the first paragraph with simply "Product."

FIGURE 11.28
Text for Main Document (Letter)

FITNESS INNOVATIONS
6651 East 30th Street
Indianapolis, IN 46206-8966

March 14, 19--

xx
xx
xx
xx
xx

Dear xx:

Thank you for your recent order of xx. We recently added the xx to our wholesale products list. We are confident that you will be completely satisfied with this new product.

We value your patronage and want to continue serving you. Our sales representative in your area, xx, will be calling on you during the week of xx to meet you and to learn more about your needs. Please let us know if the week of xx is not a convenient time for you and we will ask xx to contact you to set up an alternative time to meet with you.

Meanwhile, you can learn more about us and our product line from the enclosed catalog that describes our company and provides a complete list of products available for wholesale purchase. For your convenience, call us toll free at 1-800-555-3391 to place future orders. We look forward to the opportunity to serve you again soon.

Sincerely,

Deanna Carnes
Vice-President

FIGURE 11.29
Data Record Information for Form Letter

Mr. Steven Brightwell
Cedar Valley Fitness Center
880 Laver Road West
Springfield, MO 65808-2764
eight (Quantity)
Adjustable Slantboards (Product)
Marcia (RepFirst)
Picard (RepLast)
April 17 (DateofCall)

Ms. Pearl Robertson
Director
Lincoln Fitness Center
405 Grant Street
Woodbridge, NJ 07095-4903
one (Quantity)
Programmable Treadmill with
Electronic Incline (Product)
Donald (RepFirst)
Hawkes (RepLast)
May 8 (DateofCall)

Ms. Lola Evans
Manager
Byrnes Health Club
607 Courtwright Boulevard
Marlton, NJ 08053-3115
two (Quantity)
Abdominal/Back Machines (Product)
Donald (RepFirst)
Hawkes (RepLast)
May 8 (DateofCall)

Mr. Adrian Reyes
Lakeside Exercise Center
State Route 3
Olathe, KS 66062-2348
ten (Quantity)
Slide Exercisers (Product)
Jane (RepFirst)
Lapp (RepLast)
April 24 (DateofCall)

Mr. Hung-yen Kao
Manager
Bob's Gym
41 North Mulberry Street
Ballwin, MO 63011-3899
five (Quantity)
Double-Action Steppers (Product)
Marcia (RepFirst)
Picard (RepLast)
April 17 (DateofCall)

Ms. Vina Dykstra
Milton Trainers, Inc.
14 Walnut Street
Princeton Junction, NJ 08550-2520
two (Quantity)
Exercise Stands (Product)
Donald (RepFirst)
Hawkes (RepLast)
May 8 (DateofCall)

    e. In the second paragraph, replace the first *xx* with "RepFirst" and "RepLast" (remember to add a space between the two fields).

    f. Replace the next two occurrences of *xx* in the second paragraph with "DateofCall."

    g. Replace the last *xx* with "RepFirst."

10. Save the completed main document.

11. Preview the first two records, turn off the preview feature, and merge and print all letters.

12. Use the Mail Merge Query options to sort the data source in ascending numerical order by the "PostalCode" field.

13. Switch to the data source to verify the new order.

14. Save the changed data source as **act11-2s**.

15. Switch to the main document. Merge and print Records 1 to 3 (the New Jersey letters).

16. Filter the data source for addresses in Missouri; then merge and print.

HINT: *Select "State" and "Equal to" and key* **MO***. Be sure to click All in the Merge dialog box for Records to Be Merged.*

17. Edit the data source to add the following new record:

    Ms. Kay Thomsen
    Manager
    Redmond Fitness Center
    126 North Washington
    Kansas City, MO 64133–2099
    five (Quantity)
    Cardio Fitness Machines (Product)
    Jane (RepFirst)
    Lapp (RepLast)
    April 24 (DateofCall)

18. Save the change to the data source; then switch to the main document.

19. Merge and print again.

    Only the Missouri letters should print (including one for the new record you added for Ms. Thomsen), and the letters should print in ascending numerical order by postal code because the sort and filter options are still set.

20. Clear the screen. If prompted, save the changes to the main and data source documents.

ACTIVITY 3

1. Create the main document for merging mailing labels.

2. Create the data source using the following field names: "Title," "FirstName," "LastName," "JobTitle," "Company," "Address1," "Address2," "City," "State," and "PostalCode."

3. Save the data source as **act11-3d**.

4. Enter the data record information in Figure 11.30 on page 284.

5. View and save the data source.

6. Sort the data source in ascending numerical order by the "PostalCode" field. Then save the data source again.

7. Switch to the main document.

8. Set up the main document. Use Product Number 5162 for a laser printer or 4146 for a dot-matrix printer. Insert the fields appropriately in the sample (do not use a comma after the "City" field). Be sure to insert a postal bar code.

9. Merge and print the labels.

10. Save the main document as **act11-3m**; then clear the screen.

CREATE YOUR OWN • • • • • • • • • • • •

Create mailing labels. For the data source, create data records containing fields for names, addresses, telephone numbers, birth dates, anniversaries, children's names, and other meaningful information for your family and friends. (You can include up to 31 fields). Merge and print a set of mailing labels on plain paper for quick reference.

Keep your database current. Each time you add records to the database, print a new copy for reference. If necessary, you can add new fields by clicking the Manage Fields icon ⬚ on the Database Toolbar.

You can use your database to create personalized letters, print envelopes, or generate mailing labels. Remember that you can sort and filter your database. For example, you may want to filter for all April birth dates and print mailing labels for cards and letters to be mailed to people with those birth dates.

FIGURE 11.30
Data Record Information for Mailing Labels

MR CRAIG ZIMMERMAN
MANAGER
GLACIER GYMNASTICS AND
FITNESS CENTER
1403 SOUTH JEFFERSON
JUNEAU AK   99801-0301

MRS DEBORAH ROTH
FITNESS FOR LIFE CENTER
425 BEECHWOOD DRIVE
SUITE 1005
LAS VEGAS NV   89121-2687

MS THERESA CONNELLY
MANAGER
HEALTH AND FITNESS CLUB
880 NORTH FOURTH STREET
CORNISH ME   04020-4119

MISS VELNA MURPHY
TOTAL FITNESS CENTER
1205 EAST 18TH STREET
NEW YORK NY   10028-4834

MISS BETH GILLIS
MANAGER
SPIRITRIDGE EXERCISE CENTER
92 HARDING WAY
ATLANTA GA   30319-3288

MR PAUL SCHIMMEL
BILLINGS FITNESS CLUB
3396 STATE ROUTE 309
ASHEVILLE NC   28803-6755

MR CHARLES GARDINER
BODY BUILDERS INC
524 EAST ATWOOD
OAK RIDGE TN   37830-1402

MS VICTORIA CINTRON
CINTRON EXERCISE CLUB
7450 KENDAL STREET
DRIGGS ID   83422-3771

MR ATSUSHI WATANABE
MANAGER
TOKUDA FITNESS TRAINING
14151 KATHERINE STREET
SUITE 722
CRANSTON RI   02920-4682

MR RANDY VANDERVENNET
DIRECTOR
VANDERVENNET FITNESS CENTER
66774 ALLOWAY STREET EAST
BOULDER CO   80302-0849

MISS OKI NISHIMURA
PACIFIC FITNESS TRAINING
CENTER
1361 KINMOUNT STREET
SUITE 205
PINOLE CA   94564-3803

MR JULIO CORTEZ
THE LOCKER ROOM
2016 KINGS HIGHWAY
SUITE 1000
GRETNA LA   70056-4366

REVIEW EXERCISES

FILL IN THE BLANKS

Complete the following sentences by writing the correct word or words in the blanks provided.

1. Each row of the completed data source except the first is called a _____.

2. To begin the merge process, choose the _____ command.

3. The _____ contains the boilerplate text, with field names where variable text will be inserted.

4. The _____ contains the variable text that will be merged into the main document.

5. The top row of the data source containing all the field names is called the _____.

6. To sort or set filters, click _____ in the Mail Merge Helper dialog box.

7. Up to _____ fields can be sorted for the data source.

MATCHING

Find the icon on the right that matches the description on the left, and write the appropriate letter in the blank provided at the left margin.

____ 8. Add New Record

____ 9. Sort Descending

____ 10. View Merged Data

____ 11. Merge to Printer

____ 12. Edit Data Source

____ 13. Sort Ascending

____ 14. Mail Merge Helper

____ 15. Mail Merge

a. [A↓Z]   h. [icon]

b. [▶]   i. [icon]

c. [icon]   j. [◀]

d. (Z)   k. [icon]

e. [icon]

f. [Z↑A]

g. [«»ABC]

REFERENCE QUESTIONS

Referring to the *Microsoft Word User's Guide,* write the answers to the following questions in the space provided.

1. If you have merged to a new document rather than to the printer, how do you indicate that you want to print specific merged documents?

    _____

    _____

    _____

2. How do you change to a different data source?

    _____

    _____

    _____

COMPREHENSIVE PROJECT 1

PREPARATION

1. To complete the project activities, you will need to access the Data Disk files PROPOSAL.DOC and COMMITTE.DOC.

2. Be sure to save frequently as you work.

3. If you are unsure about how to complete an instruction, refer to the information provided in Units 1, 2, and 3.

4. If you make mistakes as you work with the project, remember to click 🔙🔽 immediately after completing the action.

5. When you have completed the project, be sure to close Word and Windows properly. If you are using the hard drive to store your completed work, back up your files onto your formatted Student Disk, and erase your files from the directory you used on the hard drive. (Do not erase the Data Disk files unless your instructor tells you to do so.)

FORMATTING

1. Open the Data Disk file **proposal.doc** and save it with a new name, **proj1a**.

2. Change the left and right margins to 1.25 inches.

3. Add a footer to print on all pages except the first page. The footer should include the title of the document ("Technology Acquisition Proposal"), the current date of printing, and the word "Page" and the page number.

4. At the end of the third sentence, which begins, "We are long overdue . . . ," add the following autonumbered footnote: **A chief goal in the new fiscal year is to maximize the potential of the fitness trainers.**

5. Add bullets to the list of needs, the list of solutions, and the list for impact.

HINT: *Each item begins a new paragraph and is indented with a tab. Under <u>NEEDS</u>, there are five items below the first paragraph; under <u>PROPOSED SOLUTION</u> , there are five items below the first paragraph (do not add bullets to any paragraph that does not begin with a tab symbol); and under <u>IMPACT OF DEFERRAL</u> , there are four items below the first paragraph.*

6. Under <u>PROPOSED SOLUTION</u>, format the two lists of hardware and software with a ½-inch left indent.

7. Format the first paragraph under the title and the first paragraph under each underlined heading with a ¼-inch first-line indent.

HINT: *Use* 🖌.

TABLES

1. Move the insertion point to the blank line under the paragraph following the heading <u>RESULTS</u>. Key the side-by-side paragraphs shown in Figure P1.1, leaving a blank row between each description. Set a ¼-inch hanging indent for both columns.

2. Move the insertion point to the blank line under the paragraph following the heading <u>PROPOSED CAPITAL EXPENDITURES</u>. Key the table illustrated in Figure P1.2 on page 290 and add a printable border. (You will need to press (**Enter**) to align the column headings as shown. But do not press (**Enter**) for the items under the headings in the first column. Be sure to center the table and adjust column widths appropriately.)

3. Sort the table by the projected costs for the new fiscal year, listing the lowest amount first.

4. Undo the sort, and sort the table by the five-year outlook, listing the highest amount first.

5. Calculate the totals for the two expense columns. Then set appropriate decimal tabs to align the amounts.

EDITING

1. Complete a spelling check.

2. Complete a grammar check. Change "affective" to **effective** in the bulleted paragraph, but click Ignore when "effective" is highlighted in the table. Click Ignore Rule for the suggestions "This main clause may contain a verb in the passive voice." and "This does not seem to be a complete sentence."

3. Move the heading and all the text under the heading <u>IMPACT OF DEFERRAL</u> (include the preceding paragraph mark), so that it follows the side-by-side paragraphs below the heading <u>RESULTS</u>.

Comprehensive member profiles.	More detailed information about each member can be maintained and managed.
Decrease in valuable and costly time that trainers spend completing paperwork and researching information.	Fitness trainers will have access to powerful tools to speed their work.
Increase in member satisfaction.	Fitness trainers will be able to update and retrieve member profiles more efficiently, thereby allowing them to spend more time assisting members with their training.
Timely and accurate feedback and recommendations to members.	Fitness trainers will be able to access member profile facts and reference data in seconds.
Increased trainer effectiveness.	Fitness trainers can focus on member needs and design effective custom training programs.
Increased cooperation between fitness trainers.	Fitness trainers will be able to manage and share information easily.

FIGURE P1.2
Table of Proposed Expenditures

Type of Investment	Projected Expense New Fiscal Year	Projected Expense Five-Year Outlook
Personal computers	160,000	200,000
Printers and cables	35,000	40,800
CD-ROM Reference Libraries and upgrades	40,000	60,000
Communication software and upgrades	10,000	15,250
Word processing software and upgrades	14,200	18,800
Database management software and upgrades	17,580	21,670
Spreadsheet software and upgrades	14,440	18,750
Scheduling and project management software and upgrades	13,750	17,500
Training programs	7,500	15,000
Maintenance	5,000	15,000
Insurance	7,020	35,100
Supplies	3,500	17,500
Total Capital Expenditure		

4. Using the initials **BDG,** add an annotation for the 40,800 amount in the table at the end of the document: **This amount should be 37,000.**

5. Using your initials, add an annotation for the title: **Change the title to all caps and bold with a larger font size and extra spacing between letters.**

6. Using your initials, add an annotation for the heading <u>NEEDS</u>: **Search and change each underlined heading to bold with a larger font size.**

7. Print a copy including annotations. Then turn off Annotations and Hidden Text for future printings.

8. Save your document as **proj1b**, then turn on revision marks so they will display when you edit the document.

9. Make the changes indicated by proofreaders' marks in Figure P1.3 on pages 292–295. (To save space, the footer, footnote, annotations, and two tables are not shown in the figure.)

10. Add an autonumbered footnote at the end of the word "benefits" above the side-by-side paragraphs. The footnote should read **Based on member and fitness trainer surveys.**

11. Search for the words "generate," "disappointed," and "discontented" and use the Thesaurus to find synonyms to replace them.

12. Search for each individual occurrence of "trainer" and change the text to **fitness trainer**. Drag the dialog box title bar to move the dialog box as needed to see the search text. (Note that "trainers" will also be changed to "fitness trainers." Be careful not to replace where the text already reads "fitness trainer.")

13. Replace all occurrences of "expense" with **cost**. (Note that "expenses" will also be changed to "costs.")

14. Search for all occurrences of text with the underline format and replace the format with 16-point bold with no underline.

HINT: *Be sure "No Underline" is listed for the format under Replace With.*

15. Turn off revision marking, save your changes, and print your document.

16. Save your document as **proj1c**. Review the revisions. As you review, accept each revision except where "expense" was changed to "cost." Reject each instance where "expense" was changed to "cost."

17. Search for and delete the annotations.

18. In the table, change 40,800 to **37,000**; then update the fields in the table so the totals will be correct.

19. Complete a final spelling check. Then proofread and make any other necessary changes.

20. Change the entire document except for the two indented lists and the two tables to double spacing.

HINT: *The quickest way to accomplish this is to select the entire document and change*

Technology Acquisition Proposal

Left-aligned, 18-point bold, all caps, expanded 2 points

The role of technology impacts both the fitness and nutrition aspects of our business. To remain competitive, we update our training equipment and modify our nutrition classes frequently because of changes in technology. We are long overdue in directing our attention to the technology available to our trainers. This proposal summarizes the current situation, focuses on several critical needs, and describes a solution. The proposal then presents the results and benefits of implementing the proposed solution versus the impact of deferring the solution. Finally, the proposal lists projected expenses for the proposed investments.

Justify

NEEDS

After careful analysis, we have identified the following needs:

- Improve the qualitative and quantitative data maintained for a member's physical analysis and progressive training performance. Although we currently maintain member profiles, they do not contain enough information to provide comprehensive assessments for designing *custom* training programs.

- Streamline the method for processing member profiles to provide more accurate assessments and more effective training programs. Trainers need a faster *and easier* way to complete the administrative

Continued on next page

tasks of creating ~and updating~ the tremendous volume of member profiles.

- Increase the timeliness and accuracy in communicating health and fitness feedback to the member. Each trainer needs quick and easy access to member information to answer questions and to improve the analysis of a member's health and fitness.

- Improve the ability for trainers to communicate with trainers at other ~sites~ *facilities* for advice and suggestions.

- Improve the ability to view the level of trainer activity and effectiveness. Accurate and reliable information is necessary for evaluation of trainer performance.

PROPOSED SOLUTION

Collectively, ~T~the following recommendations address all of the needs outlined above.

- Provide the following hardware at each of the twenty facilities for trainer use:

  Four personal computers, each equipped with an internal hard drive, a 3.5-inch floppy drive, an internal modem, and a mouse

  Four printers

  CD-ROM Disk

- Network the four computers within each facility.

- Establish *on-line* communication service among all twenty facilities.

Continued on next page

- Provide essential ~~application~~ software for each computer including the following: _(application)_

  {
  Communication
  Word processing
  Database management
  Spreadsheet
  Scheduling and project management
  }

  Alphabetical order

- Provide a CD-ROM reference library of health, fitness, and nutrition information for each facility.

RESULTS *AND BENEFITS*

Implementing the solution described above should generate the following results: *and benefits*

IMPACT OF DEFERRAL

If we do not employ the recommended solution now, *however,* we can expect the following:

- Inefficient use of trainer time.
- Unacceptable levels of customer service and disappointed members due to lack of timely *and accurate* health and fitness feedback.
- Discontented trainers because they cannot work effectively and efficiently.
- Lost membership because trainers are not able to successfully meet individual needs of members.

Continued on next page

it to double spacing. Then select each indented list under PROPOSED SOLUTION, change to single spacing, and add an additional blank line below the list. Finally, select each table and change to single spacing.

21. Adjust page breaks as needed so that headings are not separated from text. It is acceptable to carry bulleted lists and the side-by-side paragraphs onto the next page; however, do not split the list of software or the table.

22. Examine the document in print preview (zoom to a larger size if necessary to check the footer and footnotes). Save and print the document; then clear the screen.

MAIL MERGE

1. Open the Data Disk file **committe.doc**, print one copy, and clear the screen. This document is a complete list of National Family Health and Fitness Club committee members, and you will use it to create your data source in Step 5.

2. Open a new document window and change the margins to 1 inch and the font size to 12. Key the following centered and bold letter heading:

   NATIONAL FAMILY HEALTH AND FITNESS CLUB
   5 Park Street
   Boston, MA 02108-4314

3. Key the remainder of the letter, using the text illustrated in Figure P1.4 on page 297 for the body of the letter (be sure to use the 12-point font size). Include the current date in your letter,

leave several blank lines for the inside address, and supply an appropriate salutation and closing (including your initials). The author of the letter is Hanna F. Holmes, Chairperson and CEO.

4. Spell check the letter. Save it as **clubltrm** and begin the merge process with this letter as the main document.

5. Use the committee list you printed in Step 1 to create a data source and enter records. (Be sure to include fields for the committee, telephone number, and Fax number to create a database that can be used for different types of merge documents in the future.) Save the data source as **membersd**.

6. Insert appropriate merge fields for the inside address and the salutation in the main document. Add or delete extra lines as needed for the inside address and salutation. If the document is longer than one page, delete returns above and below the date as needed.

7. Save the completed main document.

8. Using Query Options, sort the data source by last name in ascending alphabetical order. Then merge and print records 1–3.

9. Edit the data source to add the following new record:

Ms. Luisa Barba
Carmel Valley Fitness and Aerobics Center
81 Devonshire Street
Boston, MA 02109-8855
Committee: Organization
Telephone: (617) 555-9988
Fax: (617) 555-9990

10. Save the changes to the data source; then filter the data source, and merge and print only the records for the Organization committee. (Be sure to change Records to Be Merged to All.)

11. Clear the screen, saving if prompted.

MAILING LABELS

1. Create a new main document for merging mailing labels.

2. Use the data source **membersd** for printing mailing labels with a postal bar code. Use Product Number 5162 for a laser printer or 4146 for a dot-matrix printer.

3. Merge and print the labels, and save the main document as **clublblm**.

We are all very proud of National Family Health and Fitness Club's commanding lead in health and fitness club membership. Sound corporate strategies and expert management have enabled National Family Health and Fitness Club to grow into a multimillion dollar business and stand out as the leader in health and fitness.

The long-range goals for the corporation are not only to maintain the current facilities, but also to increase membership and to open new facilities. To achieve this goal, our fitness trainers must be equipped with essential technology tools. Unfortunately, at this time our fitness trainers are ill-equipped for maintaining member profiles and analyzing health and fitness needs.

Our general manager and our fitness director carefully researched our fitness trainer needs and drafted the enclosed proposal. This proposal will be the topic of discussion at our board meeting next month. We are looking for an immediate resolution and are eager to discuss this proposal. Please review the proposal and carefully consider the proposed solutions. If you have any concerns or any additional recommendations, they should be expressed at the board meeting.

I am available to answer your questions and provide details and further explanation if you wish to discuss this proposal prior to our next meeting. Please contact me if I can help.

ADVANCED WORD FEATURES

PAGINATION, MULTIPLE-COLUMN DOCUMENTS, AND HYPHENATION

CHAPTER

12

OBJECTIVES
Upon completion of this chapter, you will be able to:

- Combine multiple documents.

- Adjust undesirable page breaks.

- Control spacing above and below paragraphs without adding paragraph returns.

- Add multiple-column formats.

- Add vertical lines between columns.

- Create a banner over multiple columns.

- Add borders and shading to paragraphs.

- Control column breaks and balance columns.

- Add nonbreaking spaces and nonbreaking hyphens.

- Add optional hyphens manually and automatically.

Preparation

1. To complete the chapter activities, you will need to access the Data Disk files HISTORY.DOC, RISKS.DOC, SOURCES.DOC, SYMPTOMS.DOC, PREVENT.DOC, PHARMACY.DOC, INDIANS.DOC, ALONE.DOC, HIKEBIKE.DOC, and NURSING.DOC and your Student Disk file ACT6-2.DOC.

2. For Exercises 12.15 to 12.16 and Activity 4, the Hyphenation feature must be installed.

3. Be sure to save frequently as you work; you will generally not be reminded to save until all work is completed for a document.

4. If you make mistakes as you work with the exercises in the chapter, remember to click [⤺][⤒] immediately after completing the action.

5. Be sure to close Word and Windows properly. If you are using the hard drive to store your completed work, back up your files onto your formatted Student Disk, and erase your files from the directory you used on the hard drive. (Do not erase the Data Disk files unless your instructor tells you to do so.)

Introduction

In Chapter 7 you worked with tabs to create columns. In Chapter 9 you created columns (including side-by-side paragraphs) using the Word table features. These types of columns are also known as *parallel columns.* In this chapter you will work with multiple documents and special paragraph formats. You will then add multiple-column formats to text to create *newspaper-style* (or snaking) *columns.* In newspaper-style columns, text flows down one column and begins again in the next column. You will add *banners,* paragraph borders, and *shading,* and you will use the Word hyphenation features.

Combining Multiple Documents and Pagination

Word allows you to combine multiple document files into a single document. In Exercises 12.1 and 12.2 you will combine files and apply some special paragraph formats.

EXERCISE

12.1

Combining Multiple Document Files

! **IMPORTANT:** If you are using only floppy disks before beginning this exercise, copy the following Data Disk files to your Student Disk: HISTORY. DOC, RISKS.DOC, SOURCES.DOC, SYMPTOMS.DOC, and PREVENT. DOC. You cannot insert a file from a different floppy disk than the one on which you save your work.

1. Open **history.doc** and save it in the *same* location as **chap12-1**.

! **IMPORTANT:** Before you insert files, be sure your insertion point is correct. Files are inserted at the insertion point.

2. Move the insertion point to the end of the document.

3. Choose Insert File.

TIP

If you want to work with portions of multiple documents rather than entire files, open all the necessary documents and choose Window Arrange All. Copy and paste as needed from one document to another, then close all but the final document. Before you close the final document, click [▲] to return the document window to full-size.

FIGURE 12.1
Insert File Dialog Box

File

File Name:
`*.doc`

alliance.doc
alone.doc
atlanta.doc
brochure.doc
building.doc
calendar.doc
cash.doc
ceo.doc
classes.doc
committe.doc
cts.doc
datalbl1.doc

Directories:
c:\datafile

🗁 c:\
  📁 datafile
  📁 acctg
  📁 mktg

Drives:
💾 c: disk1_vol1

List Files of Type:
Word Documents (*.doc)

Range:

OK
Cancel
Find File...
Help

☐ **Confirm Conversions**

☐ **Link to File**

4. If necessary, change to the drive and directory containing the Data Disk files (Figure 12.1).

5. Click **risks.doc** and click [OK]. The entire file is inserted at the insertion point.

6. Insert the following files in order: **sources. doc**, **symptoms.doc**, and **prevent.doc**. Do not clear the screen yet.

E X E R C I S E

12.2

Applying Special Paragraph Formats

As you have been working on documents in this text, you have added and deleted returns and hard page breaks to adjust undesirable page breaks. Each time you edit a document that is formatted in this manner, however, you may need to adjust the page breaks again. The four Pagination options in the Text Flow category of the Format Paragraph dialog box (Figure 12.2) allow you to adjust page breaks automatically:

■ **_Widow/Orphan_ Control.** Word automatically prevents widows (single lines of a paragraph at the top of a page) and orphans (single lines of a paragraph at

the bottom of a page). Unless you need a specific line count for a page (for example, in a legal document), you generally leave this option on.

■ **Keep Lines Together.** Word will keep an entire paragraph together on the same page rather than splitting it between pages.

■ **Keep with Next.** Word will keep at least the last two lines of the first paragraph with the first two lines of the next paragraph. You can combine Keep Lines Together and Keep with Next when you

FIGURE 12.2
Text Flow Category of the Format
Paragraph Dialog Box

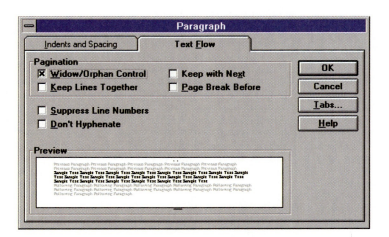

have two paragraphs you want to keep together and do not want the second paragraph to be split between pages.

- **Page Break Before.** Use this option when you have a paragraph you always want at the top of a page.

The Spacing Before and After options in the Indents and Spacing category of the Format Paragraph dialog box (Figure 12.3) allow you to key measurements to adjust the amount of paragraph spacing automatically. In the past, you pressed (Enter) to add blank lines before and after paragraphs. This meant, for example, that when you wanted to move or copy a side heading, you needed to select the blank lines along with the side heading. Instead, if you add the Spacing Before and After formats to the side heading, you can move just the side heading and not have to adjust spacing around it.

In the following steps, you will turn off widow and orphan control to see the effect on page breaks throughout your document. You will then turn widow and orphan control back on. You will also further adjust page breaks with the Keep with Next and Keep Lines Together.

1. Turn off widow and orphan control:

   a. If necessary, open **chap12-1.doc**. Select your entire document.

HINT: *Triple-click in the selection bar.*

   b. Choose Format Paragraph and click the Text Flow folder tab.

   c. Click Widow/Orphan Control to turn off the option (it should not have an X or a gray square); then click OK .

2. Print a copy of your document.

Notice that your printout shows one or all of the following undesirable page breaks:

- Single lines of a paragraph at the top or bottom of a page (widows and orphans)

- Headings separated from their associated text

- Bulleted lists split between pages (sometimes acceptable, but in most cases, you want to keep bulleted lists together on one page)

FIGURE 12.3
Indents and Spacing Category of the Format Paragraph Dialog Box

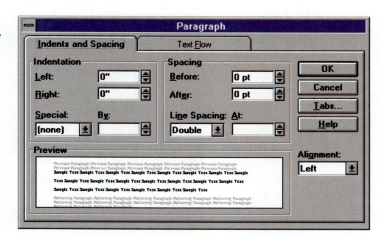

3. Click ⌢⟨⟩ to turn Widow/Orphan Control back on.

4. Change the bulleted lists and the blank lines between bulleted paragraphs to single spacing.

HINT: *Drag down the selection bar, then press* ⟨**Ctrl**⟩ + ⟨**1**⟩.

5. Add a blank line above the heading "Symptoms of Lead Poisoning." If necessary, click ⟨≡⟩ to remove the bullet from the blank line.

6. Delete one of the blank lines below the title.

7. Keep the bulleted lists together on a single page:

a. Scroll to the first bulleted list (beginning with "Lead in drinking water . . .") on the second page.

b. Select the bulleted list and blank lines between the bulleted paragraphs but do not select the last bulleted paragraph.

⚠ **IMPORTANT: When you want to keep two or more paragraphs together, do not select the last paragraph of the group, because you do not want to keep it with the next paragraph.**

c. Choose Format Paragraph.

d. If necessary, click the Text Flow folder tab. Click Keep with Next to turn it on; then click ⟨ **OK** ⟩.

e. Position the insertion point in the bulleted paragraph "Lead dust on clothing . . ." and turn on Keep Lines Together rather than Keep with Next.

f. Scroll down to the paragraph that begins "It is important that we educate the public . . ."

g. Select from this paragraph down to the last bulleted item (do not include the last bulleted paragraph but do include the blank line above it).

h. Turn on the Keep with Next format.

i. Select the last bulleted paragraph and turn on Keep Lines Together rather than Keep with Next.

With ⟨¶⟩ turned on in Normal View, Word displays a small, nonprinting, black square to the left of the bulleted items. This black square indicates that one or more of the paragraph formats Keep with Next, Page Break Before, and Keep Lines Together are turned on.

In the following steps you will format your side headings to keep them with their associated text. You will also add space above and below them so that you will not need to press ⟨**Enter**⟩ to space them properly.

8. Add paragraph formats to your side headings:

a. Move the insertion point to the side heading "History" on the first page.

b. Choose Format Paragraph and, if necessary, click Text Flow.

c. Turn on Keep with Next; then click the Indents and Spacing folder tab.

d. Under Spacing, key **12** in the Before box

and **3** in the After box. Then click $\boxed{\text{OK}}$.

e. Repeat the Keep with Next and Spacing Before and After formats for the other side headings "Environmental Risks," "Sources of Lead," Symptoms of Lead Poisoning," and "Prevention of Lead Poisoning."

9. Add a header with a page number for all pages but the first.

TIP

To add or remove 12 points of space above a paragraph, press Ctrl + the number O.

HINT: *Choose View Header and Footer.*

10. Spell check and proofread the document.

11. Save the changes to the document, print one copy, and clear the screen.

Adding a Multiple-Column Format

You can add a multiple-column format to all or part of a document. When you format text in columns, Word formats the text in a section. Sections enable you to format a document with a combination of multiple-column formats. For example, you can have a single-column, a two-column, and even a three-column format all within the same document. You can format text in columns of equal width or in columns of unequal width. The number of columns and the widths of the columns can vary from one section to the next.

EXERCISE

Removing Formats

In Exercise 12.4 you will add multiple-column formats to the document you completed in Exercise 12.2. This document has a header beginning on the second page and some special paragraph for-mats that should be removed before you begin formatting the text in multiple columns.

1. If necessary, open your Student Disk file **chap12-1.doc.** Save it as **chap12-2.**

2. Remove the header:

    a. Choose View Header and Footer.

    b. Click , turn off Different First Page, and click [**OK**].

    c. Select all the header text.

HINT: *Double-click in the selection bar to the left of the header frame.*

    d. Press (Delete).

    e. Click [**Close**].

3. Remove the special paragraph formats:

    a. Select the entire document.

HINT: *Triple-click in the selection bar.*

    b. Choose Format Paragraph.

    c. If necessary, click the Text Flow folder tab.

Notice that the Keep with Next and Keep Lines Together boxes are gray. They are gray because some paragraphs in the document are formatted with the special paragraph formats and some are not.

    d. Click the Keep with Next box twice to turn off the format for all paragraphs.

    e. Click the Keep Lines Together box twice to turn off the format for all paragraphs.

    f. Click [**OK**].

E X E R C I S E

12.4

Creating Columns of Equal Width

● ●

1. Click [▤] on the horizontal scroll bar.

Switching to Page Layout View will allow you to see the multiple-column text as it will appear when you print the document. Only single columns can be seen in Normal View.

2. Create two columns of equal width:

    a. Select the paragraph below the heading "History."

HINT: *Double-click in the selection bar.*

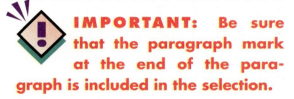

IMPORTANT: **Be sure that the paragraph mark at the end of the paragraph is included in the selection.**

    b. Click the Columns icon on the Standard Toolbar [▦]. A grid displaying four columns appears (Figure 12.4).

FIGURE 12.4
Sample Columns Grid

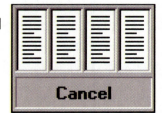

FIGURE 12.5
Completed Columns
Grid

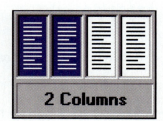

2 Columns

c. Drag across the grid until two of the columns are selected (Figure 12.5). Then release the mouse button.

d. Deselect the text and, if necessary, scroll to see the end of the paragraph.

The section should now look similar to the illustration in Figure 12.6. Notice the section break at the end of the section. Word created a new section both before and after the selected text and formatted the text in two columns of equal width.

Page 1	Sec 2	1/4

Look at the left side of the status bar where "Sec 2" is displayed. (The number of pages shown may vary.) As you work with your document,

Word displays the number of the *section* where the insertion point is located.

3. Create three columns of equal width:

a. Select the heading "Environmental Risks" and the paragraph below.

HINT: *Drag down the selection bar.*

IMPORTANT: Be sure the paragraph mark at the end of the paragraph is included in the selection.

b. Click 📑, drag to select three columns, release the mouse button, and deselect the text.

IMPORTANT: When you click 📑, Word always formats the text in columns of equal width.

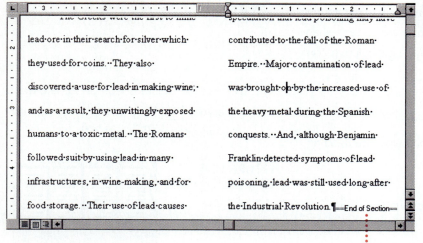

lead·ore·in·their·search·for·silver·which·
they·used·for·coins.··They·also·
discovered·a·use·for·lead·in·making·wine;·
and·as·a·result,·they·unwittingly·exposed·
humans·to·a·toxic·metal.··The·Romans·
followed·suit·by·using·lead·in·many·
infrastructures,·in·wine-making,·and·for·
food·storage.··Their·use·of·lead·causes·

speculation·that·lead·poisoning·may·have·
contributed·to·the·fall·of·the·Roman·
Empire.··Major·contamination·of·lead·
was·brought·on·by·the·increased·use·of·
the·heavy·metal·during·the·Spanish·
conquests.···And,·although·Benjamin·
Franklin·detected·symptoms·of·lead·
poisoning,·lead·was·still·used·long·after·
the·Industrial·Revolution.¶===End of Section===

FIGURE 12.6
Text Formatted in Two
Columns of Equal Width

Section Break

EXERCISE

Creating Columns of Unequal Width

You can also format columns by choosing the Format Columns command to display the dialog box shown in Figure 12.7.

If you click Two or Three under Presets, Word initially creates two or three columns of equal width, just as Word does when you click  and drag across the sample columns *grid.* You can redefine these columns, however, by keying measurements for Width and Spacing.

If you click Left or Right under Presets, two columns of unequal width are created. When Left preset is turned on, the left column is half the width of the right column. When Right preset is turned on, the left column is twice as wide as the right column.

1. Create preset columns of unequal width:

    a. Select the heading "Sources of Lead," the

paragraph below the heading, and the bulleted list below the paragraph.

IMPORTANT: Be sure that the blank line below the bulleted list is included in the selection.

    b. Choose Format Columns.

    c. Under Presets, click Left. Notice the column formats as displayed in the Preview box (Figure 12.8).

FIGURE 12.8
Preview of Columns of Unequal Width Using Left Preset

    d. Click OK; then deselect the text.

2. Create two columns of equal width and redefine their width:

    a. Select the heading "Symptoms of Lead Poisoning" and the first two paragraphs

FIGURE 12.7
Columns Dialog Box

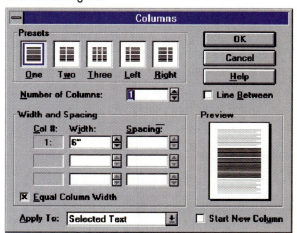

below the heading (the second paragraph begins "Lead poisoning is a health . . .").

HINT: *Drag down the selection bar. Keep dragging down past the bottom of the page; the screen will scroll to the next page as you continue to drag.*

b. Choose Format Columns. Under Presets, click Two.

c. Turn off Equal Column Width.

d. Double-click the Width box for Column 1 under Width and Spacing to select the box; then key **3.25**. Leave the Spacing box set at 0.5 inch.

e. Double-click the Width box for Column 2 until the box is selected. Word automatically changes the measurement to 2.25 inches.

f. Click [OK]; then deselect the text.

EXERCISE

12.6 Adding a Line Between Columns

1. Create two columns of equal width with a line (a vertical rule) between them:

a. Select the last three paragraphs below the heading "Symptoms of Lead Poisoning." (Begin the selection with "Children and fetuses . . .")

b. Choose Format Columns. Under Presets, click Two.

c. Turn on Line Between.

d. Click [OK]. Then deselect the text and scroll up to the paragraph "Children and fetuses . . ."

When Line Between is turned on, Word adds a line between the columns of text. The vertical rule is as long as the longest column in the *section* (Figure 12.9).

FIGURE 12.9
Columns with Line Between

→ Children·and·fetuses·are·at·the· greatest·risk·and·can·suffer·learning· disabilities,·decreased·growth,·impaired· hearing,·and·brain·damage.··Studies·of· children·show·that·lead·poisoning·causes· biochemical·effects·that·result·in· neurobehavioral·problems.··The·lead· negatively·affects·cognitive·thinking,·

occur·from·high·doses·of·lead.··Severe· retardation,·school·problems,·and· downward·shifts·in·IQ·result·from·low· doses·of·lead.··IQ·shifts·can·range·from·4· to·15·points.··At·this·time·it·is·believed· that·the·damage·from·lead·is·permanent.¶
→ Adults·are·primarily·at·risk·for· lead·poisoning·due·to·exposure·in·the·

2. Scroll down and select the heading "Prevention of Lead Poisoning," the paragraph below, and the bulleted list that follows the paragraph. Do not select below the bulleted list because the end of the document should not be formatted for multiple columns.

3. Repeat the two-column format with the vertical rule between the columns.

Changing the Width of Columns and the Spacing Between Columns

You can adjust the width of columns and the spacing between them by dragging the column markers on the ruler. If the columns you are adjusting are of equal width, changing the width of one column will change the widths of all the columns. If the columns you are adjusting are of unequal width, only the column that you are adjusting will change.

EXERCISE

12.7 Changing Column Widths and the Spacing Between

1. Adjust column widths for columns formatted with equal widths:

a. Move the insertion point to the beginning of the document. Then position the insertion point in the left column under the heading "History."

b. If necessary, choose View Ruler to display the horizontal and vertical rulers. Notice the column marker (the gray box) between the two columns on the horizontal ruler.

c. On the ruler, position the mouse pointer on the left edge of the column marker.

When you see the two-headed arrow, drag left to approximately 1.5 inches; then release the mouse button.

Notice that Word adjusted the width of both columns, so that they are still equal in width.

2. Undo this adjustment.

3. Drag the left edge of the column marker to approximately 2.5 inches on the ruler; then release the mouse button. Again, Word adjusts the width of both columns so they are equal.

4. Adjust column widths for columns formatted with unequal widths:

a. Scroll down to the heading "Sources of Lead" and position the insertion point in the right column.

b. Drag the right edge of the column marker to the right, to approximately 1 inch on the ruler; then release the mouse button.

Notice that Word adjusted the width of only the right column because the columns are formatted in unequal widths.

5. Undo this adjustment.

Deleting Section Breaks and Changing Section Formatting

In addition to column formats, sections contain formats for margins, headers and footers, page numbers, and page orientation. If you delete a section break, you also delete the formatting for the text above the section break. When a section break is deleted, the text becomes part of the section that follows.

All the sections that you created in this document are called Continuous sections. They start immediately below the preceding section on the *same* page. Sections can also be formatted to start on a new page, and they can be formatted to start on the next odd or next even page (often used when the document contains several chapters).

EXERCISE

12.8

Delete Section Breaks

1. Move the insertion point to Section 3:

a. Double-click the page number on the status bar.

b. Under Go to What, click Section.

c. Click Previous; then click [**Close**].

Word positions the insertion point at the beginning of Section 3.

2. Click the up scroll bar arrow several times.

Notice that Section 3 is formatted in three columns and that Section 2 above is formatted in two columns. The status bar displays "Sec 3."

3. Delete a section break to combine two sections.

a. Position the insertion point on the section break at the end of Section 2. (It follows the words "... after the Industrial Revolution.")

b. Press (Delete).

When the section break is deleted, the text becomes part of the section below. Now the two sections are combined into one. The status bar still displays "Sec 2;" however, the section is now formatted in three columns (Figure 12.10).

4. Go to Section 3, which now begins with the heading "Sources of Lead."

HINT: *Click Next in the Go To dialog box.*

Scroll up slightly and click on the section break at the end of Section 2.

Notice that Section 3 is formatted with a Left preset format and Section 2 is formatted with three columns. The status bar shows "Sec 2."

TIP

If you accidentally delete a section break, click .

5. Press (Delete). The two sections are combined with a Left preset format. The status bar still displays "Sec 2."

6. Go to Section 3 which now begins with the heading "Symptoms of Lead Poisoning." Scroll up slightly and click on the section break at the end of Section 2.

Notice that Section 3 is formatted with two columns of unequal width, wider than those in Section 2. The status bar shows "Sec 2."

7. Delete the section break at the end of Section 2. The columns in Section 2 are now all of the unequal width of the former Section 3.

8. Go to Section 3, which now begins with the paragraph "Children and fetuses ..." Scroll up slightly and click on the section break at the end of Section 2.

FIGURE 12.10
Two Sections Combined after Deleting Section Break

result, they unwittingly exposed humans to a toxic metal. The Romans followed suit by using lead in many infrastructures, in wine making, and for food storage. Their use of lead causes speculation

Franklin detected symptoms of lead poisoning, lead was still used long after the Industrial Revolution.¶

Environmental·Risks¶

→ Lead is commonly found in the

remains in the body and disturbs the enzyme system and the formation of hemoglobin. Hemoglobin carries oxygen through the bloodstream to organs and tissues. Although nearly all body tissue can

Section 3 is formatted with two columns of equal width, with a vertical rule between columns. Section 2 has two columns of unequal width and no vertical rule. The status bar shows "Sec 2."

9. Delete the section break at the end of Section 2.

The document now contains four sections. The first section (for the title page and the first heading) is formatted in one column. The second and third sections are formatted in two columns of equal width, with a vertical rule between columns. The fourth section contains one or two blank paragraphs at the end of the document.

EXERCISE

12.9

Changing Section Formatting

1. Go to Section 4 at the end of the document. Then scroll up and double-click the section break at the end of Section 3.

2. If necessary, click the Layout folder tab. Word displays the dialog box illustrated in Figure 12.11.

3. Open the Section Start list box, click New Page, and click ⬚ OK ⬚.

When the document is printed, this section (beginning with the heading "Prevention of Lead Poisoning" will begin at the top of a new page.

FIGURE 12.11
Layout Category of File Page Setup
Dialog Box

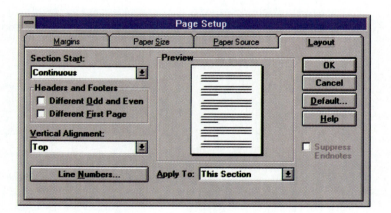

Adding a Banner over Multiple Columns

Usually, heading text is formatted as a single-column banner spreading across the multiple columns. One way to create banners automatically is to select the text below the heading and format only that text for multiple columns (you will use this procedure in Activities 3 and 4). The heading would then remain as a single-column banner. In text that is already formatted for multiple columns (such as this document), you create a banner by changing just the heading to the single-column format.

EXERCISE

Creating Banners

1. Move the insertion point to the beginning of the document. Notice that the heading "Environmental Risks" is in a section that is formatted in two columns.

2. Create a single-column banner with the bold and center formats:

   a. Select the paragraph containing the heading "Environmental Risks."

   IMPORTANT: Be sure the paragraph mark at the end of the heading is included in the selection.

   b. With the paragraph selected, click ▦, click one column, and release the mouse button.

Word creates a new section for the selected text and formats the text in one column.

   c. With the text still selected, apply the bold and center formats; then deselect.

All the headings should still be formatted 14-point Times New Roman underline. Do not remove the underlining or change the font or font size; simply add the bold and center formats. Your heading should look similar to the one in Figure 12.12.

3. Select the heading "Sources of Lead." Format

FIGURE 12.12
Single-Column Banner with Center and Bold Formats

infrastructures,·in·wine-making,·and·for-
food·storage.··Their·use·of·lead·causes·

poisoning,·lead·was·still·used·long·after·
the·Industrial·Revolution.¶══End of Section══

Environmental·Risks¶════════End of Section════════

→ Lead·is·commonly·found·in·the·

body·and·disturbs·the·enzyme·system·and·

it as a single-column banner with the bold and center formats.

4. Double-click the section break following the heading "Sources of Lead" and format the new section to always start on a new page:

HINT: *Click New Page for Section Start; then click* ⎡ **OK** ⎤ .

5. Format the heading "Symptoms of Lead Poisoning" as a single-column banner with

the center and bold formats and starting on a new page.

6. Format the heading "Prevention of Lead Poisoning" as a single-column banner with the center and bold formats. This section is already formatted to start on a new page.

7. Move the insertion point to the beginning of the document and select the heading "History." It is already formatted for a single column. Apply the bold and center formats.

Adding Borders and Shading to Paragraphs

You can enhance paragraphs by adding borders and rules. Borders and rules can be added to one or more sides of a paragraph. Also, background shading can be applied to paragraphs for special effects.

EXERCISE

Adding a Paragraph Border

1. Position the insertion point in the title, "GETTING THE LEAD OUT."

2. If necessary, click ⊞ on the Formatting Toolbar to display the Borders Toolbar (Figure 12.13).

3. Click the Outside Border icon on

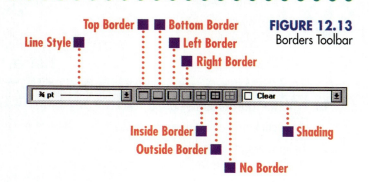

FIGURE 12.13
Borders Toolbar

the Borders Toolbar ⊞. Word adds a border on all four sides of the paragraph (Figure 12.14).

FIGURE 12.14
Paragraph with Outside Border

GETTING·THE·LEAD·OUT¶

¶

4. Click the No Border icon ⊞ to clear the outside border.

5. With the insertion point still positioned in the heading, click the down arrow next to the Line Style box. In the Line Style box (Figure 12.15), click 6 pt.

IMPORTANT: Word saves the most recent Line Style box setting, so the thickness and style displayed for this box will vary. Always check

FIGURE 12.15
Line Style Box

that the Line Style box has been set to the desired thickness and style before applying a border.

6. Click the Bottom Border icon ▢. Word adds a single rule below the paragraph (Figure 12.16).

FIGURE 12.16
Heading with 6-Point Rule Below

GETTING·THE·LEAD·OUT¶

¶

EXERCISE

Adding Paragraph Shading

● ●

1. Go to Section 6.

HINT: *Key **6** for the Section Number in the Go To dialog box, click Go To, and click* **Close** .

2. Click ▤ to switch temporarily to Normal View. (It is usually easier to select text in Normal View.)

3. Scroll down and select the bulleted list (beginning with "Lead in drinking water . . .").

IMPORTANT: Do not include the blank line below the last bulleted item in the selection.

FIGURE 12.17
Shading Box

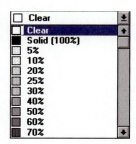

4. Click the down arrow next to the Shading box. In the Shading box (Figure 12.17), click 10%.

5. Switch back to Page Layout View and deselect the text. A light background shading has been added to the paragraphs (Figure 12.18).

6. Go to Section 10. In Normal View, select the

bulleted list beginning with "Have children tested ..."

IMPORTANT: Do not include the section break or the blank lines below the section break in the selection.

7. Add 10% background shading. Then switch back to Page Layout View and deselect the text.

FIGURE 12.18
Shaded Text

- Lead·in·drinking·water.··Lead·gets· into·the·drinking·water·because·of· corrosion·in·pipes·or·from·certain· properties·of·the·water.··The·lead·in· drinking·water·most·likely·results· from·lead·that·leaches·in·from·pipes.·· Through·the·1920s,·lead·was·used·in· household·pipes.··Newer·homes·now· have·copper·pipes.··However,·up· until·1988·lead·solder·was·legally·still·

Food·containers·and·packaging.··A· recent·study·indicated·that·the·use·of· lead-based·inks·on·bread·bags·was· harmful·because·the·lead·would· migrate·to·food·if·the·bags·are·turned· inside-out·and·reused.¶

¶

- Lead·dust·on·clothing.··Persons·who· work·with·lead·may·have·lead·dust· on·their·clothing.¶

¶═══════════End of Section═══════════

Adjusting Column Breaks

Columns above a Continuous section break are automatically balanced. Word fills each column with text and then wraps additional text to the next column. If necessary, Word shortens each column so that column lengths are approximately equal. There may be occasions, however, when you want to control column breaks. To adjust where a column ends, you add a hard column break.

On the last page of a section or document, the last column may be empty or partially filled; on such occasions, you will want to balance columns manually. To balance columns manually, you insert a Continuous section break at the end of the last column.

EXERCISE

Adding a Hard Column Break

1. Go to Section 6 (it begins "Major sources of the toxic . . .").

2. Scroll down and position the insertion point at the end of the paragraph.

3. Choose Insert Break, click Column Break, and click [OK]. The bulleted list below the paragraph is moved to the next column.

4. Scroll down until you see a dotted line across the column with the words "Column Break." (See Figure 12.19.)

Notice that there is no text below the column

take·a·closer·look·at·some·of·these·

sources.........................Column Break·························

FIGURE 12.19
Column Break

break. The text that was below the column break in this section has been moved to the next column.

5. Undo the insertion of the column break and allow Word to adjust the columns in the section evenly.

EXERCISE

Balancing Columns

1. Insert a Continuous section break at the end of the last column in Section 8:

a. Go to Section 9; then scroll up to the end of Section 8. Notice that Section 8 is currently all displayed in one column, although it is formatted for two columns.

b. Position the insertion point between the last paragraph mark and the section break in the first column (it follows the words "... extreme cases of lead poisoning.")

c. Choose Insert Break.

d. Under Section Breaks, click Continuous.

e. Click [**OK**]. Then scroll up slightly until you see two section breaks. The text is now in two approximately equal (balanced) columns (Figure 12.20).

FIGURE 12.20
Balanced Columns

main·sources·of·lead·exposure·for·adults.·"

In·adults·lead·poisoning·can·trigger·high·

blood·pressure,·anemia,·and·reproductive·

══════════End of Section═════════

and·death·can·result·in·extreme·cases·

of·lead·poisoning.¶══════End of Section═════

2. Go to the end of Section 6 (the section break is in the second column, several lines above where the first column ends). Insert a Continuous section break between the last paragraph mark and the existing section break.

3. Add a page number at the bottom center of each page.

HINT: *Choose Insert Page Numbers.*

4. Use Print Preview to see that all columns on all pages are approximately balanced.

5. If the second page has only one or two lines, delete the blank line above "History" on the first page.

6. Save the changes to the document, print one copy, and clear the screen.

Controlling Line Breaks with Hyphenation and Nonbreaking Spaces

Hyphens can be added to control where line breaks appear in a document. Hyphens can make a document more attractive by eliminating excess white space at the end of a line, or within a line if you have justified text. Nonbreaking spaces can also be added to prevent undesirable line breaks.

IMPORTANT: The Hyphenation feature must be installed for you to complete the next two exercises.

EXERCISE

12.15 Inserting Hyphens and Nonbreaking Spaces

• •

1. Open the Data Disk file **pharmacy.doc** and save it in the appropriate location for Student Disk files as **chap12-3**.

2. If necessary, turn on ¶ so that the special characters for hyphens and spaces will be displayed as you add them. Check also to make sure that the Zoom Control box on the Standard Toolbar is set at 100%. The document must be displayed at the 100 percent view to use the Hyphenation feature effectively.

3. Change to Page Layout View.

HINT: *Click* 🗏 *on the horizontal scroll bar.*

4. Select from the first paragraph "Pharmacists employed . . ." through the end of the document (except the ending paragraph mark). Format for two columns of equal width, then deselect the text.

5. Change to Normal View (scrolling is quicker in Normal View). Scroll through the document. Notice that some words may be split that should not be split (for example, B. Pharm., Pharm. D., and Smith-Hockaden).

6. Insert a *nonbreaking hyphen:*

a. With the insertion point positioned at the beginning of the document, choose Edit Find and search for "Smith-Hockaden". (Clear any formats if necessary before clicking Find Next.)

b. When Word highlights the name, click in the name in the document window and delete the hyphen. (If necessary, scroll to see the text.)

c. Press Ctrl + Shift + ⊡ . Word inserts a nonbreaking hyphen.

d. Move the insertion point to the beginning of the next word ("a") so you can see the new hyphen.

Smith—Hockaden,

Notice that the entire name (Smith-Hockaden) is now on a single line rather than split between lines. Nonbreaking hyphens are inserted to tell Word that text containing a hyphen (such as the last name Smith-Hockaden) should not be broken. The nonbreaking hyphen will look like a normal hyphen when the document is printed.

Nonbreaking hyphens can also be used in ranges (for example, 40–48). Although the ranges may not be split now in your document, editing may change where the ranges are positioned on a line. Inserting nonbreaking hyphens ensures that the ranges will not be split between lines after editing.

7. Move the insertion point to the top of the document, then search for each of the following ranges and in the document window change the hyphen to a nonbreaking hyphen.

   a. 40–48

   b. $41,500–$46,200

   c. $40,000–$42,000

   d. $22,000–$25,000

8. Insert a *nonbreaking space:*

   a. Move the insertion point to the top of the document and search for the first occurrence of "B. Pharm."

   b. In the document pane, click in the space between "B." and "Pharm." and delete the space.

   c. Press (Ctrl) + (Shift) + (Space Bar). Word inserts a nonbreaking space.

   d. Move the insertion point to the beginning of the next word so that you can see the symbol.

·B.°Pharm.│

   e. Search for the next occurrence of "B. Pharm." and in the document pane change the space to a nonbreaking space.

Notice that the entire degree name ("B. Pharm.") is now on the same line of the paragraph rather than split between two lines. Nonbreaking spaces are used to indicate words that should be kept together, such as degrees, dates, and measurements. Note that although Word will leave a space between the two words when the document is printed, the symbol for the nonbreaking space will not print.

When you need to insert special symbols (such as nonbreaking hyphens or nonbreaking spaces) for the same text throughout a document, you can use the replace function with Word's special menu for symbols.

9. Replace the space in all other occurrences of "B. Pharm." with a nonbreaking space:

   a. Click Replace. (If necessary, choose Edit Find, then click Replace.)

   b. If necessary, key **B. Pharm.** in the Find What box.

   c. Key **B.** in the Replace With box (do not press (Space Bar)).

   d. Click Special, then click Nonbreaking Space. Word inserts the symbol for a nonbreaking space (^s).

   e. Without spacing, key **Pharm.**

   f. When the dialog box looks like Figure 12.21 on page 323, click Replace All, then click [OK] when all replacements are made.

10. As shown in Figure 12.22 on page 323, replace the space in all occurrences of "Pharm. D." with a nonbreaking space, then close the dialog box.

In the following steps you will insert hyphens so that the words "medical," "medication," and "medications" will be divided between the letters "i" and "c" when the words fall at the end of a line.

FIGURE 12.21
Replacing the Space in B. Pharm. with a Nonbreaking Space

FIGURE 12.22
Replacing the Space in Pharm. D. with a Nonbreaking Space

11. Insert an *optional hyphen*:

a. Move the insertion point to the top of the document. Choose Edit Find and search for the first occurrence of "medic." (Be sure that Match Case and Find Whole Words Only are turned off.)

b. Position the insertion point between the "i" and the "c" in the document window and press **Ctrl** + ⊙. Word inserts an optional hyphen.

c. Move the insertion point to the next word ("but") so you can see the new hyphen.

medi¬cations,

An optional hyphen tells Word that if a word will wrap to a new line, it can be divided at the location of the optional hyphen. Optional hyphens print only when they fall at the end of a line. When printed, optional hyphens look like normal hyphens.

12. Replace all other occurrences of "medic" with "medi," an optional hyphen, and "c":

    a. Click Replace. (If necessary, choose Edit Find and click Replace.)

    b. If necessary, key **medic** in the Find What box.

    c. Key **medi** in the Replace With box (do not key a space).

    d. Click Special, then click Optional Hyphen.

Word inserts the special character for the nonbreaking hyphen (^-) in the Replace With box.

    e. Without spacing, key **c**.

    f. Click Replace All, then click   OK   and   Close   when all the replacements are made.

13. Save the changes to your document but do not clear the screen.

EXERCISE
12.16

Hyphenating Documents Using the Tools Hyphenation Command

Although you can insert optional hyphens using the keyboard or using search and replace, as you did in the previous exercise, it is usually quicker to insert them using the Tools Hyphenation command.

1. If necessary, move the insertion point to the top of the document. Select the entire document and change to the Courier New font, then deselect the text.

2. Manually hyphenate the document:

    a. Choose Tools Hyphenation. Word displays the hyphenation box (Figure 12.23).

    b. Click Manual. A dialog box similar to the one shown in Figure 12.24 on page 325 is displayed.

 IMPORTANT: Hyphenation may vary from printer to printer. If Word hyphenates at points other than those indicated in this exercise, consult a

FIGURE 12.23
Tools Hyphenation Dialog Box

Hyphenation

☐ <u>A</u>utomatically Hyphenate Document

☐ Hyphenate Words in <u>C</u>APS

               OK

               Cancel

Hyphenation <u>Z</u>one: 0.25"   <u>M</u>anual...

<u>L</u>imit Consecutive Hyphens To: No Limit   <u>H</u>elp

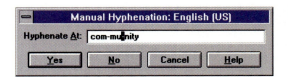

FIGURE 12.24
Manual Hyphenation Dialog Box

dictionary or a word division manual to decide on proper hyphenation.

As shown in Figure 12.24, Word stops at "community" and shows two optional hyphens. A blinking highlight indicates Word's preferred choice for the division. A dotted vertical line indicates the right margin. You can click Yes to accept Word's hyphenation choice, or you can click No to indicate that the word is not to be hyphenated. You can also change the hyphenation point.

c. Click on the first hyphen to move the hyphenation point, then click Yes.

d. When Word stops at "career," click No. (In long documents, to prevent an excessive number of hyphens, avoid a two-letter syllable division and avoid dividing words with five or fewer letters.)

e. When Word stops at "profession," click Yes.

f. When Word stops at "educational," move the hyphenation point to the first hyphen, then click Yes.

g. Click Cancel (you do not need to manually hyphenate the entire document).

In most cases, it is more efficient to let Word automatically hyphenate a document, in which case you are not asked to confirm any hyphens. The automatic hyphenation process should be the very last step before paginating and printing your document, because any editing changes you make can change line endings and require you to rehyphenate the entire document.

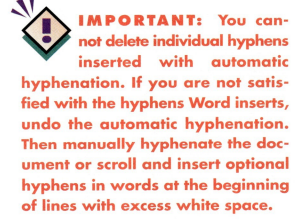 **IMPORTANT:** You cannot delete individual hyphens inserted with automatic hyphenation. If you are not satisfied with the hyphens Word inserts, undo the automatic hyphenation. Then manually hyphenate the document or scroll and insert optional hyphens in words at the beginning of lines with excess white space.

3. Click the underlined arrow for ⌢⬆, then drag down to select Manual Hyphenation and Hyphenation.

4. Select the entire document and click ▤, then deselect the document and center just the title.

5. Automatically hyphenate the document:

a. Choose Tools Hyphenation.

b. Turn on Automatically Hyphenate Document.

c. Click OK .

Word automatically hyphenates the document without stopping to confirm hyphenation points.

6. Insert page numbers at the bottom center of each page.

7. Save and print the document, then clear the screen.

8. If you want to, save the document with a new name and experiment with different margins, fonts, font sizes, and number of columns to see how hyphenation is affected.

COMPUTER ACTIVITIES

ACTIVITY 1

1. Open a new document window and change the font size to 12-point.

2. Change to double spacing and key the text illustrated in Figure 12.25 below. (Be sure to leave a blank line at the end of the document.)

FIGURE 12.25
List of Courses to
Be Keyed

        The following is a list of courses that will be offered Spring Quarter in the Nursing program.

Nursing for Health

Wellness Lifestyles

Human Existence

Health-Impaired Individuals

Health Care Trends

Conceptual and Theoretical Nursing

Professional Nursing Practices

Nursing Assessment

Nursing Diagnosis

The Research Process

        See your departmental adviser for information about enrollment restrictions, requirements, or special course information.

3. Spell-check and proofread the document; save it as **act12-1**.

4. In Page Layout View, select the list of courses, beginning with "Nursing for Health" and ending with "The Research Process." Format for two equal columns with no line between the columns.

5. Add another blank line at the end of the document (there should be two blank paragraph marks), move the insertion point to the next-to-last paragraph mark, and add a Continuous section break.

6. Save the changes, print one copy, and clear the screen.

ACTIVITY 2

1. Open your Student Disk file **act6-2.doc** and save it as **act12-2**.

2. Search for and delete any hard page breaks.

HINT: *Choose Edit Replace. If necessary, click No Formatting for both the Find What and Replace With boxes. In the Find What box, click Special and Manual Page Break. Leave the Replace With box blank.*

3. Change to Page Layout View.

4. Remove the page numbers:
   a. Scroll to the bottom of the second page. Double-click the page number to display the Header and Footer Toolbar.
   b. Click 📖, turn off Different First Page, and click | **OK** |.
   c. Select the number in the entire footer pane and press (**Delete**). If either the page number or the centered paragraph mark remains, select again and delete.
   d. Click | **Close** |.

5. Select the entire document and change to single spacing with justified alignment.

6. With the document still selected, format it as two columns of equal width with a line between.

7. Center the title "HOME REMEDIES," then format 18-point bold, all caps, with expanded character spacing of 2 points.

8. Select the title "HOME REMEDIES" and the blank line below the title. Format them as a single-column banner; then deselect the heading and blank line.

9. Select each of the following headings (include the paragraph mark) and change the heading to a single-column banner with bold but no underline:

- "Insect Bites"
- "Poison Ivy/Poison Oak"
- "Congestion"
- "Tension Headaches"
- "Hiccups"

HINT: Click [U] to remove the underlines.

10. Select the heading "Insect Bites" and apply centered alignment, 12-point Spacing Before, 3-point Spacing After, and Keep with Next.

11. Repeat the format for the remaining headings.

12. Drag to select the ending paragraph mark in the document and format it for one column. (The text above the ending paragraph mark should still be in two columns.)

13. Change the section format for the heading "Congestion" so that it starts on a new page. (Be sure to double-click the section break following the heading, not the one preceding the heading.)

14. Insert a Continuous section break immediately preceding the section break at the bottom of the first page, so that the columns in that section will balance.

15. Insert page numbers at the bottom center of each page.

16. Save the changes to your document, print one copy, and clear the screen.

ACTIVITY 3

1. Open the Data Disk file **indians.doc** and save it in the appropriate location for Student Disk files as **act12-3**.

2. Move the insertion point to the end of the document, press (Enter) twice, and insert the Data Disk file **alone.doc**.

HINT: Choose Insert File.

3. With the insertion point at the end of the document, press (Enter), and insert the Data Disk file **hikebike.doc**.

4. Move the insertion point to the top of the document and press **Enter**. Then move the insertion point into the new blank paragraph and format the paragraph with a 3-point top border.

HINT: *Click the Top Border icon* .

5. Change the heading "THE POTAWATOMI PATH" to centered and bold with 20 percent shading.

6. Change to Page Layout View.

7. Select the text below the banner heading "THE POTAWATOMI PATH" and the first blank line below the text (Do not select the blank line that precedes the text.)

8. Format the text in two columns of equal width with a line between.

9. Change the heading "THE HEALTH RISKS OF LIVING ALONE" to centered and bold with 20 percent shading.

10. Select the three paragraphs that follow the banner heading "THE HEALTH RISKS OF LIVING ALONE" and the first blank line that follows. Format the selection in three columns of equal width.

11. Change the heading "HIKING AND BIKING ADVENTURES" to center and bold with 20 percent shading.

12. Select the two paragraphs that follow the banner heading "HIKING AND BIKING ADVENTURES" and the first blank line below. Format the selection with a Left preset.

13. Position the insertion point in the blank paragraph at the end of the document and add a 3-point bottom border.

14. Save the changes to your document, print one copy, and clear the screen.

ACTIVITY 4

IMPORTANT: The Hyphenation feature must be installed in order for you to complete this activity.

1. Open the Data Disk file **nursing.doc** and save it in the appropriate location for Student Disk files as **act12-4**.

2. Make sure that Zoom Control is set at 100%.

3. Change to Page Layout View.

4. Format all text but the title, the blank line below the heading, and the blank line at the end of the document as two columns of equal width.

5. Replace the hyphens in the following with nonbreaking hyphens:

   "$20,000–$24,000"
   "$38,800–$42,500"
   "Gisela Sjostedt-Smith"
   "Shelby-Richland Hospital"

6. Replace the spaces in the following with nonbreaking spaces:

   fifteen percent
   sixty percent
   twenty percent
   sixty-five percent

HINT: *In the Find What box, key a space and* **percent.** *In the Replace With box, click Special, click Nonbreaking Space, key* **percent,** *and click Replace All.*

7. Move the insertion point to the top of the document. Hyphenate the document automatically.

8. Insert page numbers at the bottom center of each page.

9. Save the changes to your document, print one copy, and clear the screen.

CREATE YOUR OWN • • • • • • • • • • • • • •

Write a one-page newsletter article about recent developments in office technologies. For example, you can write about portable fax machines and hand scanners. Key and format your article in newspaper-style columns with a banner over the columns. You can decide whether the columns are to be of equal or unequal width. Add paragraph borders and shading for special emphasis.

REVIEW EXERCISES

TRUE / FALSE

Each of the following statements is either true or false. Indicate your answer on the left by circling T if the statement is true or F if the statement is false.

T   F   **1.**   You must format all of a document in sections before you can add multiple-column formats.

T   F   **2.**   The number of columns is a paragraph format.

T   F   **3.**   Multiple columns can be seen in Normal View.

T   F   **4.**   The section break controls the format of the preceding section.

T   F   **5.**   To change a Continuous section break to a New Page section break, you must choose the Insert Break command.

T   F   **6.**   Newspaper-style columns can only be of equal width.

T   F   **7.**   The character for nonbreaking spaces never prints.

FILL IN THE BLANKS

Complete the following sentences by writing the correct word or words in the blanks provided.

8.   To control column breaks manually (add hard column breaks), choose the _____ command.

9.   To format with multiple columns of different widths and to add vertical lines between columns, choose the _____ command.

10. To combine all text from one file with another, choose the _____ command.

11. A(n) _____ hyphen is used to tell Word not to break a hyphenated word at the end of a line.

12. If _____ is selected in the Hyphenation dialog box, Word stops each time it reaches a word to be hyphenated and shows optional hyphens in the Hyphenate At box.

13. A(n) _____ is used to indicate two words that should be kept together.

14. A(n) _____ prints only when the word falls at the end of a line and needs to be split.

15. To control page breaks and paragraph spacing, choose the _____ command.

MATCHING

Find the key(s) or icon in the right column that matches the description in the left column, and write the appropriate letter in the blank provided at the left margin.

____ 16. nonbreaking hyphen

____ 17. nonbreaking space

____ 18. optional hyphen

____ 19. Page Layout View

____ 20. Columns

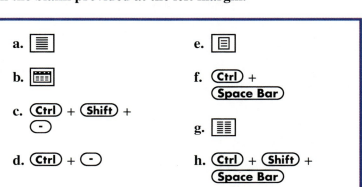

a.
b.
c. Ctrl + Shift + -
d. Ctrl + -
e.
f. Ctrl + Space Bar
g.
h. Ctrl + Shift + Space Bar

REFERENCE QUESTIONS

Referring to the *Microsoft Word User's Guide,* write the answers to the following questions in the space provided.

1. How can you adjust the distance between a paragraph border and the paragraph text?

_____

_____

_____

2. If you are hyphenating a document but have one or more paragraphs that you do not want hyphenated, how do you instruct Word not to hyphenate those particular paragraphs?

_____

_____

_____

GRAPHICS AND FRAMES

CHAPTER

13

OBJECTIVES
Upon completion of this chapter, you will be able to:

- Insert, crop, and scale a graphic.

- Add a frame to a graphic.

- Move and size frames.

- Wrap text around frames.

- Change text to a graphic.

- Format drop caps.

- Use WordArt.

- Use the drawing tools.

Preparation

1. To complete the chapter activities, you will need to access the Data Disk files TREES.DOC, GREENWAY.DOC, and FACTS.DOC.

2. To complete the chapter activities, you will need to have the Word for Windows clip art files installed. Check the *c:\winword\clipart* subdirectory to see if you have any files listed before you begin the chapter. For Exercise 13.7, you also need to have WordArt installed. WordArt is most likely installed in the *c:\windows\msapps* subdirectory.

3. You should complete all chapter exercises and activities in Page Layout View. If Word prompts you to switch to Page Layout View, click Yes.

4. Be sure to save frequently as you work; you will generally not be reminded to save until all work is completed for a document.

5. If you make mistakes as you work with the exercises in the chapter, remember to click ⟲⬇ immediately after completing the action.

6. Be sure to close Word and Windows properly. If you are using the hard drive to store your completed work, back up your files onto your formatted Student Disk, and erase your files from the directory you used on the hard drive. (Do not erase the Data Disk files unless your instructor tells you to do so.)

Introduction

Word has a number of ways to make documents more attractive. You can *import clip art,* use WordArt to shape and rotate text, add dropped capital letters *(drop caps),* and draw your own pictures. In addition to creating graphics, you can add *frames* to position graphics anywhere in a document.

Working with Graphics

One way to make your documents more attractive is to add graphics. You can insert graphics that are already prepared, known as clip art.

13.1 **Inserting a Graphic**

● ●

You can insert an entire graphics file, or you can copy and paste a graphic that is a portion of another file. In this text you will only insert entire clip art graphics files.

1. Open the Data Disk file **trees.doc** and save it in the appropriate location for Student Disk files as **chap13-1**.

2. Move the insertion point to the end of the document.

3. Insert a graphic:

a. If necessary, click Tab so you will have a full-size view of how your graphics will look when printed.

b. Choose Insert Picture. Word displays the Insert Picture dialog box.

c. If necessary, change the drive and directory so that *c:\winword\clipart* is displayed under Directories (Figure 13.1).

d. Under File Name, scroll down and click **leaf.wmf**. (If you do not see leaf. wmf, change the File Name box to *.*.)

e. If necessary, turn on Preview Picture. Word displays the graphic in the Preview box (Figure 13.2).

f. Click [**OK**]. Word inserts the graphic in your document at the insertion point.

4. Save your document, but do not print or clear the screen.

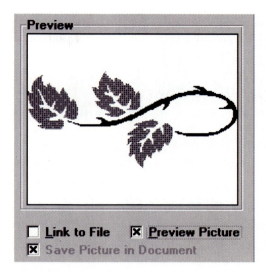

FIGURE 13.2
Preview Box in
Insert Picture
Dialog Box

FIGURE 13.1
Clipart Subdirectory
in Insert Picture
Dialog Box

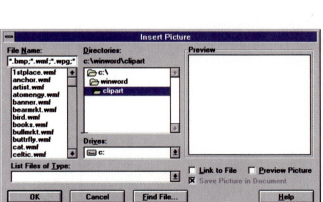

13.2

Scaling and Cropping a Graphic

When you *scale* a graphic proportionally, you change all dimensions of the graphic approximately equally. You can also scale a graphic just vertically or just horizontally, which distorts the graphic. When you *crop* the graphic, you cut off portions of the graphic that you do not want to show. Word also enables you to add white space around the graphic.

1. Click on the graphic to select it.

Eight small squares called *handles* appear. The graphic should now look like Figure 13.3.

2. Scale the graphic proportionally from the bottom right corner:

a. Position the mouse pointer on the bottom right corner handle of the graphic until the pointer changes to the diagonal sizing arrow ↖.

b. Hold down the mouse button until you see "100% High and 100% Wide" on the status bar.

c. With ↖ still displayed, drag the corner handle down and to the right until the scaling dimensions are approximately 200% High and 200% Wide; then release the mouse button. Figure 13.4 illustrates the scaled graphic.

> **TIP**
>
> To restore an imported graphic to its original size or to "uncrop" it, choose Format Picture, click Reset, and click **OK**.

IMPORTANT: Do not be concerned about scaling graphics exactly in this chapter. If you should ever need exact scaling, you can choose Format Picture and specify scaling measurements for width and height.

3. If necessary, click the down scroll bar arrow so that all of the graphic is visible on your screen.

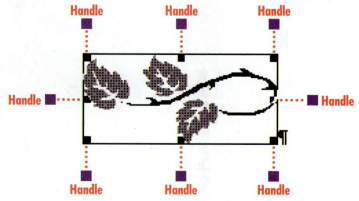

FIGURE 13.3
Selected Graphic

FIGURE 13.4
Graphic Scaled
Proportionally

4. Scale the graphic proportionally from the bottom left corner:

a. Position the mouse pointer on the bottom left corner handle.

b. When you see ↘, drag the corner handle up and to the right until the graphic is scaled at approximately 150 % High and 150 % Wide; then release the mouse button.

When you drag any corner handle of a graphic, Word scales the graphic approximately proportionally.

5. Scale the graphic disproportionally:

a. Position the mouse pointer on the middle handle on the bottom side of the graphic.

b. When the pointer changes to the vertical sizing arrow ↕, drag the handle down until the status bar displays approximately "200% High." Then release the mouse button.

When you drag any middle handle of a graphic, Word sizes the graphic disproportionally. Figure 13.5 illustrates the scaled graphic.

6. Crop the graphic to show only the first leaf on the left with its stem:

a. Position the mouse pointer on the middle handle on the right side of the graphic. (The handle appears as a white square so it can be distinguished from the dark line in the graphic.)

b. When the pointer changes to the horizontal

FIGURE 13.5
Graphic Scaled
Disproportionally

sizing arrow ↔, hold down (Shift) to display a cropping box that surrounds the handle.

c. Continue to hold down (Shift) with the cropping box displayed. Then hold the mouse button down and notice that the status bar displays "Cropping: 0" Right."

d. Still holding down (Shift), drag the handle to the left until the status bar displays approximately "Cropping 1.05" Right." Then release the mouse button. Figure 13.6 illustrates the cropped graphic.

e. Position the mouse pointer on the middle handle on the bottom side of the graphic, hold down (Shift), and drag the handle up to crop some of the white space below the leaf. When you have the bottom at the

desired location (approximately "0.2" Bottom" in the status bar), release the mouse button. Word crops the bottom side of the graphic (Figure 13.7).

7. Add white space to the graphic:

a. Position the mouse pointer on the middle handle on the left side of the graphic.

b. Hold down (Shift), and drag the handle just slightly to the left until the status bar displays "Cropping –0.05" Left." Figure 13.8 illustrates the cropped graphic.

When you hold down (Shift) and drag a handle out and away from the graphic, Word adds white space to the side of the graphic.

FIGURE 13.6
Graphic Cropped from Right

FIGURE 13.7
Graphic Cropped from Bottom

FIGURE 13.8
Cropping to Left To Add White Space

EXERCISE 13.3

Adding a Border to a Graphic

You can use the Borders Toolbar to add a border to a graphic.

1. If necessary, click [icon] on the Formatting Toolbar to display the Borders Toolbar.

2. If necessary, click on the graphic to select it (eight handles should be displayed).

3. Click the down arrow next to the Line Style box and click 1½ pt. → [1½ pt ▼]

4. Click the Outside Border icon [icon]; then click

outside the graphic to see the border (Figure 13.9).

FIGURE 13.9
Outside Border
Added to Graphic

Working with Frames

Frames can be added to graphics, objects, and text. In this chapter, you will add frames to graphics. In order to position a graphic in a particular place on the page, you must add a frame around the graphic. Once a frame is added to a graphic, the graphic can be moved anywhere within the printable area of the page. When you insert a frame, Word adds a nonprinting, simple line border around the frame. When working with frames, it is best to display the document in Page Layout View.

EXERCISE 13.4

Adding a Frame to a Graphic and Moving and Sizing the Frame

When you add a frame to a graphic, the frame is the same size as the graphic, and it includes a

nonprinting line border. You can move a frame anywhere within the document by dragging it, and you can scale (size) a frame the same way you scale a graphic.

1. If necessary, click (Tab) to switch to Page Layout View.

2. Add a frame to a graphic:

   a. Click on the graphic to select it. The eight handles should be displayed around the graphic.

   b. Choose Insert Frame.

The graphic now has a crosshatched border with sizing handles on each side (Figure 13.10). You will also notice an anchor ⚓ displayed to the right of the frame. The anchor indicates that the frame is anchored to the paragraph. When you move the frame, the anchor will move to the nearest paragraph.

FIGURE 13.10
Graphic with Frame

Anchor

3. Move the frame:

   a. If necessary, scroll up so you can see the four paragraphs of text.

   b. Position the pointer on a border of the frame.

TIP

To remove a *frame*, select the *frame* in Page Layout View, choose Format Frame, and click Remove Frame.

   c. When the pointer changes to a four-headed positioning pointer ⌖, drag the frame to the middle of the page (with the top of the frame on the blank line below the second paragraph); then release the mouse button. Word displays a dotted frame as you drag.

4. If necessary, click the left scroll bar arrow so that you can see the left margin and the anchor (Figure 13.11).

FIGURE 13.11
Frame Repositioned in Text

⚓ ¶
Planting·trees·can·help·solve·
help·reduce·erosion,·restore·
habitat·for·wildlife.¶
¶
For·information·on·national·and·
555-TREE.¶
¶
enviro
damag

local·t

When you moved the *frame*, the anchor also moved. It is now located in the left margin, to the left of the blank paragraph in which the top of the frame is positioned. (Your frame position may be slightly different from the position shown in Figure 13.11.) If you add text above the paragraph with the anchor, the graphic will move down the page with the paragraph. Notice also that the text of the following paragraph in which you positioned part of the frame is wrapped around the frame. If you want text to wrap around a graphic, you must add a frame to the graphic.

5. Format the frame for no text wrap:

a. With the frame still selected, choose Format Frame. Word displays the Frame dialog box (Figure 13.12). (Your measurements may vary.)

b. Click None; then click [**OK**]. The frame is now positioned between lines of text; text does not wrap around it (Figure 13.13).

6. Click ⌢▣ to restore the format to wrap the text around the frame.

7. Move the frame to the bottom right corner of the document by dragging it so that the bottom border of the frame aligns with the last line of text and the right border of the frame aligns with the right margin (Figure 13.14).

FIGURE 13.12
Format Frame Dialog Box

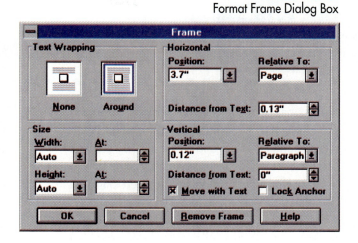

FIGURE 13.13
Frame with No Text Wrap

Trees·cool·the·atmosphere·in·hot·weather·and·provide·welcome·shade·on·a·hot·sur day.··They·render·shelter·for·wildlife.··Numerous·recreational·parks·are·situated·in

Planting·trees·can·help·solve·environmental·problems.··New·trees·can·help·reduce· erosion,·restore·damaged·ecosystems,·and·provide·habitat·for·wildlife.¶

FIGURE 13.14
Frame Positioned at
Right Margin

:s·can·help· it·for·wildlife.¶

11·1-800-555-

until the status bar displays approximately "200% Wide," then release the mouse button.

9. Delete the hyphens in the telephone number in the last paragraph and insert nonbreaking hyphens.

HINT: *Press* (Ctrl) + (Shift) + (-).

8. Scale the frame:

a. Position the mouse pointer on the middle handle on the left side of the frame.

b. When the pointer changes to ↔, drag

Inserting an Empty Frame

Many types of documents—newsletters, for example—include pictures that relate to the subject matter. Depending on available resources, pictures are either scanned and saved as graphics files to be imported or are physically pasted onto the completed document. To leave space for pictures when you are composing a document, you can insert a blank frame (also called a *placeholder*) and position it appropriately on the page. Placeholders can be inserted for any picture, text, or graphic that is to be added later.

1. Move the insertion point to the top of the document. If necessary, switch to Page Layout View.

2. If necessary, choose View Ruler to display horizontal and vertical rulers.

3. Choose Insert Frame. The pointer changes to a cross hair. ╋

4. Position the cross hair just above and to the left of the word "Whether" in the first line of the first paragraph.

5. Using the rules to guide you, hold down the mouse button, and drag down and to the right to create a frame approximately 3 inches wide and 1 inch high. Then release the mouse button. Figure 13.15 illustrates the frame you inserted.

FIGURE 13.15
Empty Frame Inserted

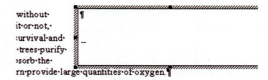

Adding Special Effects

You can also make your document more attractive by adding special effects, including dropped capital letters (drop caps), WordArt, and drawings that you create.

EXERCISE

Formatting a Drop Cap

The drop-cap format can be added to the first letter in the first word of a paragraph, or it can be added to the entire first word.

1. Format a *drop cap* for the first letter of a paragraph:

    a. Position the insertion point in the word "Can" in the first paragraph, which begins "Can you imagine . . ."

    b. Choose Format Drop Cap.

Word displays the Drop Cap dialog box (Figure 13.16). Notice that the default setting is None.

FIGURE 13.16
Format Drop Cap Dialog Box

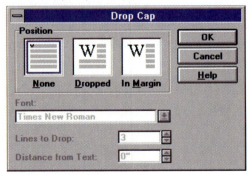

    c. Under Position, click Dropped.

    d. Open the Font box in the dialog box. Scroll up and click Arial.

    e. For the Lines to Drop box, click the down increment arrow to change the number to

2. This setting specifies the height of the *drop cap.*

    f. For Distance from Text, click the up increment arrow to change the distance to 0.1". This setting controls the amount of space between the *drop cap* and the text that follows it.

    g. Click OK .

Notice that when you have not selected text, Word automatically formats just the first letter of the paragraph as a *drop cap.* Notice also that the *drop cap* is formatted in a frame in the top left corner of the paragraph. Although you may not see the anchor clearly, the frame is anchored to the paragraph, and the text in the paragraph wraps around the frame (Figure 13.17).

FIGURE 13.17
Drop Cap in Frame

2. Format the first letter of a paragraph as a *drop cap* in the margin:

    a. Position the insertion point anywhere in the second paragraph, which begins "Trees cool the . . ."

    b. Choose Format Drop Cap, click In Margin, and click OK .

The *drop cap* is in the margin to the left of the paragraph (Figure 13.18). This option is not available for multiple-column text.

FIGURE 13.18
Drop Cap in Margin

3. Apply a border and shading to the frame:

  a. If necessary, click on the *drop cap* to select it (the crosshatched border should appear).

  Top of screen → **b.** Change the Line Style box to ¾ pt.

  c. Change the Shading box to 25%.

  d. Click the Top Border icon ▢ and the Left Border icon ▢.

  e. Deselect the *drop cap* to see the format (Figure 13.19).

FIGURE 13.19
Shaded, Bordered Drop Cap

You can apply borders and shading to any selected frame, just as you did with graphics.

4. Remove the drop-cap format:

  a. Click on the frame to select it; then choose Format Drop Cap.

  b. Under Position, click None.

  c. Click [**OK**].

5. Format the first word in a paragraph as a *drop cap:*

  a. Select the first word, "Planting" in the third paragraph, which begins "Planting trees can . . ."

  b. Choose Format Drop Cap.

  c. Click Dropped, and click [**OK**].

When you select the first word (instead of positioning the insertion point in the word), the entire word is formatted as a *drop cap* (Figure 13.20).

FIGURE 13.20
Word Formatted as Drop Cap

6. Click [icons].

7. Create *drop caps* with a border and shading for the first letter of the second and third paragraphs (be sure no text is selected before you begin this step):

  a. Position the insertion point in the second paragraph and choose Format Drop Cap.

  b. Click Dropped.

  c. Change the font to Arial, Lines to Drop to 2, and Distance from Text to 0.1".

  d. Click [**OK**].

  e. If necessary, change the Line Style box to ¾ pt.

  f. Change the Shading box to 25%.

  g. Click ▢ and ▢.

h. Repeat Steps a–g for the third paragraph.

8. Add 25 percent shading and a top and left border to the *drop cap* for the first paragraph.

9. Save the changes to your document, but do not print or clear the screen.

EXERCISE

Creating Text in WordArt

 IMPORTANT: WordArt must be installed to complete this exercise.

WordArt is a feature that you can use to enhance your documents. WordArt enables you to alter text that you key quickly and easily by changing shapes, rotating the text, and adding shadows and shading. This exercise will introduce you to many WordArt features. You may want to explore more of them on your own after you complete the exercise.

1. Position the insertion point in the blank paragraph at the beginning of the document.

2. Press ⟨Enter⟩ eight times.

3. Without moving the insertion point, choose Insert Object. Word displays the Insert Object dialog box.

4. If necessary, click the Create New folder tab to display the Create New category of the Insert Object dialog

box, as shown in Figure 13.21. (Your Object Type box may vary slightly.)

5. In the Object Type box, click Microsoft Word-Art 2.0; then click [**OK**].

Word displays the WordArt Toolbar, text entry box, and menu bar (Figure 13.22 on page 348).

6. In the text box, key **The Value of Trees**.

FIGURE 13.21
Insert Object Dialog Box

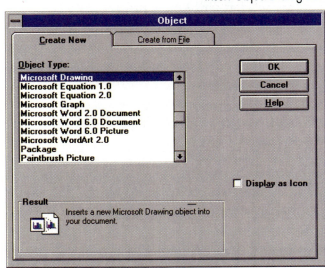

FIGURE 13.22
WordArt

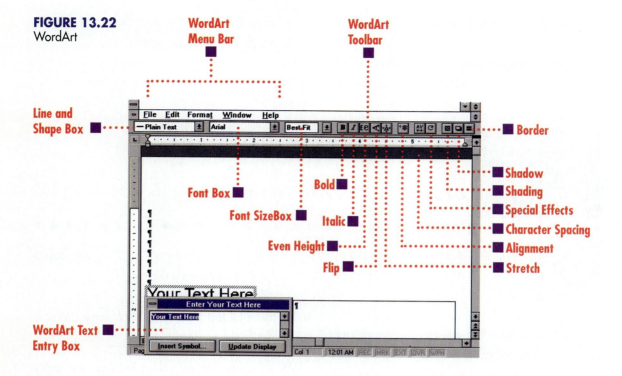

WordArt Menu Bar

WordArt Toolbar

Line and Shape Box

Border

Font Box

Bold

Shadow

Shading

Font SizeBox

Italic

Special Effects

Even Height

Character Spacing

Alignment

Flip

Stretch

WordArt Text Entry Box

7. Click the down arrow next to the Line and Shape box (currently showing "—Plain Text") to display the options shown in Figure 13.23.

8. Click the first icon in the second row. Arch Up (Curve) will be displayed in the Line and Shape box.

9. Click **B**.

10. Click the Shading icon. In the Shading dialog box (Figure 13.24 on page 349), click the first option in the second row under Style, and click **OK**.

11. Click in the document to exit WordArt.

12. Double-click the WordArt object to return to WordArt.

FIGURE 13.23
WordArt Line and Shape Options

Arch Up (Curve) (Exercise 16.7)

Button (Pour) (Comprehensive Project 2)

Wave 1 (Activity 3)

FIGURE 13.24
WordArt Shading Dialog Box

■ **Click this style icon for
Exercise 13.7 and Activity 3.**

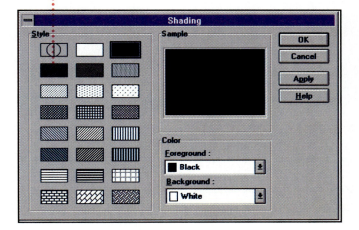

FIGURE 13.25
WordArt Shadow Box

■ **Click this style icon
for Exercise 13.7.**

■ **Click this
icon for
Comprehensive
Project 2.**

13. Click the Shadow icon [⬜]. In the Shadow box (Figure 13.25), click the second option in the first row.

14. Click in the document to exit WordArt.

15. With the WordArt object still selected, insert a frame.

16. Drag the frame approximately to the center of the page and up to the top of the document (align the top of the frame with the first blank paragraph on the page); then release the mouse button (Figure 13.26).

17. Save the changes to your document, but do not print or clear the screen.

FIGURE 13.26
WordArt Object Positioned
at Top Center of Document

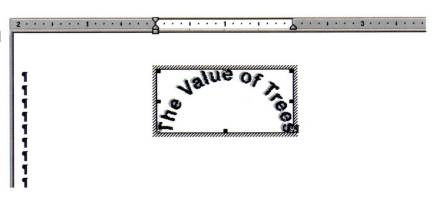

Using the Drawing Tools

Exercise 13.8 will introduce you to a few of the Word drawing features. Exercise 13.9 will describe several more functions. After you practice using the features introduced in these exercise, you may want to explore more of them on your own.

EXERCISE

13.8

Using the Drawing Tools

In this exercise you will use the drawing tools to add a tree to the WordArt object, as shown in Figure 13.27.

FIGURE 13.27
Tree Trunk and Branches

1. If necessary, click the Drawing icon on the Standard Toolbar ⬚ to display the Drawing Toolbar (Figure 13.28).

2. Create a straight line:

   a. Click the Line icon ◺ on the Drawing Toolbar. The pointer changes to a cross hair.

   b. Position the cross hair right under the middle of the arch you created in WordArt, drag down about 1½ inches (to just above the empty frame), and release the mouse button. This line will be the trunk of the tree.

   c. Click the Line Style icon ▦ on the Drawing Toolbar, and click the fourth line from the top (the thickest line). Word changes the trunk of the tree to a thick line.

FIGURE 13.28
Drawing Toolbar

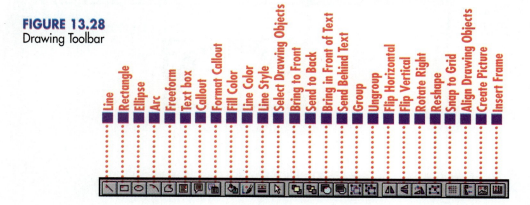

IMPORTANT: All drawings you create will now have the new line style until you change the line style.

3. Click .

4. Position the cross hair in the middle of the tree trunk, and drag out and up about 1 inch to create a branch.

5. Click ⌨ and click the third line from the top. Word changes the branch to a thickness less than the trunk.

6. Create several more branches on both sides of the trunk similar to Figure 13.27. Word will apply the same line style to all branches. (You must, however, click ◲ to create each branch.)

7. Save the changes to your document, print one copy, and clear the screen. (Be patient; WordArt may take some time to print.)

EXERCISE

Further Exploring the Drawing Tools

This exercise will guide you through other drawing features.

1. Open a new document window. If necessary, click ◲ to display the drawing tools.

2. Draw a rectangle:

a. Click the Rectangle icon ▢ on the Drawing Toolbar; then move the pointer into the document window. The pointer changes to a cross hair.

b. Position the cross hair where you want the drawing to begin.

c. Drag the cross hair to the right and then

down. Release the mouse button. Word creates a perfectly proportioned rectangle.

3. Draw an ellipse:

a. Click the Ellipse icon ◯ on the Drawing Toolbar; then move the pointer into the document window. The pointer changes to a cross hair.

b. Position the cross hair where you want the drawing to begin.

c. Drag the cross hair to the right and then down. Release the mouse button. Word creates a perfectly proportioned ellipse.

4. Draw an arc:

a. Click the Arc icon ⬒ on the Drawing Toolbar; then move the pointer into the document window. The pointer changes to a cross hair.

b. Position the cross hair where you want the drawing to begin.

c. Drag the cross hair in the directions you want to arch the arc (in this case, drag to the right and then down), and release the mouse button. Word creates an arc.

5. Fill in a square, rectangle, circle, or ellipse drawing:

a. Select the drawing that you want to fill.

HINT: *Move the mouse until you see ⬉; then click on an edge of the graphic.*

b. Click the Fill Color icon 🖌 on the Drawing Toolbar. Word displays a color

box as shown in Figure 13.29. (Colors shown may vary.)

If you have a color monitor, you will see colors for options. If your printer has the capability to print colors, you can print your drawings in color.

FIGURE 13.29
Fill Colors

c. Click one of the boxes to add shading or a color. Word fills the drawing with your selection.

IMPORTANT: All shapes you draw except lines and arcs will have the new fill color until you change it again. Click None if you prefer no fill color for other drawings.

6. Draw a free-form shape:

a. Click the Freeform icon 🖉 on the Drawing Toolbar; then move the pointer into the document window. The pointer changes to a cross hair.

b. Position the cross hair where you want the drawing to begin.

c. Drag the cross hair anywhere on the screen to create your drawing. You can draw a picture or even write your name.

d. Double-click when you are ready to stop drawing in free-form.

TIP

Press (**Backspace**) to delete the last line segment as you draw a free-form shape.

7. If desired, click [icon], the Line Color icon [icon], or [icon] to change the appearance of your graphic.

8. Clear the screen. It is not necessary to save this document.

COMPUTER ACTIVITIES

ACTIVITY 1

1. Open the Data Disk file **dream.doc** and save it as **act13-1**.

2. Delete the default tabs at the beginning of each paragraph.

3. Add a blank line between the two paragraphs of text and change the document to single spacing.

4. If necessary, change to Page Layout View.

5. Position the insertion point at the end of the document and insert the clip art file **jet.wmf**.

6. Scale the graphic to approximately 50% High and 50% Wide.

7. Add a frame to the graphic.

8. Reposition the frame so that the top left corner of the frame is aligned at the top left corner of the second paragraph. If necessary, choose Format Frame and wrap the text around the frame.

9. Save the changes to the document, print one copy, and clear the screen.

ACTIVITY 2

1. Open your Data Disk file **greenway.doc** and save it as **act13-2**.

2. If necessary, change to Page Layout View.

3. With the insertion point positioned at the beginning of the document, insert the clip art file **cityscpe.wmf**.

4. Crop the graphic so that only the top view of the city is displayed.

HINT: *Crop from the bottom up to the horizontal line that divides the views of the city.*

5. Add a frame to the graphic.

6. Move the frame, aligning it so that the top half of the frame is positioned above the first para-

graph and the lower half is positioned within the paragraph (about halfway across the paragraph).

7. Format the first letter in the paragraph as a *drop cap*. Use the Dropped position, and change the font to Arial, Lines to Drop to 2, and Distance from Text to 0.1".

8. Add a top and left border to the *drop cap,* and add 20% shading.

9. Save the changes to your document, print one copy, and clear the screen.

ACTIVITY 3

1. Open your Data Disk file **facts.doc** and save it as **act13-3**.

2. With the insertion point at the top of the document, press **Enter** ten times.

3. If necessary, change to Page Layout View.

4. Move the insertion point up to the sixth blank paragraph from the top.

5. Insert a WordArt object and key **Did You Know?**

6. Use the icons and options to change the appearance as follows:
   a. Line and Shape: fifth option in the fifth row. ("Wave 1" will show in the Line and Shape box after the icon has been selected.)
   b. Bold
   c. Shading: first option in the second row under Style.

7. Insert a frame around the WordArt object.

8. Reposition the object so that it is centered above the first paragraph.

9. Save the changes to your document, print one copy, and clear the screen.

CREATE YOUR OWN ● ● ● ● ● ● ● ● ● ● ● ●

Use Word's drawing tools to create your own graphic. If you want to, key text and use your drawing to accompany the text.

REVIEW EXERCISES

TRUE / FALSE

Each of the following statements is either true or false. Indicate your answer on the left by circling T if the statement is true or F if the statement is false.

T   F   1. When a graphic is scaled, its dimensions are always changed proportionally.

T   F   2. Frames can be positioned anywhere within the printable area of the page.

T   F   3. When you drag a corner handle of a graphic, the graphic dimensions change proportionally.

T   F   4. In order to position a graphic in a particular place on the page, you must add a frame around the graphic.

T   F   5. You must drag across a graphic to select it.

T   F   6. Graphics can be resized, but frames cannot.

FILL IN THE BLANKS

Complete the following sentences by writing the correct word or words in the blanks provided.

7. Frames can be inserted as _____ for pictures, text, or graphics that are to be added later.

8. To insert an empty frame, choose the _____ command.

9. To insert a clip art graphic in a document, choose the _____ command.

10. Resizing graphics is called _____.

11. Cutting off portions of a graphic is called _____.

12. To wrap text around the frame, choose the _____ command.

13. To format a letter as a dropped capital letter, choose the _____ command.

14. To create text in WordArt, choose the _____ command.

MATCHING

Find the icon on the right that matches the description on the left, and write the appropriate letter in the blank provided at the left margin.

____ **15.** Positioning Pointer

____ **16.** Cross hair

____ **17.** Vertical Sizing Arrow

____ **18.** Drawing

____ **19.** Freeform

____ **20.** Arc

a. +

b. ⌨

c. ⬉

d. ⬂

e. ▤

f. ⬀

g. ↕

h. ⌐

i. ⬔

j. 🖌

REFERENCE QUESTIONS

Referring to the *Microsoft Word User's Guide,* write the answers to the following questions in the space provided.

1. Graphics files are generally quite large; and when you insert a graphic in a document, the graphic increases the size of the document substantially. How can you reduce the size of the document after the graphic is inserted?

_____

_____

_____

2. Can you add a frame around a table cell or an entire table?

_____

_____

_____

MORE ON GRAPHICS AND FRAMES

OBJECTIVES
Upon completion of this chapter, you will be able to:

- ■ Insert empty frames, insert text in frames, and frame text.

- ■ Position a frame exactly and with a reference point.

- ■ Print side headings in the left margin.

- ■ Create sidebars.

- ■ Add shading to the contents of frames.

- ■ Create a pull quote.

- ■ Repeat frame contents on multiple pages.

Preparation

1. To complete the chapter activities, you will need to access the Student Disk files CHAP12-2.DOC, ACT12-3.DOC, CHAP6-3.DOC, and ACT12-2.DOC. You will also need to access the Data Disk files BROCHURE.DOC and HEALTH.DOC.

2. You should complete all chapter exercises and activities in Page Layout View. If Word prompts you to switch to Page Layout View, click Yes.

3. Be sure to save frequently as you work; you will generally not be reminded to save until all work is completed for a document.

4. If you make mistakes as you work with the exercises in the chapter, remember to click ⟲⊡ immediately after completing the action.

5. Be sure to close Word and Windows properly. If you are using the hard drive to store your completed work, back up your files onto your formatted Student Disk, and erase your files from the directory you used on the hard drive. (Do not erase the Data Disk files unless your instructor tells you to do so.)

Introduction

In Chapter 13 you learned to insert frames around graphics so you could position the graphics anywhere on the page. You also learned to insert empty frames as placeholders for graphics. In this chapter you will insert frames as placeholders, insert frames and key text in the frames, and frame text.

In Chapter 13 you dragged frames to position them approximately where you wanted the graphics to appear. You can position a frame in an exact location by selecting preset positions or keying measurements in the Format Frame dialog box. A frame can be positioned both horizontally and vertically. As shown in Figure 14.1, for preset horizontal positions you can select left, right, or center. For mirror (facing) pages you can select inside or outside. As shown in Figure 14.2, for preset vertical positions you can select top, bottom, or center. In addition to selecting a preset position or keying a measurement, you can set the frame relative to a reference point such as a margin, a page, a paragraph, or the edge of a column. In Exercises 14.1 and 14.2, you will finalize a document that will be printed as a mailing brochure.

FIGURE 14.1
Fixed Horizontal Frame Positioning

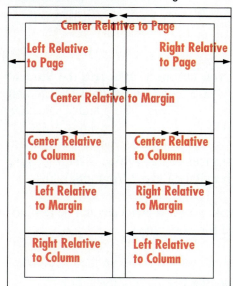

FIGURE 14.2
Fixed Vertical Frame Positioning

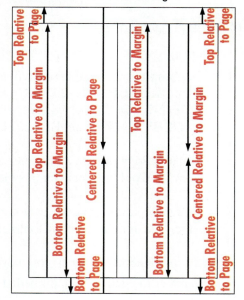

EXERCISE

14.1 Positioning Frames Exactly with a Reference Point

1. Open the Data Disk file **brochure.doc** and save it in the appropriate location for Student Disk files as **chap14-1**.

2. If necessary, switch to Page Layout View.

3. Go to Section 4.

HINT: *Double-click the page number on the status bar.*

The insertion point should now be in the left column that begins with the paragraph "So that is what we are doing . . ."

4. Insert a frame approximately 1 inch wide by 1 inch high, starting toward the middle of the paragraph that begins, "So that is what we are doing . . ."

HINT: *Choose Insert Frame and drag to draw the frame, using the rulers as your guideline.*

IMPORTANT: You do not need to be concerned with exact sizing or placement of any empty frame you insert in this chapter. All empty frames you insert in this chapter will initially be 1 by 1 inch, but you will

adjust their size and placement after you insert them.

IMPORTANT: Although size and placement of the frames you insert is not important, the position of the *anchor* is critical. The anchor for the frame should be displayed at the top left corner of the paragraph in which you just inserted a frame. Scroll left if necessary to verify the position of the anchor. If the *anchor* for any frame you insert in this chapter is attached to the wrong location, simply drag the anchor to the correct location.

5. With the frame selected, choose Format Frame. The dialog box shown in Figure 14.3 on page 362 appears, although your settings will be different.

6. Under Size, make the following changes:

   a. If necessary, click the down arrow next to the Width box and click Exactly.

   b. Double-click the measurement in the At box (for Width) to select it; then key **1.75**.

   c. Click the down arrow next to the Height box and click Exactly.

d. Double-click the measurement in the At box (for Height) to select it; then key **1.2**.

Word will size the frame to exactly 1.75 inches wide and 1.2 inches high.

7. Under Horizontal, make the following changes:

  a. Click the down arrow next to the Position box and click Center.

  b. Click the down arrow next to the Relative To box and click Column.

  c. Leave the default setting of 0.13" in the Distance from Text box.

Word will position the frame horizontally in the center of the column and will leave 0.13 inch of white space between the text and the left and right sides of the frame.

8. Under Vertical, make the following changes:

  a. Double-click the measurement in the Position box to select it; then key **.65**.

  b. If necessary, click the down arrow next to the Relative To box and click Paragraph.

  c. Double-click the measurement in the Distance from Text box to select it; then key **.13**.

  d. If necessary, turn on Move with Text.

Word will position the frame 0.65 inch down from the top of the paragraph and will leave 0.13 inch of white space between the text and the top and bottom sides of the frame. By turning on Move

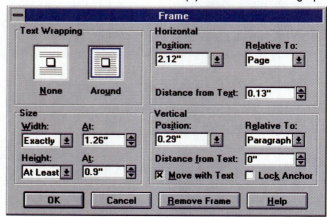

with Text, you instruct Word to move the frame up or down on the page as you insert or delete paragraphs above or below the frame.

9. When the dialog box looks like Figure 14.4, click **OK**.

Word sizes and places the frame exactly as instructed in the left column. If necessary, scroll to

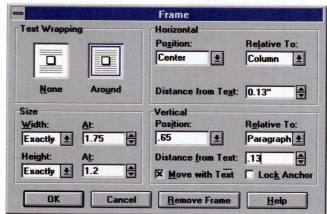

the left and notice that the frame is still anchored to the paragraph (Figure 14.5).

FIGURE 14.5
Frame Positioned in First Paragraph

So·that·is·what·we·are·doing--helping· our·members·to·exercise·properly,·

achieve·a·healthful·diet,·and·ultimately· improve·their·health·and·well-being.··We·

IMPORTANT: Page lay-outs vary, depending on your selected printer. As you work with positioning frames with exact measurements in this chapter, you may find that the frame would look better at a different position. If necessary, drag the frame or change the position measurements in the Format Frame dialog box.

10. Scroll down and position the insertion point in the right column, in the paragraph that begins, "You can still count . . ."

11. Insert a frame approximately 1 by 1 inch, starting toward the middle of the paragraph.

IMPORTANT: The *anchor* for the frame should be displayed next to the specified paragraph in the right column.

12. With the frame selected, choose Format Frame and format the frame as follows:

   a. Under Size, set the width exactly at **1.5"**, and set the height exactly at **.75"**.

   b. Under Horizontal, position the frame at the center relative to the column. Distance from Text should be 0.13".

   c. Under Vertical, position the frame at the bottom relative to the margin. Distance from Text should be 0".

   d. Do not turn on Move with Text. (If you want the frame positioned at the bottom, you do not want the frame to move if the text moves.)

   e. Click OK .

Word positions the frame horizontally in the center of the column. Vertically, the frame is positioned so that the bottom of the frame is aligned with the bottom margin (Figure 14.6). (The text shown may vary.)

FIGURE 14.6
Frame Positioned at
Bottom Center of Second Column

You·can·still·count·on·our·fitness· trainers·to·assist·you·with·the·new·health·

13. Move the insertion point to the end of the document and insert a frame approximately 1 by 1 inch somewhere to the right of the company address.

IMPORTANT: The anchor for the frame should be displayed next to one of the paragraphs containing the company address at the left.

14. With the frame selected, choose Format Frame and format the frame as follows:

   a. Under Size, set the width exactly at **1**", and set the height exactly at **1**".

   b. Under Horizontal, position the frame at **6.45**" relative to the page. Distance from Text should be **0.13**".

   c. Under Vertical, position the frame at **5.7**" relative to the page. Distance from Text should be 0".

   d. Do not turn on Move with Text.

   e. Click [OK].

Word positions the frame horizontally 6.45 inches from the left edge of the page and vertically 5.7 inches from the top edge of the page.

15. Scroll to the right. Position the insertion point in the frame and key the following lines, centered and single-spaced, as shown in Figure 14.7. Press (Enter) after each line except the last:

Bulk Rate
U.S. Postage
PAID
Columbus, OH
Permit No. 851

FIGURE 14.7
Keying Text in a Frame

16. Save the changes to your document, but do not clear the screen.

Adding Side Headings in the Left Margin

1. Go to page 3.

2. Choose File Page Setup. If necessary, click the Margins folder tab.

Notice that the left margin in this section of the document is set at 2.45 inches. This wide left margin can accommodate side headings positioned in the left margin.

3. Click [Cancel].

4. Select the first paragraph heading, "Body Strength." Do not include the period or the two blank spaces in the selection.

5. Apply the bold format.

6. With the text still selected, choose Insert Frame.

Word inserts a frame the same size as the selected text and places a simple line border around the frame (Figure 14.8).

FIGURE 14.8
Framed Heading within a Paragraph

Body·Strength¶ ⚓Many·of·you·
strength.··Our·f
achieve·strength·gains·quickly.··Y

7. With the frame selected, choose Format Frame and format the frame as a side heading:

   a. Under Size, set the width exactly at **1.2"**. If necessary, click the down arrow next to the Height box and click Auto.

   b. Under Horizontal, position the frame at the left relative to the page. Distance from Text should be 0.13".

   c. Under Vertical, position the frame at **0"** relative to the paragraph. Distance from Text should be 0".

   d. If necessary, turn on Move with Text.

   e. Turn on Lock Anchor.

   f. When the dialog box looks like Figure 14.9, click OK .

Word will position the frame horizontally in the left margin, aligned with the page. Vertically, the frame is positioned 0 inches down from the top of the paragraph to which it is anchored. With Height set at Auto, Word adjusts the frame size vertically so that all the text will fit within the frame.

   Turning on Lock Anchor locks the anchor to the paragraph. If the paragraph is moved to the next page, the frame will also move to the next

page. A Locked Anchor ⚓ is displayed to the left of the paragraph to which the frame is anchored. You cannot reposition a locked anchor.

8. You do not want a printed border around your side headings, so remove the border from the frame.

HINT: Click [▦] on the Borders Toolbar.

9. Click in the paragraph to the right to ensure that the printable border has been removed. (A border still displays on the screen when the frame is selected.)

FIGURE 14.9
Settings for Side Headings Framed in Margin

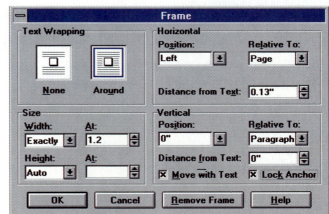

10. Delete the period and two blank spaces at the beginning of the paragraph (Figure 14.10).

FIGURE 14.10
Completed Side Heading in Left Margin

¶
¶
Body·Strength¶   Many·of·you·
              trainers·know·

11. Repeat Steps 4 through 10 to format each remaining side heading as bold text in frames positioned in the left margin. If a heading ends on a different page than its associated text, add one or two blank lines above the heading.

12. Select the blank paragraph above and the paragraph containing text to the right of the margin side heading "Body Toning."

When you select the two paragraphs, the frame containing the side heading is automatically selected, because the frame is anchored and locked to the paragraph.

13. Cut the paragraph and paste it on the blank line below "Body Strength."

The frame anchor was locked to the paragraph, so when the paragraph was moved to a new page, the frame moved with the paragraph.

14. Save the changes to your document, print one copy, and clear the screen.

14.3 Creating a Sidebar with a Border and Shading

A *sidebar* is supplemental text that is added to a main document such as a magazine or newspaper article. It is usually displayed in a boxed area and sometimes is shaded.

1. Open your Student Disk file **chap12-2.doc** and save it as **chap14-2**.

get test the size you want it first.

2. Select the first heading, "History," and the paragraph mark that follows the heading. Do not select the section break.

3. Press ⟨Delete⟩.

4. Select the paragraph beginning "The Greeks were the first . . ."

HINT: *Double-click in the selection bar next to the paragraph.*

5. Insert a frame around the text.

6. Choose Format Frame and position the frame as follows:

    a. Under Size, set the width exactly at **4.5**", and set the height to at least **4.5**".

    b. Under Horizontal, position the frame at the right relative to the margin. Distance from Text should be 0.13".

    c. Under Vertical, position the frame at the bottom relative to the margin. Distance from Text should be 0".

    d. Do not turn on Move with Text or Lock Anchor.

e. Click [OK].

Word will size the frame to exactly 4.5 inches wide and at least 4.5 inches high. The frame is positioned next to the right and bottom margins.

7. With the frame still selected, apply 10%

shading. Figure 14.11 illustrates the bottom portion of your sidebar. (The text next to the frame may vary.)

8. Save the changes to your document, but do not clear the screen.

FIGURE 14.11
Position of Sidebar
Article

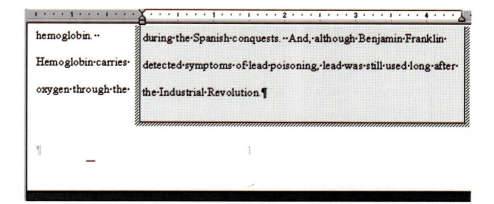

EXERCISE

14.4 Creating Pull Quotes

A *pull quote* emphasizes a passage from a document such as a magazine article. To create a pull quote, you copy the text that you want to emphasize and insert the text in a frame. The frame can be positioned anywhere on the page and may even include a border and shading. For further emphasis, you can add a bold format and increase the font size of the pull-quote text.

1. Move the insertion point to the top of the document.

2. Search for the sentence that begins. "Lead poisoning is a health problem …" When Word locates the sentence, cancel the dialog box and drag to select the sentence.

3. Click 🖹 to copy the text to the Clipboard.

4. Scroll up and position the insertion point in the first paragraph in the left column, under the heading "Symptoms of Lead Poisoning."

5. Insert a frame approximately 1 inch by 1 inch, starting toward the middle of the paragraph.

IMPORTANT: The anchor should be to the left of the paragraph, not the heading.

6. If necessary, position the insertion point in the frame. Click 🗐 to insert the contents of the Clipboard.

Notice that the frame size automatically adjusts to fit the pasted text.

7. Select the text in the frame and change the text to 14-point bold. Again, the frame size automatically adjusts.

8. Remove the border from the frame.

9. Format the frame as follows:

a. Under Size, set the width exactly at **1.9"**, and set the height at Auto.

b. Under Horizontal, center the frame relative to the page. Distance from Text should be 0.13".

c. Under Vertical, center the frame relative to the page. Distance from Text should be **0.13"**.

d. Do not turn on Move with Text or Lock Anchor.

e. Click [OK]. Your pull-quote frame should now look similar to that in Figure 14.12. (The text on both sides may vary.)

10. Move the insertion point to the top of the document.

11. Search for the sentence that begins, "At this time . . ." and copy the entire sentence to the Clipboard.

HINT: *The sentence may be split between pages and may appear in two different columns. Hold* Ctrl *and click to select the sentence.*

12. Deselect the sentence, then insert a frame approximately 1 inch by 1 inch, starting somewhere toward the middle of the next paragraph that begins, "Adults are primarily at risk . . ." Be sure the anchor is to the left of the paragraph.

13. Paste the contents of the Clipboard in the frame, and change the text to 14-point bold.

14. Remove the border from the frame.

FIGURE 14.12
Pull Quote

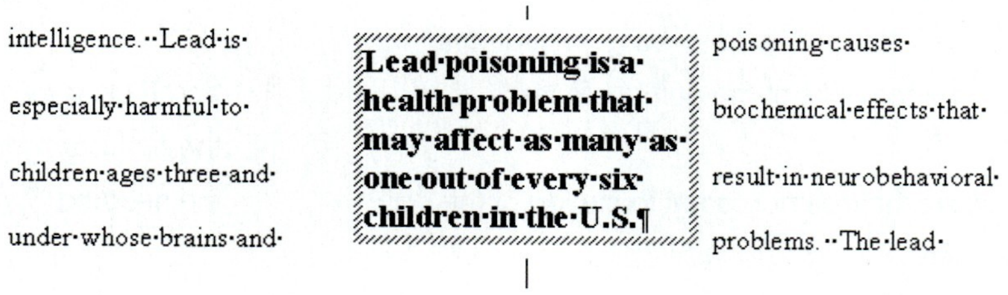

intelligence. · · Lead · is ·
especially · harmful · to ·
children · ages · three · and ·
under · whose · brains · and ·

Lead·poisoning·is·a·health·problem·that·may·affect·as·many·as·one·out·of·every·six·children·in·the·U.S.¶

poisoning · causes ·
biochemical · effects · that ·
result · in · neurobehavioral ·
problems. · · The · lead ·

15. Format the frame as follows:

a. Under Size, set the width exactly at **1.9** ", and set the height at Auto.

b. Under Horizontal, center the frame relative to the page. Distance from Text should be 0.13".

c. Under Vertical, set the position at **1**" relative to the margin. Distance from Text should be **0.13**".

d. Do not turn on Move with Text or Lock Anchor.

e. Click [OK]. Your second pull quote should look similar to the one in Figure 14.13. (The text on both sides may vary.)

16. Save the changes to your document, but do not clear the screen.

FIGURE 14.13
Second Pull Quote

→ Adults·are·primarily·
at·risk·for·lead·poisoning·
due·to·exposure·in·the·
workplace.··Standards·exist·to·limit·lead·

**At·this·time·it·is·
believed·that·the·
damage·from·lead·is·
permanent.¶**

In·adults·lead·poisoning·can·
trigger·high·blood·pressure,·
anemia,·and·reproductive·
system·disorders.··Lead·poisoning·can·

E X E R C I S E

Repeating Frame Contents on Multiple Pages

You can repeat frame contents on every page of a document by inserting a framed item in a header or footer and positioning the frame where you want the contents to print.

1. Move the insertion point to the top of the document.

2. Choose View Header and Footer and click the Show/Hide Document Text icon 🖹 on the Header and Footer Toolbar.

The document will no longer be displayed on the screen, making it easier for you to work with the framed graphic you will insert.

3. Open the Data Disk file **health.doc**, which contains a framed graphic created in Word-Art.

4. Click on the frame to select it; then click 🖺 to copy the frame and its contents to the Clipboard.

5. Close HEALTH.DOC.

6. With the insertion point positioned in the header pane, click 🖺 to insert the contents of the Clipboard.

7. Drag the graphic to the left out of the header pane.

8. With the frame still selected, format the frame as follows:

    a. Under Size, set the width and height at Auto.

    b. Under Horizontal, position the frame **0.5**" relative to the page. Distance from Text should be 0.13".

    c. Under Vertical, center the frame relative to the page. Distance from Text should be 0".

    d. Do not turn on Move with Text or Lock Anchor.

    e. Click | OK |.

9. Click 🗗 so you can see your repeating frame header next to the dimmed text (Figure 14.14).

10. Close the header pane. The framed graphic is dimmed in the left margin next to the text.

IMPORTANT: **This frame is contained within the header for the document. If you want to change the position of the frame, you must first choose View Header and Footer before you can select the frame and begin to work with it.**

FIGURE 14.14
Repeating Frame Header

End of Section

Header and Footer
Close

al·Risks¶

→ Lead·is·commonly·found·in·the·
modern·environment·in·air,·soil,·food,·
drinking·water,·and·house·paint. ··Lead·is·
a·heavy·metal·that·affects·human·health·

bloodstream·
Although·nea
absorb·lead,·i
in·the·bones.¶

11. Click 🔍.

12. Click ▦ and drag across the grid until you see "1 x 5 Pages" (or 2 x 3 Pages if your document has 6 pages). Then release the mouse button to display a reduced view of all five or six pages (Figure 14.15).

Notice that the WordArt graphic appears in the left margin on every page of the document.

13. Close Print Preview, save the changes to your document, print one copy, and clear the screen.

FIGURE 14.15
Reduced View of Five Pages in Print Preview

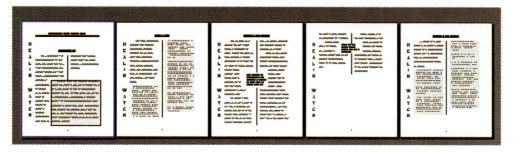

COMPUTER ACTIVITIES

ACTIVITY 1

1. Open your Student Disk file **act12-3.doc** and save it as **act14-1**.

2. Insert an empty frame (approximately 1 by 1 inch) as a placeholder toward the middle of the first column, under the article entitled "THE POTAWATOMI PATH." The anchor should be to the left of the paragraph, not the heading.

3. Format the frame as follows:

    a. The frame should be exactly 0.75" wide and exactly 0.75" high.

    b. The frame should be positioned horizontally left relative to the margin, with a distance from text of 0.13".

    c. The frame should be positioned vertically at 0" relative to the paragraph, with a distance from text of 0".

    d. Move with Text should be turned on, but Lock Anchor should be off.

4. Insert an empty frame (approximately 1 by 1 inch) as a placeholder toward the middle of the first paragraph in the first column under the article entitled "THE HEALTH RISKS OF LIV-ING ALONE." The anchor should be with the paragraph, not the heading.

5. Format the frame as follows:

    a. The frame should be exactly 1.25" wide and exactly 1.25" high.

    b. The frame should be positioned horizontally centered relative to the page, with a distance from text of 0.13".

    c. The frame should be positioned vertically at 3.3" relative to the margin, with a distance from text of 0".

    d. Move with Text and Lock Anchor should be off.

6. Insert an empty frame (approximately 1 by 1 inch) as a placeholder toward the middle of the paragraph that begins, "Each year we help . . ." under the article entitled "HIKING AND BIK-ING ADVENTURES." The anchor should be with the paragraph, not the heading. Do not be concerned if the frame itself appears in the previous section.

7. Format the frame as follows:

    a. The frame should be exactly 1" wide and at least 0.5" high.

b. The frame should be positioned horizontally right relative to the margin, with a distance from text of 0.13".

c. The frame should be positioned vertically at 8.5" relative to the page, with a distance from text of 0".

d. Move with Text and Lock Anchor should be off.

8. Save the changes to your document, print one copy, and clear the screen.

ACTIVITY 2

1. Open your Student Disk file **chap6-3.doc** and save it as **act14-2**.

2. If necessary, delete any hard page breaks.

3. Remove the header and footer:

   a. Choose View Header and Footer.

   b. Click [📖], turn off Different First Page, and click | **OK** |.

   c. Delete the text in the header pane.

   d. Click [📄] and delete the footer text.

   e. Click | **Close** |.

4. Position the insertion point on the first blank line below the heading "The Effects of Physical Activity on Health and Fitness," and insert a Continuous section break.

5. Insert another Continuous section break in the blank line directly above the company name and address at the end of the document.

6. Move the insertion point up to Section 2 above the section break, and change the left margin to 2.5" to accommodate side headings in the left margin.

HINT: *Choose File Page Setup and click the Margins folder tab.*

7. Remove the underline format for each side heading.

8. In Page Layout View, select each side heading (but not the following paragraph marks). Insert a frame and format the contents of each frame as follows:

   a. Change the text to 14-point bold.

   b. Add 20% shading.

9. Deselect the frame; then delete the two paragraph marks following each frame (not the one right next to the frame for the anchor).

10. Size and position each frame so that the side heading is positioned in the left margin:

    a. Size each frame exactly at 1.25" wide, and select Auto for the height.

    b. Position the frame horizontally left relative to the page, with a distance from text of 0.13".

    c. Position the frame vertically 0" relative to the paragraph, with a distance from text of 0".

    d. Turn on Move with Text and Lock Anchor.

HINT: *After you format the first frame, select each remaining frame and choose Edit Repeat.*

11. Insert a page number at the bottom center of each page.

12. Save the changes to your document, print one copy, and clear the screen.

ACTIVITY 3

1. Open your Student Disk file **act12-2.doc** and save it as **act14-3**.

2. Search for the sentence that begins, "Home remedies make everyday . . ."

3. Copy the sentence except for the tab to the Clipboard, then deselect the sentence.

4. Create a pull quote by inserting a frame (approximately 1 by 1 inch) in the first paragraph in the first column and pasting the contents of the Clipboard into the frame.

5. Format the contents of the frame as follows:

    a. Remove the border from the frame.

    b. Format the text in 14-point bold.

    c. Add 10 percent shading.

6. Format the frame as follows:

    a. Size the frame so that it is exactly 2" wide, and select Auto for height.

    b. Position the frame horizontally centered relative to the page, with a distance from text of 0.13".

    c. Position the frame vertically 1" relative to the paragraph with a distance from text of 0.13".

    d. Lock Anchor should be off.

7. Save the changes to your document, print one copy, and clear the screen.

CREATE YOUR OWN

Design a one- or two-page newsletter describing events at your school. Use appropriate headings and column formats. Insert placeholders for pictures of people mentioned in your newsletter. Include at least one pull quote in the newsletter and a sidebar article. Use WordArt, borders, shading, and the drawing tools as desired. Size and position frames as needed.

REVIEW EXERCISES

TRUE / FALSE

Each of the following statements is either true or false. Indicate your answer on the left by circling T if the statement is true or F if the statement is false.

T   F   **1.**   Frames can only be positioned relative to a margin or to a column.

T   F   **2.**   Frames can be positioned in headers and footers.

T   F   **3.**   Pull quotes can be framed and set off with larger font sizes.

T   F   **4.**   To repeat frame contents on every page of a document, you insert the framed item in the document and then choose View Header and Footer.

FILL IN THE BLANKS

Complete the following sentences by writing the correct word or words in the blanks provided.

5.   If you want a frame to move as you insert or delete paragraphs above or below the frame, turn on _____.

6.   To position a frame in an exact location, choose the _____ command.

7.   To format a frame in the left margin, you must position the frame horizontally relative to the _____.

8.   When a passage in an article is emphasized in a frame, it is called a(n) _____.

9.   Supplemental text that is added to a magazine or newspaper article is called a(n) _____.

10.   To lock an anchor to a paragraph, choose the _____ command.

REFERENCE QUESTIONS

Referring to the *Microsoft Word User's Guide,* write the answers to the following questions in the space provided.

1. After inserting a frame at the top of a document, you decide you want to add text above the frame. What should you do?

   _____

   _____

   _____

2. How do you print side headings in the margins on facing pages?

   _____

   _____

   _____

COMPREHENSIVE PROJECT 2

PREPARATION

1. To complete the project activities, you will need to access the Data Disk files NATURE5. PCX, THOMPSON.DOC, POISON.DOC, CEO.DOC, VITAMINS.DOC, ALLIANCE.DOC, EXPO.DOC, NUTRIENT.DOC, TELLUS.DOC, and FAX.DOC.

2. The Hyphenation feature must be installed in order to complete one of the steps in the project.

3. To install some of the graphics in this project, the PC Paintbrush (PCX) filter and WordArt must be installed.

4. Remember to save frequently as you work.

5. You should complete all of the project in Page Layout View. If Word prompts you to switch to Page Layout View, click Yes.

6. If you are unsure about how to complete an instruction, refer to the information provided in Unit 4.

7. If you make mistakes as you work with the project, remember to click ⟲⟳ immediately after completing the action.

8. When you have completed the project, be sure to close Word and Windows properly. If you are using the hard drive to store your completed work, back up your files onto your formatted Student Disk, and erase your files from the directory you used on the hard drive. (Do not erase the Data Disk files unless your instructor tells you to do so.)

PREPARING A NEWSLETTER

In this project you will format a three-page newsletter. All of the articles for the newsletter are stored in separate Data Disk files. To begin the newsletter, you will follow a layout with information regarding the number of columns and descriptions for placeholders. Specific instructions are also provided for creating the newsletter banner, adding graphics, borders, shading, a pull quote, a sidebar, and a footer.

1. In a new document window, change all margins to 1 inch.

2. Select the paragraph mark and set paragraph spacing after to 5 points and change the font size to 12, then save the file as **project2**.

3. Press **Enter** seven times to create some blank lines at the top of the document. Then position the insertion point in the first blank line.

4. Use WordArt to create part of the newsletter banner as follows:

   a. Insert a WordArt 2.0 object.

   b. In the text box, key **FITNESS WORLD**, press **Enter** twice, and key **REPORT**.

   c. In the Line and Shape box (Figure P2.1), click the fourth icon in the third row. The Line and Shape box will show Button (Pour).

   d. Select the text in the text box and add the bold format.

   e. In the Shadow box (Figure P2.2), click the third icon in the first row.

   f. Exit to Word. Then scale the graphic proportionally to approximately 65 percent Wide and 65 percent High.

   g. If necessary, select the graphic. Insert a frame around the graphic, and position the frame so that it is horizontally centered relative to the page and vertically .5 inch relative to the page. Leave size and width at auto, leave the default distance from text, and do not turn on Move with Text or Lock Anchor.

5. Add a graphic to the center of the WordArt as follows:

   a. Position the insertion point in a blank paragraph to the left of the WordArt frame. Insert the clip art graphic **nature5.pcx** that is stored on the Data Disk. (Change the drive and directory, then key **nature5.pcx** in the File Name box.)

   b. Select the graphic and scale proportionally to approximately 95 percent wide and 95 percent high. Then crop from the right to delete most of the white space.

   c. Add a frame to the graphic. Then drag the frame so that it is positioned in the center of the WordArt frame. If necessary, rescale the graphic to fit within the WordArt frame and reposition the frame for the graphic to fit the graphic in the center.

FIGURE P2.1
Line and Shape Box

Button (Pour) button

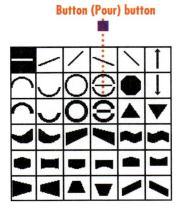

FIGURE P2.2
Shadow Box

Click this shadow option.

6. Complete the banner by adding the city, volume number, date, and issue number as follows:

   a. Position the insertion point in the fifth blank line and key **Chicago, Illinois**. Center the text, make it bold, and add a 3 pt bottom border to the paragraph. (If the border does not extend the full width of the page, add a blank line above the text.)

   b. Position the insertion point in the first blank line below the border and key **Volume 4** at the left margin.

   c. Set a center-aligned tab in the middle of the page (3.25 inches), press (**Tab**), and key **March 1995**.

   d. Set a right-aligned tab at the right margin (6.5 inches), press (**Tab**), and key **Number 3**.

HINT: *To set the tab at the right margin, choose Format Tabs.*

7. Position the insertion point on the next line and add 20 blank lines. (You will need blank lines below each section break you add in the following step, but you can delete any extra blank lines later.)

8. Figure P2.3 on pages 381–383 shows the layout for each page of the newsletter. Follow the instructions in the layout for inserting the files containing the newsletter articles, formatting the articles in multiple columns, and adding frames as placeholders. Reposition frames and anchors as needed to fit the layout.

HINT: *You may find it easier in some cases to drag frames to reposition them appropriately if you turn off Move with Text.*

   a. Position the insertion point in the first blank paragraph below the volume number for the banner.

   b. Key the first heading illustrated in the layout (use two lines for just the THOMPSON title in the newsletter, with a NEWLINE character at the end of the first line).

   c. Change the heading to 14-point Courier New bold, centered with 3-point spacing before and after the paragraph.

   d. Insert and format the article as described in the layout.

9. Position the insertion point on the first blank line below the article, and repeat Step 8 until all articles have been inserted into the newsletter as shown in the layout. Insert hard page breaks before headings when necessary.

10. Search for and select the following text in the article "NATIONAL ALLIANCE MEETING": "inform, educate, and motivate the general public about health, fitness, and nutrition to achieve wellness." (Be sure to include the period.)

11. Copy and paste the selected text as a pull quote in a frame approximately 1¾ inches wide and 1 inch high in the middle column of the article. (Be sure to deselect the text before inserting the frame and pasting.)

(NEWSLETTER BANNER)

THOMPSON RECEIVES
DISTINGUISHED SERVICE AWARD

- Insert the Data Disk file THOMPSON.DOC on the line below the heading.
- Select and format the article text (not the heading) in two columns of equal width.
- Insert an empty frame (1.5 inches wide by 1 inch high) as a placeholder for a picture of Dr. Thompson. Position the frame somewhere in the last paragraph.

LEAD POISONING: CHILDREN ARE AT RISK

- Insert the Data Disk file POISON.DOC on the line below the heading.
- Format the article text (not the heading) in three columns of equal width with a vertical line between the columns.

Continued on next page

NATIONAL FAMILY HEALTH AND FITNESS CLUB CEO RESIGNS

- Insert the Data Disk file CEO.DOC on the line below the heading.
- Format the article text (not the heading) in three columns of equal width.
- Insert an empty frame (1.5 inches wide by 1 inch high) as a placeholder for a photo of Hanna Holmes. Center the frame horizontally within the first column and vertically 0 inches relative to the first paragraph so that the positioned frame is immediately above the first paragraph.
- Insert a second empty frame (1.5 inches wide by 1 inch high) as a placeholder for a photo of Manuel Guerrero. Center the frame horizontally within the second column and vertically 0 inches relative to the paragraph about Mr. Guerrero so that the positioned frame is somewhere above the paragraph.

VITAMINS THAT FIGHT DISEASE

- Insert the Data Disk file VITAMINS.DOC on the line below the heading.
- Format the article in two columns of equal width with a vertical line between the columns.
- If necessary, insert a column break before the third item so that there are two items in each column.

NATIONAL ALLIANCE MEETING

- Insert the Data Disk file ALLIANCE.DOC on the line below the heading.
- Format the article in three columns of equal width with a vertical line between the columns.

Continued on next page

FITNESS EXPO SCHEDULE

- Insert the Data Disk file EXPO.DOC on the line below the heading.
- Leave the heading and the article text formatted in one column.

KNOW YOUR NUTRIENTS

- Insert the Data Disk file NUTRIENT.DOC on the line below the heading.
- Format the article in two columns of equal width with a vertical line between the columns.

TELL US WHAT YOU THINK

- Insert the Data Disk file TELLUS.DOC.
- Leave the heading and article text formatted in one column.

12. Change the first letter to a capital letter, and change the entire pull-quote to bold. If the article fits on one page, change the font size to a larger font size appropriate for a pull quote. If you want to, remove the border of the frame, and/or add shading.

13. Add a 2¼ pt border above the heading and below the last paragraph in the "FITNESS EXPO SCHEDULE" article.

14. Insert the Word clip art graphic **disk.wmf** anywhere within the article "KNOW YOUR NUTRIENTS." Add a frame and position the frame horizontally at the right margin and vertically approximately 4 inches down on the page. (Vertical position may vary.)

15. Insert the Word clip art graphic **mail.wmf** anywhere within the article "TELL US WHAT YOU THINK," and format the graphic as follows:

    a. Crop approximately .9 inch from the top of the graphic so that the flap on the open envelope at the top of the graphic is not visible.

    b. Scale the graphic to approximately 50 percent Wide and 50 percent High.

    c. Add a frame and position the frame in the upper left corner of the article.

16. Create a sidebar to the article "TELL US WHAT YOU THINK:"

    a. Insert an empty frame anchored to the first paragraph in the article.

    b. Size the frame to exactly 3.5 inches wide; use Auto for height.

    c. Position the frame in the lower right corner of the article so that it is horizontally right-aligned relative to the margin and vertically aligned within the article.

    d. Position the insertion point in the frame and insert the Data Disk file **fax.doc**.

    e. Delete any unnecessary blank lines in the frame.

    f. Add shading to the sidebar frame. (Use shading from 5 to 20 percent for all shading in the newsletter; experiment to see what looks best for your printer.)

17. Create a sidebar to list the national executive board members as follows:

    a. Insert an empty frame anchored to the heading "THOMPSON RECEIVES DISTIN-GUISHED SERVICE AWARD."

    b. Size the frame with a width of exactly 1.4 inches and Auto for height.

    c. Position the frame at the left margin, aligned slightly down from the paragraph to which it is anchored.

    d. Position the insertion point in the frame and if necessary change the font to 10-point and paragraph spacing after to 5 points.

    e. Center and key the heading **NATIONAL EXECUTIVE BOARD** in bold. Press (Enter) twice and change to left alignment.

    f. The list of officers is illustrated in Figure P2.4 on page 385. Each officer's title should be keyed with the bold format and followed with the NEWLINE character ((Shift) +

(**Enter**)). Each officer's name should be keyed without the bold format and followed by a hard return ((**Enter**)). (Do not press (**Enter**) after the last name.)

g. Add a ¾ pt outside border to the frame and add shading.

18. Format the first letter of the article text for each of the articles listed below as a dropped capital letter in the Dropped style, dropping down two lines. If desired, add shading and a top and left border to each dropped capital letter.

a. LEAD POISONING: CHILDREN ARE AT RISK

b. NATIONAL FAMILY HEALTH AND FIT-NESS CLUB CEO RESIGNS (Add a blank line above the first paragraph before adding the drop cap.)

c. NATIONAL ALLIANCE MEETING

d. KNOW YOUR NUTRIENTS

19. Add shading to the headings that were formatted with 14-point Courier New bold, except for "FITNESS EXPO SCHEDULE."

20. Move the insertion point to the top of the document and add a footer as follows:

a. The footer text should be keyed in 10-point and should include the name of the newsletter, "FITNESS WORLD REPORT."

b. Insert the graphic **nature5.pcx** at the left edge of the footer.

c. Crop the graphic by .4 inch at the right.

d. Scale the graphic to 75 percent Wide and 75 percent High. Then add a frame.

e. Position the frame in the left margin next to the footer.

HINT: *Drag the picture out of the footer frame.*

f. Format the footer so that it does not print on the first page of the document. (Be sure to change Apply To to Whole Document.)

21. If necessary, add or delete blank lines before the headings over the articles to format the pages attractively. Delete all but one blank line at the end of the document.

FIGURE P2.4
List of Officers for Sidebar

President
Mary Ann Edwards

Vice President
Marcus Groves

Secretary
Merritt Ogle

Treasurer
Troy Lumadue

Historian
Eric Hubbard

Membership
Chairperson
Wanda Sheadel

Newsletter Editor
John Kearfott

22. In the article entitled "THOMPSON RECEIVES DISTINGUISHED SERVICE AWARD," change the space to a nonbreaking space in "March 13." Add a nonbreaking hyphen in Ultra-Tech.

23. In the article entitled "NATIONAL FAMILY HEALTH AND FITNESS CEO RESIGNS," change the space in "March 1" to a nonbreaking space.

24. In the article entitled "NATIONAL ALLIANCE MEETING," add a nonbreaking space between "January" and "28" and change the hyphen to a nonbreaking hyphen.

25. Position the insertion point at the beginning of the document and manually hyphenate the entire document (or scroll and add optional hyphens to reduce excess white space). Consult a dictionary or a word division manual to decide on proper hyphenation. Do not hyphenate in the sidebar article on page 1.

26. Save your document, print one copy, and clear the screen.

USING THE MOUSE

Somewhere on your screen you should see a mouse pointer. Generally, this mouse pointer is shaped like an arrowhead. In text the pointer is shaped like the letter *I* and is called the *I-beam*. Moving the mouse controls both the shape and the position of this pointer.

To move the mouse pointer, simply slide the mouse around on the surface of your desk. If you run out of desk space on which to move the mouse, pick up the mouse and put it down where you have sufficient space to move it. Lifting the mouse does not move the mouse pointer.

Some terms with which you should become familiar are:

- *Point.* To position the tip of the mouse pointer on an item. Do not push any mouse buttons when you are instructed only to point. Because you always need to point to something before you take any other mouse action, such as clicking, you may not always be instructed to point first.

- *Click.* To press and release the mouse button quickly. Do not move the mouse as you click. Clicking instructs the computer to perform an action. Clicking generally refers to the left mouse button unless you are otherwise instructed.

- *Double-click.* To press and release the mouse button twice in rapid succession. Do not move the mouse as you double-click. Double-clicking is often used to tell your computer to select an item and carry out a command at the same time. For example, double-clicking a filename in the Open dialog box automatically selects and carries out the command to open the file without your having to click **OK** .

- *Triple-click.* To press and release the mouse button three times in rapid succession. Do not move the mouse as you triple-click. Triple-clicking is used to select text.

- *Drag.* To hold down the mouse button as you slide the mouse. Dragging is used to highlight (select) blocks of text or to reposition items. When you release the mouse button, the action (such as selecting) is completed.

- *Release.* To stop holding down the mouse button.

Scrolling

Approximate Horizontal Position Drag the scroll box on the horizontal scroll bar to the approximate position.

Approximate Vertical Position Drag the scroll box on the vertical scroll bar to the approximate position.

Scroll Down Point to the down scroll bar arrow and click. To advance several lines, click the scroll bar arrow continuously.

Scroll Up Point to the up scroll bar arrow and click. To advance several lines, click the scroll bar arrow continuously.

Scroll Up/Down One Screenful Click above or below the scroll box.

Scroll Left/Right One Screenful Click to the left or right of the scroll box.

When you have scrolled to the desired location, click to move the insertion point.

Selecting Text

Cell in Table Click in the cell selection bar at the left edge of the cell.

Character Drag across the letter.

Column in Table Click in the column selection bar at the top of the column.

Column in Text Set Up With Tabs Point to a corner of the column, hold down (Alt) and drag to the opposite corner.

Line Click in the selection bar to the left of the line.

Paragraph Double-click in the selection bar to the left of the paragraph.

Paragraph Position the mouse pointer on the paragraph and triple-click.

Row in Table Click in the row selection bar to the left of the row.

Sentence Point to the sentence, hold down (Ctrl), and click.

Whole Document Point to the selection bar and triple-click.

Whole Document Point to the selection bar, hold down (Ctrl), and click.

Word Double-click the word.

Edit Functions

Copy Selected Text Hold down Ctrl and drag the selected text to the desired location for the copy.

Move Selected Text Drag the selected text to the desired location.

Formatting Toolbar Functions

Apply a Character Emphasis Click $\boxed{\mathbf{B}}$, $\boxed{I}$, or $\boxed{\underline{U}}$ on the Formatting Toolbar.

Apply a Font Click the arrow next to the Font box on the Formatting Toolbar, then click the desired font.

Apply a Font Size Click the arrow next to the Font Size box on the Formatting Toolbar, then click the desired point size.

Apply a Style Click the arrow next to the Style box on the Formatting Toolbar, then click the desired style.

Change Paragraph Alignment Click ▤, ▤, ▤, or ▤ on the Formatting Toolbar.

Ruler Functions

Tab Stops

Clear Tab Stop Drag the marker down off the ruler.

Move Tab Stop Drag the marker on the ruler to the desired location.

Set Tab Stop Click the desired tab alignment icon at the left end of the ruler, then click on a tick mark on the ruler.

Indents

First Line Indent Drag ▽.

Hanging Indent Drag the top portion of ⌂.

Left Indent Drag the bottom portion of ⌂.

Right Indent Drag △.

Changing Margins Switch to Print Preview or Page Layout View. If necessary, choose View Ruler or click ⬚ (in Print Preview) to display horizontal and vertical rulers. Position the mouse pointer on the appropriate ruler at the left, right, top, or bottom. When you see a two-headed arrow, drag to the desired margin setting (holding **Alt** as you drag will allow you to see measurements).

Outline Commands

If necessary, change to Outline View. Point to the icon and click.

Window Commands

Close Application Double-click ▭.

Close Document Window Double-click ▭.

Maximize Window Click ▲ in the upper right corner of the window.

Minimize Window Click ▼ to the left of ▲ or ⬍ in the upper right corner of the window.

Move Window Drag the title bar to the desired position.

Open Annotation Pane Double-click the annotation mark.

Open Footnote Pane Double-click the footnote reference mark.

Resize Window Drag the window border to the desired size.

Restore Maximized Window Click ⬍ in the upper right corner of the window.

Split Window Into Panes Double-click ▬ on the vertical scroll bar or drag ▬ down the vertical scroll bar.

Close Split Window Panes
Double-click ▬ on the vertical scroll bar.

Zoom Click the arrow for the Zoom Control box on the Standard Toolbar and click the desired zoom (for example, 50%, 100%, or Page Width).

APPENDIX
b

USING DIALOG BOXES

A command in an open menu that is followed by three dots (. . .) called an ellipsis mark opens a dialog box such as the ones shown below in Figures B.1 and B.2. A dialog box asks for information necessary to complete the command (such as printing options). If at any point you accidentally open the wrong dialog box or decide not to change any of the settings, click **Q** to exit the dialog box. If you should need to see something in a document that is

FIGURE B.1

Dialog Box Options

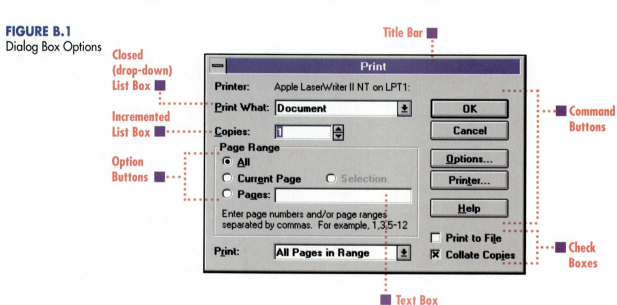

FIGURE B.2

Dialog Box with Open List Box and Folder Tabs

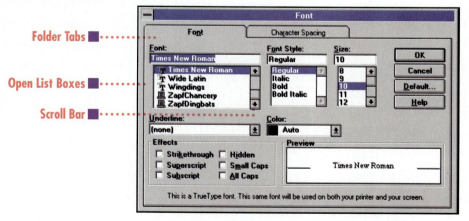

hidden by the dialog box, drag the title bar for the dialog box to move it out of the way but leave it open.

When you move around in a dialog box, your position is indicated by a highlight (a dotted rectangle, a blinking dark rectangle, or a blinking vertical line known as the insertion point). You can change as many settings (options) as desired before you close a dialog box.

Option buttons are arranged in groups. The selected option button contains a dark circle. Only one option button in a group can be selected. Click the button to select an option.

Check boxes are toggle items that can be turned on and off. An *X* indicates that the check box is turned on (selected). You can select more than one check box at a time in a dialog box. To turn a check box on or off, click the check box.

Incremented list boxes allow you to click increment arrows to gradually increase or decrease the measurement shown in the text box next to the arrows. Click the up or down increment arrows until the desired measurement is displayed, or click in the text box and key a measurement.

A closed (drop-down) list box shows only a single item (the current selection) from a list. Click the arrow next to the closed list box to display more items; then click the desired item to select it and close the list box again. If the arrow is detached from the box, you have a choice of keying an entry or opening the list box and clicking an item in the list.

Text boxes are boxes into which you enter text. When you point to a text box, the arrow pointer becomes an I-shape called the *I-beam.* Once you click in the text box, the highlight becomes the insertion point. In empty text boxes, you simply click and key the desired text. In text boxes that contain text, you click in the box, delete the existing entry, and key a new entry.

Choosing a command button carries out the command listed on the button. If the command button has no ellipsis mark, the command is immediately executed. For example, | **OK** | means to accept all the existing entries in a dialog box and close it and | **Cancel** | means to exit the dialog box without making any changes. | **Cancel** | becomes | **Close** | in some dialog boxes when an immediate change takes place in the document with the dialog box remaining open (for example, after you replace text in your document). A command button with an ellipsis (such as Options in Figure B.1) opens a related dialog box. A command button with an arrow, such as the Format button, opens a submenu. To select a command button, click it.

Folder tabs are used in dialog boxes with more than one category (Figure B.2). Each category displays a different dialog box with different options. To switch categories, simply click the folder tab. The selected category will have the bold folder tab.

Open list boxes (Figure B.2) display as many choices as will fit in the box. If there are more options than what will fit in the box, a vertical scroll bar is displayed so you can scroll down to see the other items. To select from an open list box, simply click the desired item. Double-clicking an item will generally select the item and close the dialog box at the same time.

General Troubleshooting

Throughout the course, unless otherwise indicated, capitalization does not need to match in order for a command to work (for example, you can key either **win** or **WIN** to load Windows).

If you load Windows and your screen shows only the Program Manager icon at the bottom of the screen, double-click the icon to restore the Program Manager window.

If the Program Manager window or any group window shows ◆ rather than ▲ , click ◆ to return to the default window size.

If at any point during the Introduction an application other than the Program Manager shows on your screen and you have not been instructed to switch to or load that application, press **Alt** + **Tab** (do not release **Tab**). Then release both keys when the Program Manager returns.

If you need to exit Word and Windows before you complete a chapter, double-click each application's Application Control Menu box ▭ , then in Windows, click **OK** at the prompt to exit.

If you see the Exit Windows box and you are not ready to exit Windows, click **Cancel** .

It is not necessary for screens to match exactly in the Introduction. For example, the Window menu illustrated in Figure I.4 in the Introduction may vary from yours. You may have a different number of windows, you may have different numbers assigned to the windows, and so on. You may also have different icons than those illustrated in the Introduction.

If your windows are arranged like floor tiles (side by side and vertically) and you would prefer to see them layered, click Window and then Cascade.

The Microsoft Word icon may be found in the Microsoft Office window or in another window; installation will vary from system to system. To load Word, open windows until you find the icon; then double-click the icon.

If you load Word and do not see a menu bar, click the Full Screen icon ▣ at the bottom of the screen to restore all screen elements.

After you load Word, if you see a screen showing "Quick Preview" (which appears the first few times the software is used), click Return to Word.

After you load Word, if the Word window does not occupy the entire screen, click the Maximize icon ▲ for the application window.

If the title bar does not show both Microsoft Word and a document name or number, click ▲ for the document window.

System Defaults and Common Settings

You may occasionally have difficulty completing exercises in this text. Sometimes this may be because your system defaults have been changed. Unless otherwise instructed, Figures C.1 to C.11 illustrate the settings you should use.

FIGURE C.1
View Menu with Defaults

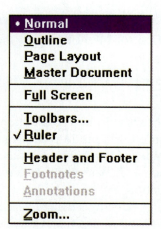

FIGURE C.2
View Toolbars Dialog Box
with Defaults

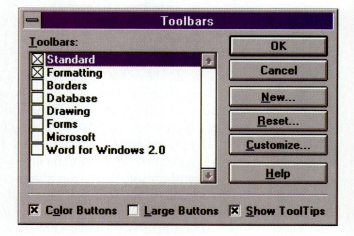

FIGURE C.3
Zoom Control Box on
Standard Toolbar

FIGURE C.4
Tools Options View Category

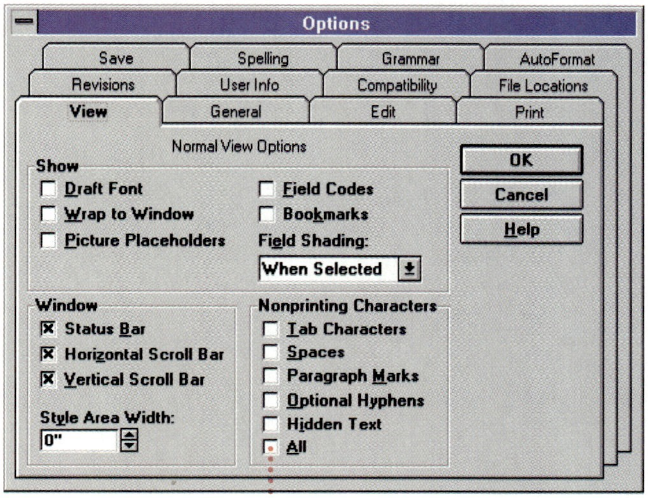

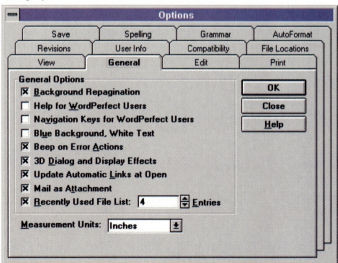

**■ Beginning with Exercise 1.6, the
All check box will be selected**

FIGURE C.5
Tools Options General
Category

FIGURE C.6
Tools Options Edit Category

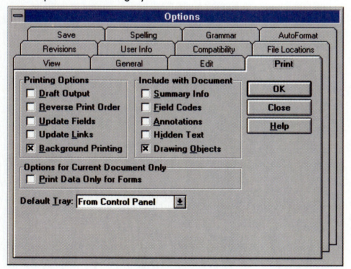

FIGURE C.7
Tools Options Print Category

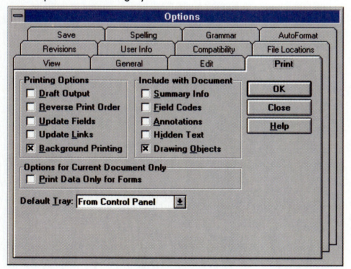

FIGURE C.8
Tools Options Revisions Category
(Colors shown may vary.)

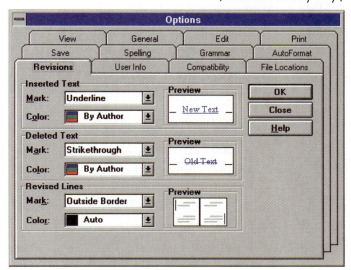

FIGURE C.9
Tools Options User Info Category

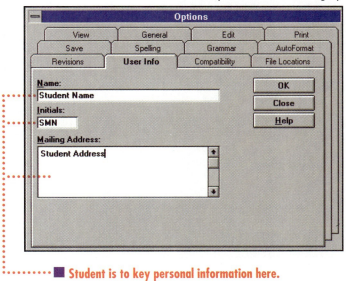

■ Student is to key personal information here.

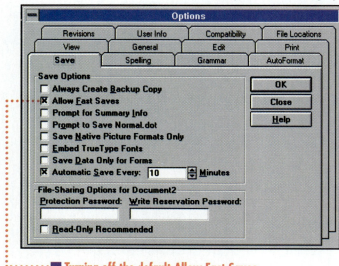

FIGURE C.10
Tools Options Save Category

■ Turning off the default Allow Fast Saves
option will conserve disk space.

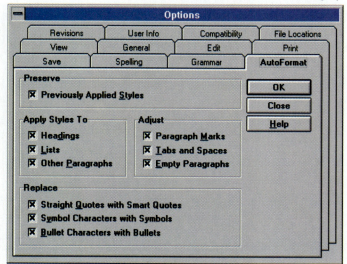

FIGURE C.11
Tools Options AutoFormat Category

Do not add words to a dictionary or to AutoCorrect unless your instructor asks you to do so.

Creating and Using Custom Dictionaries

Creating a Custom Dictionary

If you frequently use proper names and acronyms that are not in the main dictionary, you will find it helpful to add those names to a custom dictionary. You can create several custom dictionaries. For example, you can create one for legal terms, one for medical terms, and another for engineering terms.

1. Choose Tools Options and select the Spelling folder tab to display the dialog box shown in Figure D.1.

2. Click New in the Custom Dictionaries box to display the dialog box in Figure D.2 on page 402.

3. Key a dictionary name that identifies its contents (Word will automatically add the .DIC extension).

FIGURE D.1
Spelling Category of Tools Options Dialog Box

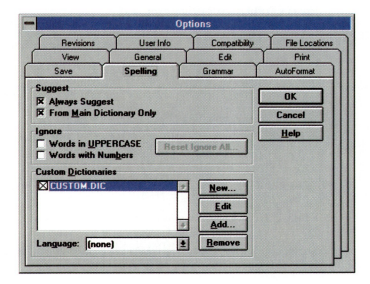

FIGURE D.2
Create Custom Dictionary
Dialog Box

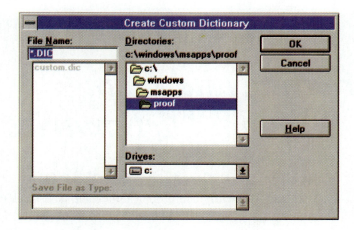

4. Click [**OK**].

5. Click the name of the new custom dictionary twice in the Custom Dictionaries box (it should be highlighted and have an *X*), then click Edit.

6. Click Yes when prompted to edit the custom dictionary, then click Cancel.

Word displays an open document with the dictionary name.

7. Add, delete, and edit the terms you want to include in this dictionary. Press **Enter** after each term.

8. Save the file with the same filename (Word saves the dictionary as a text-only file), then clear the screen.

Opening a Custom Dictionary

If you open the custom dictionary before you begin spell checking a document, Word will check both the main dictionary and the custom dictionary before presenting unknown terms in the spell check. If desired, you can have several different custom dictionaries open at the same time.

1. Choose Tools Options and click the Spelling folder tab.

2. Turn on the check box for all desired dictionaries under Custom Dictionaries.

3. Click [**OK**].

   Note that if you want to close a custom dictionary, turn off the check box for that dictionary in the Custom Dictionaries box.

4. Click [✓ABC] to begin spell-checking the document with the main document and the selected custom dictionaries.

Adding Words to a Custom Dictionary During a Spell-Check

1. When Word presents a term as an unknown word during a spell-check, select the desired custom dictionary in the Add Words To list box.

2. Click Add.

   Word adds the new term to the custom dictionary and continues the spell-check.

Editing Words in a Custom Dictionary

1. Choose Tools Options and click the Spelling folder tab.

2. Click to highlight the desired custom dictionary in the Custom Dictionaries box (do not turn off any of the check boxes).

3. Click Edit.

4. When prompted to edit the custom dictionary, click Yes.

   Word opens the custom dictionary behind the Tools Options dialog box.

5. Click Cancel to close the Tools Options dialog box so that you can work with the dictionary.

6. Make the necessary changes in the document and save the file (with the same filename), then clear the screen.

Using AutoCorrect

AutoCorrect allows you to create entries for text and graphics you use repeatedly in your documents such as your company name, company logo, short phrases, and technical terms. You can also use AutoCorrect for words you often misspell.

Viewing AutoCorrect Options

1. Choose Tools AutoCorrect. The dialog box shown in Figure D.3 appears.

   The AutoCorrect dialog box appears. If the check box Replace Text as You Type is turned on, Word will make changes automatically as you key.

2. Notice the check boxes for items Word can automatically correct:

   ■ Word can automatically change "straight" (typewriter-style) apostrophes and quotation marks to "smart quotes"(curly apostrophes and quotation marks).

   ■ If you key two capital letters at the beginning of a word, Word can automatically change the second capital letter to a lowercase letter.

FIGURE D.3
Tools AutoCorrect
Dialog Box

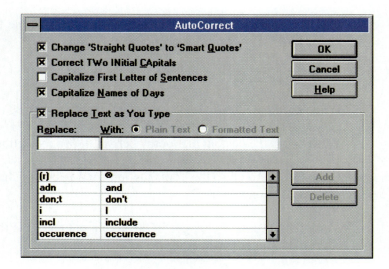

- If you forget, Word can automatically capitalize the first letter of sentences (this option is off by default).

- Word can also automatically capitalize names of days.

3. Notice also the list box with the scroll bar. These are entries that Word already automatically corrects if you make typographical errors, such as keying "adn" rather than "and" and keying "teh" rather than "the."

Adding a New AutoCorrect Entry

1. Choose Tools AutoCorrect.

2. In the Replace box, key an entry abbreviation (up to 31 characters, but no spaces). For example, you might include:

- **asap** (for "as soon as possible")

- **ot** (for "to")

- other common misspellings you make

- your first and last initials (to be replaced with your full name); do not include your middle initial or you will not be able to key reference initials in letters and memos

- **adr** (for your address)

 IMPORTANT: Do not use common words (with the correct spelling) in the Replace box for AutoCorrect or Word will replace these common words with the entry you designate for With. Instead, use abbreviated forms of words (for example "adr" rather than "address" if you plan to create an AutoCorrect entry for your address).

3. In the With box, key the full text for the entry (up to 255 characters, including spaces and punctuation) For example:

- **as soon as possible**

- **to**

- corrections for words you misspell

- ■ your full first and last name (and your middle name if desired)
- ■ your address

4. Click Add.

5. Click [**OK**] .

 IMPORTANT: You can also add entries to AutoCorrect during a spelling check by clicking AutoCorrect.

Multiple File Management

Finding Files

You can use the File Find File command to search for files and to view their contents without even opening the files.

1. Choose File Find File to display the dialog box in Figure E.1.

2. If the desired file(s) are not listed, choose Search; then do the following in the dialog box shown in Figure E.2 on page 408:

    a. Under Search For, key the filename in the File Name box (include an extension if the file is not a Word document file). To search for all files with the same extension, key an asterisk and the extension (for example *.PCX to search for all PC Paintbrush files) or open the FileName list box and select an option.

    b. If necessary, select the appropriate drive in the Location list box, or key the path you want to search. To search multiple paths, separate the paths with semicolons. If you want to search subdirectories, turn on Include Subdirectories.

FIGURE E.1
File Find File Dialog Box

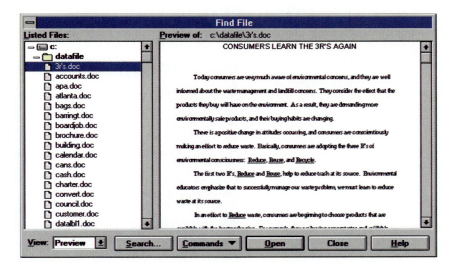

FIGURE E.2
Search Dialog Box

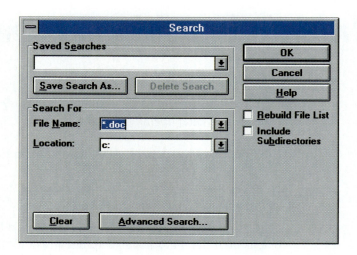

c. To specify additional search criteria about the document, click Advanced Search, then click the Summary folder tab to display the dialog box in E.3 or click the Timestamp folder to displaythe dialog box shown in Figure E.4. Key or select the appropriate criteria, then click [**OK**].

d. If desired, click Save Search As to save the search criteria (the dialog box in E.5 appears), key a name in the Search Name box, and click [**OK**].

e. Click [**OK**] to begin the search.

FIGURE E.3
Summary Category of Advanced Search Dialog Box

FIGURE E.4
Timestamp Category of Advanced Search Dialog Box

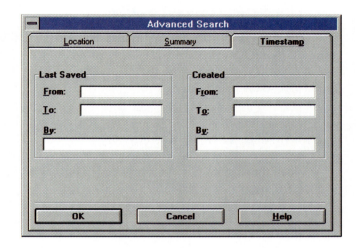

Word lists the files in the specified drive or path alphabetically by filename.

3. If necessary, select Preview in the View box.

As shown in Figure E.1, some of the contents of the first file in the list are shown in the Preview of box. The other two options in the View box display the file information and statistics about the selected file.

4. Do one of the following:

    a. Click Open to open the file.

    b. Click Commands to open a read-only copy of the file, print a copy, display summary information, delete the file, copy the file, or sort the list of files in a different order.

    c. Click Search to look for different file(s).

5. If necessary, choose Close to close the Find File dialog box.

FIGURE E.5
Save Search As Dialog Box

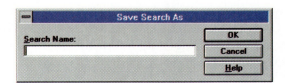

Working with Multiple Files

The File Find File command also enables you to open, copy, delete, or print multiple files at once.

1. Choose File Find File.

2. If necessary, click Search and change the search criteria to search for the desired files as explained above under Finding Files.

3. When the desired files are displayed in the Listed Files box, select the files as follows:

    a. Click once on the filename with which you want to work (double-clicking automatically opens the file).

    b. Hold down (Ctrl) and click on each additional filename until all the files with which you want to work are highlighted.

4. Do one of the following:

    a. Click Open.

    Word opens all of the selected files.

    b. Click Command and select the desired command (Open Read Only, Print, Summary, Delete, Copy, or Sorting).

5. If necessary, choose Close to close the Find File dialog box.

Document Summary Information and Statistics

By maintaining summary information for each of your documents, you can find documents easily and quickly. Summary information includes a title and subject of the document, the name of the person who created the document, keywords that identify important information in the document, and comments about the document.

Adding Summary Information to a Document

1. To add summary information to a document, choose File Summary Info to display a dialog box similar to the one shown in Figure E.6.

2. Key the information in the boxes provided. Note that Word uses the name in the User Info category of the Tools Options dialog box for the Author name but you can change this name.

It is not necessary to complete all of the summary information, but the more information you provide, the easier it will be for you to locate this document in the future.

TIP

You can tell Word to prompt you for summary information each time you save a new document. Choose Tools Options, click the Save folder tab, and turn on Prompt for Summary Info.

Viewing and Editing Document Summary Information and Statistics

Even if you choose not to add summary information when you save your documents, Word automatically keeps track of several kinds of statistical data each time you work with a document.

1. View the document statistics by doing one of the following:

   a. If you already have a document open, choose File Summary Info and click Statistics.

FIGURE E.6
Summary Info Dialog Box

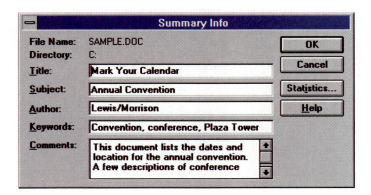

b. If you do not have a document open, choose File Find File (search for the desired file if necessary), select a completed document for which you want to view the statistics, click Commands, click Summary, and click Statistics.

2. Word provides the following information as shown in Figure E.7:

■ filename, directory, the attached template, and the title

■ the date created, date last saved, and date last printed

■ who saved the document last

■ the number of revisions (calculated by totaling the number of times the document was saved)

■ the total editing time (calculated by totaling the number of minutes the document has been open during all editing sessions since it was created, with the exception of read-only access)

■ the document size in terms of bytes, pages, paragraphs, lines, words, and characters (hidden text is included in the total characters)

FIGURE E.7
Document
Statistics Dialog
Box

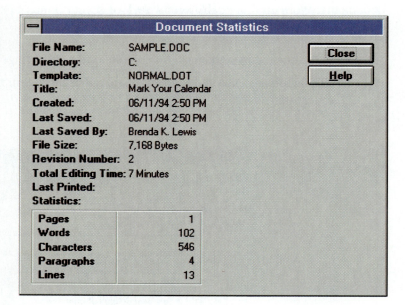

3. Edit summary information (statistics cannot be edited) by doing one of the following:

    a. In an open document, choose File Summary Info, make the desired changes, and click OK.

    b. Choose File Find File, locate the desired file, then do the following:

    ■ Click Commands.

    ■ Click Summary.

    ■ Make the necessary changes.

    ■ Click OK.

Printing the Summary Information

1. Choose File Print and do one of the following:

    a. To print the summary information with the document, select Document in the Print What box, click Options, turn on Summary Info under Include With Document, and click OK.

    b. To print only the summary information, select Summary Info in the Print What box.

2. Click OK.

KEYBOARD SHORTCUTS

Note: Do not hold (Shift) unless indicated.

Position the Insertion Point

Left One Character	(←)	Up One Paragraph	(Ctrl) + (↑) twice
Right One Character	(→)	Down One Paragraph	(Ctrl) + (↓)
Down One Line	(↓)	Beginning of Table Row	(Alt) + (Home)
Up One Line	(↑)	Last Cell in Table Row	(Alt) + (End)
Beginning of Line	(Home)		
End of Line	(End)		
Top of Window	(Ctrl) + (Page Up)	Top of Table Column	(Alt) + (Page Up)
Bottom of Window	(Ctrl) + (Page Down)	Bottom of Table Column	(Alt) + (Page Down)
Up One Window	(Page Up)		
Down One Window	(Page Down)	Next Table Cell	(Tab)
Beginning of Document	(Ctrl) + (Home)	Previous Table Cell	(Shift) + (Tab)
		Next Column	(Alt) + (↓)
End of Document	(Ctrl) + (End)	Previous Column	(Alt) + (↑)
Left One Word	(Ctrl) + (←)	Top of Previous Page	(Alt) + (Ctrl) + (Page Up)
Right One Word	(Ctrl) + (→)		
Top of Current Paragraph	(Ctrl) + (↑)	Top of Next Page	(Alt) + (Ctrl) + (Page Down)

Select Text

Extend Selection	(F8)	Shrink Selection	(Shift) + (F8)
Extend Selection	(Shift) + Positioning Insertion Point Key Combination (above)	Select Column	(Ctrl) + (Shift) + (F8) + direction keys

Select Entire Document	**Ctrl** + **A**	Select Table	**Alt** + **5** (keypad; NUMLOCK off)
Select Entire Document	**Ctrl** + **5** (keypad; NUMLOCK off)	Table Update AutoFormat	**Alt** + **Ctrl** + **U**

Edit Functions

Activate Menu Bar	**F10**	Edit Cut (to Clipboard)	**Shift** + **Delete**
Cancel	**Esc**	Edit Find	**Ctrl** + **F**
Column Break	**Ctrl** + **Shift** + **Enter**	Edit Go To	**Ctrl** + **G**
Copy	**Shift** + **F2**	Edit Go To	**F5**
Copy Format	**Ctrl** + **Shift** + **C**	Edit Paste (from Clipboard)	**Ctrl** + **V**
Delete Next Word	**Ctrl** + **Delete**	Edit Paste (from Clipboard)	**Shift** + **Insert**
Delete Previous Word	**Ctrl** + **Backspace**	Edit Paste Format	**Ctrl** + **Shift** + **V**
Edit AutoText	**F3**	Edit Redo (after Undo)	**Ctrl** + **Y**
Edit AutoText	**Alt** + **Ctrl** + **V**	Edit Redo (after Undo)	**F4**
Edit Bookmark	**Ctrl** + **Shift** + **F5**	Edit Redo (after Undo)	**Alt** + **Shift** + **Backspace**
Edit Clear	**Delete**	Edit Repeat (last edit or format)	**Ctrl** + **Y**
Edit Copy (to Clipboard)	**Ctrl** + **C**	Edit Repeat (last edit or format)	**F4**
Edit Copy (to Clipboard)	**Ctrl** + **Insert**	Edit Repeat (last edit or format)	**Alt** + **Enter**
Edit Cut (to Clipboard)	**Ctrl** + **X**		

Edit Replace	**Ctrl** + **H**
Edit Undo	**Ctrl** + **Z**
Edit Undo	**Alt** + **Backspace**
Go Back	**Shift** + **F5**
Go Back	**Alt** + **Ctrl** + **Z**
Go to Annotation	**Alt** + **F11**
Insert Annotation	**Alt** + **Ctrl** + **A**
Insert Footnote	**Alt** + **Ctrl** + **F**
Insert Merge Field	**Alt** + **Shift** + **F**
Mail Merge Check for Errors	**Alt** + **Shift** + **K**
Mail Merge Edit Data Source	**Alt** + **Shift** + **E**
Mail Merge to Document	**Alt** + **Shift** + **N**
Mail Merge to Printer	**Alt** + **Shift** + **M**
Mark Index Entry	**Alt** + **Shift** + **X**
Move	**F2**
Move Table Down/ Move Paragraph Down	**Alt** + **Shift** + **↓**

Move Table Row Up/ Move Paragraph Up	**Alt** + **Shift** + **↑**
New Page	**Ctrl** + **Enter**
Overtype	**Insert**
Paste from Clipboard	**Ctrl** + **V**
Repeat Find	**Shift** + **F4**
Repeat Find	**Alt** + **Ctrl** + **Y**
Show All Non-printing Characters	**Ctrl** + **Shift** + **8**
Spelling	**F7**
Spike	**Ctrl** + **F3**
Split Table	**Ctrl** + **Shift** + **Enter**
Tab Character (Table)	**Ctrl** + **Tab**
Toggle All Fields Display	**Alt** + **F9**
Thesaurus	**Shift** + **F7**
Unspike	**Ctrl** + **Shift** + **F3**
Update Field(s)	**F9**

Character Formats

Format Font dialog box	**Ctrl** + **D**	Bold	**Ctrl** + **B**
All Caps	**Ctrl** + **Shift** + **A**	Bold	**Ctrl** + **Shift** + **B**

Change Case	**Shift** + **F3**	Normal Text	**Ctrl** + **Space Bar**
Double Underline	**Ctrl** + **Shift** + **D**	Optional Hyphen	**Ctrl** + **-**
Ellipsis	**Alt** + **Ctrl** + **.**	Reset Character (normal text)	**Ctrl** + **Space Bar**
En Dash	**Ctrl** + **-** (keypad; NUMLOCK off)	Reset Character (normal text)	**Ctrl** + **Shift** + **Z**
Em Dash	**Alt** + **Ctrl** + **-** (keypad; NUMLOCK off)	Shrink Font	**Ctrl** + **<**
Font Box on Formatting Toolbar	**Ctrl** + **Shift** + **F**	Shrink Font One Point	**Ctrl** + **[**
Font Size Box on Formatting Toolbar	**Ctrl** + **Shift** + **P**	Small Caps	**Ctrl** + **Shift** + **K**
		Subscript	**Ctrl** + **=**
Grow Font	**Ctrl** + **>**	Superscript	**Ctrl** + **Shift** + **=**
Grow Font One Point	**Ctrl** + **]**	Symbol Font	**Ctrl** + **Shift** + **Q**
Hidden Text	**Ctrl** + **Shift** + **H**	Underline (Continuous Single)	**Ctrl** + **U**
Italics	**Ctrl** + **I**		
Italics	**Ctrl** + **Shift** + **I**	Underline (Continuous Single)	**Ctrl** + **Shift** + **U**
Nonbreaking Hyphen	**Ctrl** + **Shift** + **-**	Word Underline	**Ctrl** + **Shift** + **W**
Nonbreaking Space	**Ctrl** + **Shift** + **Space Bar**		

Paragraph Formats

Apply List Bullet Style	**Ctrl** + **Shift** + **L**	Close Paragraph Spacing (Space Before 0 pt)	**Ctrl** + number **0**
Centered Alignment	**Ctrl** + **E**	Double Space Lines	**Ctrl** + **2**
		Format AutoFormat	**Ctrl** + **K**

Format Header/ Footer Link	**Alt** + **Shift** + **R**	Reset Paragraph (to applied style definitions)	**Ctrl** + **Q**
Hanging Indent	**Ctrl** + **T**	Right Alignment	**Ctrl** + **R**
Justified Alignment	**Ctrl** + **J**	Show Style for Paragraph	**Shift** + **F1**, click text
Left Alignment	**Ctrl** + **L**	Single Space Lines	**Ctrl** + **1**
Nest (Left Indent)	**Ctrl** + **M**	Style Box on Formatting Toolbar	**Ctrl** + **Shift** + **S**
NEWLINE	**Shift** + **Enter**		
New Paragraph	**Enter**	Format Style dialog box	**Ctrl** + **Shift** + **S** twice
Normal Style	**Ctrl** + **Shift** + **N**		
Normal Style	**Alt** + **Shift** + **5** (keypad; NUMLOCK off)	Unhang Indent	**Ctrl** + **Shift** + **T**
		Unnest (Reduce Left Indent)	**Ctrl** + **Shift** + **M**
1.5-Space Lines	**Ctrl** + **5**		
Open Paragraph Spacing (Space Before 12 pt)	**Ctrl** + number **0**		

Outline Commands

Collapse	**Alt** + underscore	Collapse to Level	**Alt** + **Shift** + (a level number)
Collapse	**Alt** + **Shift** + minus on keypad (NUMLOCK off)	Demote	**Alt** + **Shift** + **→**
Collapse All Body Text	**Alt** + **Shift** + **A**	Demote to Body Text	**Alt** + **Shift** + **5** (keypad; NUMLOCK off)
Collapse All Body Text	***** on keypad (NUMLOCK off)	Demote to Body Text	**Ctrl** + **Shift** + **N**
		Expand	**Alt** + **+**

Expand	**Alt** + **Shift** + plus on keypad (NUM-LOCK off)	Move Up	**Alt** + **Shift** + **↑**
		Promote	**Alt** + **Shift** + **←**
Expand All Body Text and Headings	**Alt** + **Shift** + **A**	Toggle First Line of Body Text/All Body Text	**Alt** + **Shift** + letter **L**
Expand All Body Text and Headings	ASTERISK on keypad (NUMLOCK off)	Apply Heading 1	**Alt** + **Ctrl** + **1**
Expand to Level	**Alt** + **Shift** + (a level number)	Apply Heading 2	**Alt** + **Ctrl** + **2**
		Apply Heading 3	**Alt** + **Ctrl** + **3**
Move Down	**Alt** + **Shift** + **↓**		

File Management

File New	**Ctrl** + **N**	File Print Preview	**Ctrl** + **F2**
File Open	**Ctrl** + **O**	File Print Preview	**Alt** + **Ctrl** + **I**
File Open	**Ctrl** + **F12**	File Save	**Ctrl** + **S**
File Open	**Alt** + **Ctrl** + **F2**	File Save	**Shift** + **F12**
File Print	**Ctrl** + **P**	File Save	**Alt** + **Shift** + **F2**
File Print	**Ctrl** + **Shift** + **F12**	File Save As	**F12**

Window Commands

Close Application Window (Exit Word)	**Alt** + **F4**	Close Document Window	**Ctrl** + **W**
Close Document Window	**Ctrl** + **F4**	Close Pane	**Alt** + **Shift** + **C**

Maximize Appli-cation Window	**Alt** + **F10**	Restore Application Window	**Alt** + **F5**
Maximize Document Window	**Ctrl** + **F10**	Restore Document Window	**Ctrl** + **F5**
Move Document Window	**Ctrl** + **F7**, direction key, **Enter**	Size Document Window	**Ctrl** + **F8**, direction key, **Enter**
Next Pane	**F6**	Split Document Window	**Alt** + **Ctrl** + **S**, direction key, **Enter**
Next Window	**Ctrl** + **F6**		
Next Window	**Alt** + **F6**	View Normal	**Alt** + **Ctrl** + **N**
Previous Pane	**Shift** + **F6**	View Outline	**Alt** + **Ctrl** + **O**
Previous Window	**Ctrl** + **Shift** + **F6**	View Page Layout	**Alt** + **Ctrl** + **P**
Previous Window	**Alt** + **Shift** + **F6**		

Fields and Miscellaneous

Do Field Click	**Alt** + **Shift** + **F9**	Insert Field Char-acters (braces)	**Ctrl** + **F9**
Help (Contents)	**F1**	Insert Page Field	**Alt** + **Shift** + **P**
Context Help in a dialog box	**Shift** + **F1**	Insert Time Field	**Alt** + **Shift** + **T**
Context Help in doc-ument window	**Shift** + **F1**, click command or icon	Lock Fields	**Ctrl** + **3**
		Lock Fields	**Ctrl** + **F11**
Insert Date Field	**Alt** + **Shift** + **D**	Mark Citation	**Alt** + **Shift** + **I**
Insert Endnote	**Alt** + **Ctrl** + **E**	Mark Table of Contents Entry	**Alt** + **Shift** + **O**
Insert Field	**Ctrl** + **F9**		

Microsoft System Information	(**Alt**) + (**Ctrl**) + (**F1**)	Previous Object	(**Alt**) + (↑)
Next Field	(**F11**)	Toggle Single Field Display	(**Shift**) + (**F9**)
Next Field	(**Alt**) + (**F1**)	Unlink Fields	(**Ctrl**) + (**6**)
Next Object	(**Alt**) + (↓)	Unlink Fields	(**Ctrl**) + (**Shift**) + (**F9**)
Previous Field	(**Shift**) + (**F11**)	Unlock Fields	(**Ctrl**) + (**4**)
Previous Field	(**Alt**) + (**Shift**) + (**F1**)	Unlock Fields	(**Ctrl**) + (**Shift**) + (**F11**)

CREATING AND PRINTING ENVELOPES

1. Do one of the following:

   a. If you want to key the delivery address for an envelope when no document is open, choose Tools Envelopes and Labels. The dialog box in Figure G.1 will open.

   b. If you want to create an envelope using an address contained within a document, open the document containing the delivery address, then choose Tools Envelopes and Labels. Word automatically locates the address in the document and displays it in the Envelopes and Labels dialog box.

 IMPORTANT: If the document contains more than one address, you may need to select the delivery address.

2. If necessary, click the Envelopes folder tab.

3. If necessary, key the delivery address in the Delivery Address box.

TIP

If you want the delivery address to be formatted in all caps with no punctuation, delete the punctuation from the address in the document, select the address and change the text to all caps, then choose Tools Envelopes and Labels.

FIGURE G.1
Tools Envelopes and Labels Dialog Box

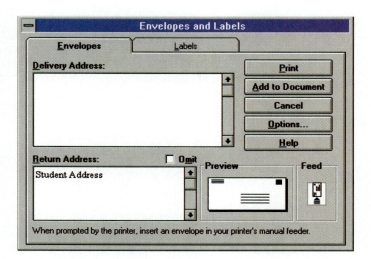

4. If desired, change the return address in the Return Address box. If you do not want to print a return address, turn on Omit.

Word automatically inserts the address specified in the User Info category of the Tools Options dialog box, but you can change this address by simply keying a new one. If you key a new return address, Word will store the new address as the default return address.

5. Click Options and, if necessary, click the Envelopes Options folder tab to display the dialog box in Figure G.2. Then make any of the following selections:

    a. Select the correct envelope size in the Envelope Size list box.

    b. Turn on Delivery Point Bar Code to print a POSTNET bar code.

    To use the bar code option, your printer must be able to print graphics. Word prints a machine-readable bar code representing a U.S. Zip Code and the street address for delivery point.

    c. Turn on FIM-A Courtesy Replay Mail to print a code to identify the front of the envelope.

    To use this option, your printer must be able to print graphics and you must first turn on Delivery Point Bar Code. The Facing Identification Mark is

FIGURE G.2
Envelope Options
Dialog Box

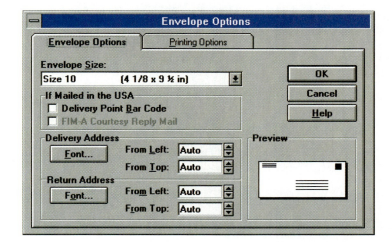

printed on the front side of a courtesy reply envelope that is preprinted with the sender's name and address.

    d. Change the font and/or font size of the delivery address by clicking Font in the Delivery address box. Change the spacing from the left edge or the top edge of the envelope by clicking the up or down increment arrow.

    e. Change the font and/or font size of the return address by clicking Font in the Delivery address box. Change the spacing from the left or the top by clicking the up or down increment arrow.

6. Click the Printing Options folder tab to display the dialog box in Figure G.3. Then make the following selections:

    a. Click the appropriate icon for the Feed Method.

    b. Click Face Up or Face Down.

    c. If necessary, click Clockwise Rotation.

Printers handle envelopes in different ways. Check your printer manual for information about the feed method recommended for your printer.

    d. Select the appropriate option for feeding the envelope in the Feed From box.

FIGURE G.3
Printing Options Category of the Envelope Options Dialog Box

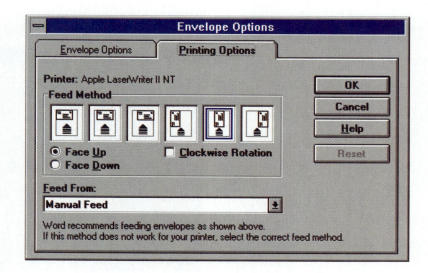

7. Click [**OK**] to exit the Printing Options dialog box.

8. If desired, click Add to Document.

    When you click Add to Document, Word stores the envelope address in a separate section at the beginning of the document. Word prints the envelope first, then the document. When Word begins printing, you may be prompted to insert an envelope into the printer.

9. If you add the envelope to the document, you can add special text and graphics as follows:

    a. Switch to Page Layout View.

    b. Position the insertion point in the envelope section of the document and key the special text and/or insert or create a graphic.

10. Click Print.

PROOFREADER'S MARKS

DEFINED		EXAMPLES
Paragraph	¶	¶ Begin a new paragraph at this point. Insert a letter here.
Insert a character	∧	
Delete	ℛ	Delete ~~these words~~ Disregard the previous correction. To
Do not change	*stet or* ⋯⋯	
Transpose	*tr*	transpose is to around turn.
Move to the left	[	[Move this copy to the left.
Move to the right	]	Move this copy to the right.
No paragraph	*No* ¶	*No* ¶ Do not begin a new paragraph here. Delete the hyphen from
Delete and close up	ℐ	pre-empt and close up the space.
Set in caps	*Caps or* ≡	a sentence begins with a capital
Set in lower case	*lc or* /	letter. This Word should not
Insert a period	⊙	be capitalized. Insert a period⊙
Quotation marks	∨∨ ∨∨	Quotation marks and a comma
Comma	∧	should be placed here, he said.
Insert space	#	Space between these/words. An
Apostrophe	∨	apostrophe is what's needed here.
Hyphen	=	Add a hyphen to Afro/American. Close
Close up	⌒	up the extra spa ce.
Use superior figure	∨	Footnote this sentence. Set
Set in italic	*Ital. or* ———	the words, sine qua non, in italics.
Move up	⊓	This word is too low. That word is
Move down	⊔	too high.

A

Alignment Positioning text so that all lines are even at the left margin, even at the right margin, even at both margins, or centered.

Alphanumeric Sorted first by numbers, then by letters.

Anchor A symbol indicating the paragraph to which a frame is attached.

Annotation Note (comment) added within a document by the author and reviewer(s) of the document, formatted as hidden text.

Ascending Order From the beginning of the alphabet, the lowest number, or the earliest date.

Autofit A command that allows Word to automatically adjust table column widths to the size of the largest entry in the column.

B

Banner Full-width headline such as the title for a newsletter or report.

C

Case-Sensitive In sorting, places uppercase before lowercase letters.

Cell Selection Bar Unmarked area slightly to the right of the left border of a table cell used for selecting the entire cell.

Cells Rows and columns of boxes in a table.

Change Bar Mark displayed and/or printed to indicate which lines of a document contain revisions; also called revision bar.

Character Format Format affecting a single selected character or a group of selected characters; includes the following: font, font size, style (such as bold or italic), position (superscript or subscript), and kerning.

Click Position the mouse pointer; then quickly press and release the left mouse button.

Clip Art Prepared art files you can import into a document.

Clipboard Temporary storage area for text that is to be moved (cut) or copied and then pasted to another location.

Column Selection Bar Unmarked area at the top border of a column used for selecting the entire column.

Crop Trim a graphic.

D

Data Disk Disk containing some of the documents on which exercises and activities in this textbook are based.

Data Record Each row or paragraph in a data source containing information to be merged into a single copy of the form document.

Data Source Document containing the records with variable information to be merged into a main document.

Default Preset option or variable to which the program reverts if the setting is not specified.

Descending Order From the end of the alphabet, the highest number, or the latest date.

Deselect Remove the highlight from selected text.

Dialog Box Submenu displayed in a rectangular box containing options for carrying out a command.

Directory Group of files (often a convenient category); directories provide an organized file structure and often contain lower-level directories known as subdirectories.

DOS (Disk Operating System) An operating system that provides the basic procedures for a disk-oriented computer.

Double-click Position the mouse pointer; then quickly press and release the left mouse button twice in rapid succession.

Drag Position the mouse pointer, press down and hold the left mouse button while moving the mouse to the desired position, and release.

Drag and Drop Drag the mouse to move or copy selected text to a new location.

Drop Cap Enlarged capital letter used to emphasize the first letter in a paragraph; also called a display capital letter.

E

Endnotes References printed at the end of a section or document.

F

Field Set of codes to tell Word to insert items into a document; one piece of information in a data source record; or a column to be sorted.

Field Name Indicates variable text to be inserted in a main document; also called a merge field.

Filter Specifying criteria for which data records are to be merged and printed.

Font General shape of a set of characters.

Font Size Height and width of a character font measured in points.

Font Style Bold and italic formats for a selected font.

Footer Printed lines (running head) appearing at the bottom of each document page.

Formatting Arranging the page and paragraph layout and emphasizing characters.

Formula Instruction for how to calculate totals of table rows and columns.

Frame Box that can be bordered and repositioned to arrange text and graphics at specific locations.

G

Grid A sample with boxes to drag across and specify the number of rows and columns; or a blank table.

Gridlines Nonprinting dotted lines surrounding a table cell.

H

Handles Small squares surrounding a graphic, indicating that it is selected.

Hanging Indent All lines but the first "hang" (are indented) to the right of the first line; commonly used for enumerations, bulleted lists, and bibliographies.

Hard Page Breaks Manual page breaks.

Header Printed lines (running head) appearing at the top of each document page.

Header Row Contains all the field names to be used in a data source.

Hidden Text Formatted text that is not visible; it can be viewed or printed only if the Hidden Text option is turned on in the

Tools Options View or Tools Options Print category.

Highlight Select text for editing or formatting or select a menu, command, or dialog box option. Highlighted items are generally shown in reverse video; in dialog boxes, the highlight can be reverse video, a blinking vertical line, or a dotted rectangular outline.

I

I-Beam When positioned on text, the mouse pointer becomes an I-shaped pointer known as the I-beam.

Icon Pictorial representation of a function or window.

Iconizing Reducing (minimizing) an application or window to an icon.

Import Bring a graphic or text into the application from another source.

Indent Distance between paragraph boundaries and page margins or column boundaries; controls the width of the paragraph and the horizontal boundaries of the paragraph.

INSERT In the default INSERT mode, new text is inserted between existing characters.

Insertion Point Blinking vertical bar indicating where text will next be inserted.

J

Justified Alignment of text flush with both left and right margins; extra space is added between words as needed.

K

Keep with Next Format to keep at least the last two lines of a paragraph with the next paragraph on the same page.

Kerning Adjustment of spacing between pairs of characters to affect visual impact of text; space can be increased or decreased.

L

Landscape Orientation Document prints sideways with the long edge of the page at the top; also called horizontal orientation.

M

Main Document Form document that contains boilerplate text and variable text.

Menu List of available operations. Dimmed options are not available; shortcut keys are indicated when available.

Menu Bar Located near the top of the window; lists all the menus available in the application.

Merge Field Indicates variable text to be inserted in a main document; also called a field name.

Merging Cells Combining two or more table cells into a single cell. Used to create a heading that spans several columns.

Multi-Task To run more than one software application at a time.

N

Nest Indent a paragraph of text to set it off from surrounding paragraphs.

Newspaper-Style Columns Text flows down one column and begins again in the next column; also called snaking columns.

Nonbreaking Hyphen Used to indicate that a hyphenated word should not be broken (for example, a hyphenated last name such as Navarro-Cruz).

Nonbreaking Space Used to indicate two words that should be kept together on one line (for example, "3 inches").

O

Optional Hyphen Used to indicate where a word should be hyphenated if it falls at the end of a line (for example, "manu-facturing").

OVERTYPE In OVERTYPE mode, new text replaces existing characters.

P

Page Layout Full page view is displayed, with elements (page numbers, headers and footers, and so on) displayed as they will be printed.

Panes Separate windows into which footnotes and annotations are entered.

Paragraph Format Format affecting the paragraph containing the insertion point; includes one or more of the following: alignment, indents, tabs, borders, spacing before and after, line spacing, pagination (such as keep with next or page break after), and line numbers.

Parallel Columns Columns created with tabs or the table feature (also side-by-side paragraphs).

Placeholder Empty frame used to leave space in a document for text, pictures, or scanned graphics to be inserted later.

Point Position the tip of the mouse pointer on or next to an item.

Points Unit of measure for fonts (1 inch equals approximately 72 points).

Portrait Orientation Document prints with the short edge of the page at the top; also called vertical orientation.

Print Preview Reduced view of the layout of a completed page, including page breaks.

Pull Quote Text highlighted in a special format to emphasize a point made in an article.

R

Redo Feature that permits reversing editing and formatting actions that have been undone.

Redlining Applying the strikethrough format to text that is to be deleted or moved.

Retrieve Open (load) an existing file and display it on the screen.

Revision Marks Formats, such as strikethrough and underline, added to text to indicate editing changes that were made.

Row Selection Bar Unmarked area slightly to the left of the far left column border of a row, used for selecting the entire row.

Ruler Located near the top of the window; contains symbols and markers to format indents and tabs.

S

Scale Resize graphics.

Scroll Move through the pages of a document on the screen without repositioning the insertion point.

Scroll Bar Displayed along the right side or bottom of a window, a scroll bar can be used to view information beyond the borders of the window. In the Style, Font, and Font Size boxes on the Formatting Toolbar and in some dialog box list boxes, scroll bars allow for viewing additional options.

Section Division in a document that separates various page formats (such as margins, page numbers, and columns).

Select Change settings in a dialog box or in the Style, Font, or Font Size boxes on the Formatting Toolbar; highlight text for editing or formatting.

Selection Bar Invisible area to the left of the left margin that is used to select lines, paragraphs, or the entire document.

Shading Patterns used to shade the background of paragraphs and cells.

Sidebar Supplemental text added to a main document such as a magazine or newspaper article.

Side-by-Side Paragraphs Paragraphs printed in two parallel columns and aligned side by side.

Soft Page Breaks Automatic page breaks Word adds as needed when text reaches the bottom margin.

Status Bar Shows information about a document or selected command, including page number, section number, vertical and horizontal position, and status of several functions, such as Overtype and revision marking.

Student Disk Formatted disk containing files for completed exercises and activities in this textbook.

Subdirectory Directory created under the root (or top) directory.

Subscript Text formatted so that it is positioned slightly below the line of type.

Superscript Text formatted so that it is positioned slightly above the line of type.

T

Thesaurus Word tool for looking up synonyms for a word or group of words.

Title Bar Located at the top of the window; displays the name of the application, document, or group window.

Toggle Turn an option on and off using the same procedure.

Toolbar Located near the top of the window; contains icons and list boxes for the most frequently used Word commands.

Triple-click Position the mouse pointer; then quickly press and release the left mouse button three times in rapid succession.

U

Undo Feature that permits reversing editing and formatting actions.

W

Widow/Orphan When turned on, this option prevents the printing of single lines separated from the remainder of the paragraph; a widow is a single line at the top of a page; an orphan is a single line at the bottom of a page.

Window Rectangular area of the screen that appears in the screen work area; contains a running application or a document.

Word Art Program for creating special effects with text such as rotating and shadows.

Word Wrap Text automatically moves to the next line when it reaches the right margin.

Z

Zoom Control List that allows magnifying or reducing the view of a document.

Show/Hide icons, 25, 369

Side headings in left margin, 305–306, 364–366

Sidebar, 366–367

Side-by-side paragraphs, 222–224

Single-spacing of paragraphs, 107, 109

Sizing of windows, 2, 5–8

Soft page breaks, 124, 125

Sort Descending icon, 267

Sort Options dialog box, 235

Sort Text dialog box, 235–237

Sorting
  data sources, 267–269
  multiple-column lists, 234–237
  paragraphs, 241–242
  single-column lists, 234–237
  tables, 240–241

Spaces
  characters, spacing of, 114–116
  between columns, 212, 311–312
  lines in paragraphs, spacing of, 24, 107–109
  nonbreaking, 320–323
  paragraph spacing on page, 303–306

Special characters, searching and replacing, 194

Spelling, checking
  custom dictionaries, 78, 81
  entire document, 80–83
  interrupting spelling check, 81–82
  single words, 78–80

Spelling dialog box, 79–82

Spelling icon, 79

Square, drawing, 352

Standard Toolbar, 19, 206–209

Status bar, 19

Strikethrough format, 178

Student Disk, 18, 41

Styles, searching for, 189

Switch Between Header and Footer icon, 131

Switching applications, 10–11

Symbols, special menu for, 322

T

Tab Stop Alignment icons, 152

Table AutoFormat dialog box, 218

Table Cell Height and Width dialog box, 211

Table Formula command, 242, 245

Table Formula dialog box, 243

table grid, 207

Table Insert Rows dialog box, 243

Table menu, 206

Table Select Table command, 211

Table Sort Text dialog box, 234–237

Table(s)
  borders, 217–218
  calculating in, 243–244
  columns in, See Columns
  converting text to, 221–222
  editing text in cells, 212–213
  formatting, 215–218
  parts of, 206

rows, See Rows

shading, 217–218

sorting, 240–241

title, 215

unformatted, 155

updating, 245

using Toolbar to create, 206–209

Tabs
  deleting, 154–155
  moving, 154–155
  setting for tables, 215–216
  setting with Ruler, 152–154
  using, 152–157

Template(s), style sheet, See Style sheet

Text
  blocks of text, selecting, 48–52
  converting to tables, 221–222
  copying within document, 64–67
  creating in WordArt, 347–349
  deselecting, 101, 188
  entering, 21
  frames for, 341
  indenting, See Indenting
  moving, See Moving text
  replacing, 190–194
  searching for, 186–188
  selecting, See Selecting
  sorting, 234–242

Thesaurus, 87–89

Thesaurus dialog box, 88

Time, inserting, 30, 131

Time icon, 131

Title, table, 215